REBEL WITHOUT A PAUSE:

There's no justice. Just us.

And what we choose to do about it

Hank Roberts

"The Lesson" by Roger McGough from "In the Classroom" (© Roger
McGough, 1976) is printed by permission of United Agents
(www.unitedagents.co.uk) on behalf of Roger McGough

Rebel Without a Pause: There's no justice. Just us.

Thank you for buying this book. I hope you enjoy it. 50% of any profits will go to supporting the founding of the National Education Museum. The rest I just might need for legal actions!

Acknowledgements

Jean: without you I wouldn't achieve anything. Without you I am useless. You have put up with more than any human should. You played a major role in helping to write the book and the hours of editing. All my love and thanks. My kids **Kathy and Brendan** – thank you for still talking to me. Hopefully you still will when you have read the book. I love you though I don't say it often enough. Profound thanks to my chief editor **Brendan Foley,** a good friend and comrade. To **Lynda Woodruffe** for her assistance with my English grammar. To **Lucy** my Granddaughter for all her typing. To **Phil Katz**, another good friend and comrade for all his professional expertise on design and layout. To all those friends who read parts or all of the book and made useful comments. And **Eoin MacMahon** who suggested the main title. It was taken from a song title from the group, Public Enemy. **Brendan**, my son, came through with *Head Butts and Headteachers* amongst others. Valiant effort mate.

All those I have known and those that I have loved and those that have known or loved me. The **Camden Crew** I love you all because you are mad. **Ex school colleagues** from **Sladebrook** and **Copland**. Your bravery and solidarity were magnificent. **Union and political friends and comrades**; too many to mention but you know who you are. We have all done our best. I have learnt so much from you. We know it has not been enough but overwhelmingly it is not our fault. The state of Britain would have been worse still without our sacrifice and efforts. To the **Royal Institution,** a beacon of light.

To those who have gone before. We all stand on the shoulders of giants. But even more importantly no man or woman is an island. We are the most social of species and it is our collective endeavour that makes progress.

Introduction

The greatest stories in the world – both fact and fiction – have never been written. For every death-defying heroic adventurer that survived to write their tale, most didn't get past the defying death part of the process. Their tale will have gone with them to the grave. Of those that have survived most will never put pen to paper.

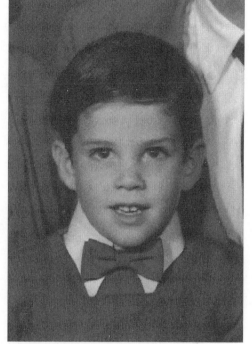

Everyone has a story in them, but the vast majority never even try to write it. Of those that start, most don't finish. And those that finish? Most don't get published.

The world's most fantastic stories, its greatest potential literature, have been confined to their owners' minds, at best merely glimpsed by those that knew them as friends, lovers or family. All consigned to the void alongside their mortal remains.

This is one that made it. Interesting? I hope so - why else would I have written it? Funny? Well, I certainly laughed. Fantastic? No, I assure you – it's all true. Will this book find itself on lofty shelves beside the world's greatest literature? No. Then again, I think some of Dickens' writing is rather dull. I guess his forte is the stereotype Mr Gradgrind in Hard Times. "*Facts, facts and more facts*". What an inspiration.

This book was written over a period of many years, mainly when I was travelling to and from holidays. Accounts are given of the events as known at the time. I have chosen to keep it like that rather than update them, to try and add immediacy and to reflect my feelings and knowledge at the time.

For example, the amount taken by my headteacher Sir Alan Davies and others which I write as £1.9 million was subsequently discovered to be £2.7 million. But what's £800,000 between mates, or in this case freemasons, eh?

If you think this book is bearable, after telling all your friends to buy it, or buying it for them, then do me, your friends and yourself a favour - **write one yourself**.

Chapter One
IT BEGINS

I have lived in a church cellar, stolen firearms, been a central committee member of a Communist Party - subsequently expelled, gained a black belt in karate 2nd Dan, slept with three women at once - no money changed hands, attended a military boarding school - expelled, been in a band - my mother used to say that I was the vocalist – she couldn't bring herself to say that I was a singer.

I've been the President of one student union and been awarded honorary life membership of another. As a teacher, I led an all-day sit in of 20 teachers in the Headteacher's office. It made the first item on the BBC six o'clock news. I've drunk bleach, put a couple of people in hospital via head butts – if forced to fight, highly recommended. I've committed credit card fraud down Oxford Street[1], and been suspended from school as a teacher - twice. I've been suspended from the National Union Teachers (NUT) once. I was an elected member of the national executive of two teaching unions, the NUT and ATL at the same time and missed being elected General Secretary of the ATL by 104 votes but subsequently was elected as National President.

I lived with, i.e. was looked after by, a teacher at my school, Mr Connor and his family after being thrown out of home as an unruly school boy.

I worked on a farm and used the money to live by myself in rented accommodation while studying for A-levels in the sixth form.

Led an occupation of Brent's education office. Later I lived in a tent for six months to stop an academy, a privately run but state funded school. I have been poor. I've been vaguely rich. I have slept in the gutter and at some of the best hotels including at The Lanesborough, which provided a personal butler – she was charming.

I twice faced someone with a knife. Well, three times if you include Jean, the missus. Mind you, the really scary one was when Jean hurled a jar of mayonnaise at me – Hellman's of course. Only the best.

---

[1] Most people have done things in their youth that they are ashamed of.

"It's f.....g freezing" I say to Jean as I emerge from my swim in the Antarctic ocean.

I've swum with marine iguanas in the Galapagos and with penguins in Antarctica, swum at the North Pole, snorkelled in the Maldives, scuba dived in Bermuda, ridden camels in the Sahara and the Gobi and elephants in Zimbabwe, Cambodia and Sri Lanka. I've seen a geezer in Iceland – actually it should be geyser but when we were there it wasn't working properly – more like an old geezer. We were told that they added washing up liquid to encourage it, but it sounded a bit odd to me.

I appeared before a High Court judge at the Old Bailey. I once had an angry person with a gun searching for me, an associate of the notorious Adams family of London. No. They didn't find me, or you wouldn't be reading this.

I won an award for chess and I'm a patron of the Royal Institution. It sounds great, but you just have to give them money.

I certainly haven't been everywhere and done everything, but I did get the T-shirt. Interested? The story as they say gets better. Or should that be worse. There are many things I would not do now, but they are too numerous to mention.

Oh, and by the way, although this account is to a large degree autobiographical, I have tried hard to impart some useful knowledge. I couldn't resist, could I? After all I am a teacher … Onwards.

Chapter Two
BERMUDA, PARADISE ISLAND

It all began for me in Bermuda. Not a bad place to start, as you have to start somewhere. Certainly a good thing to drop into a conversation, unless of course you happen to be in Bermuda and surrounded by Bermudians. But as there are over 7 billion people on the planet and only just over 60,000 Bermudians living on the island, it's a pretty good conversation piece. You're not that likely to be chatting to too many people who will say "Bermuda? Me too".

Before I tell you anything about Bermuda, my growing up there and my family, let me first debunk one thing. There is no such thing as the Bermuda Triangle. It's a myth. The claim is that a triangular area of ocean stretching between Florida, Bermuda and Puerto Rico has more ships and aircraft disappearing than would be statistically expected. This is untrue. The capacity of people, or at least many, to believe in bullshit is a never-ending source of amazement to me. I am not alone – many scientists have explored this, the best of which I think was the late Carl Sagan in *A Demon Haunted World*, which I recommend.

The nonsense of the Bermuda Triangle was best exposed by Larry Kusche in a book *The Bermuda Triangle Mystery – Solved*, that was first written as early as 1975 then revised in 1995. In the epilogue he writes *"Many theories have been proposed to solve the mystery of the Bermuda Triangle. Time warps, reverse gravity fields, witchcraft, atmospheric aberrations, magnetic and gravitational anomalies, seaquakes, waterspouts, tidal waves, freak seas, death rays from Atlantis, black holes in space, underwater signalling devises to guide invaders from other planets, UFOs collecting earthlings and their vehicles for study in other galaxies ..."* We have entered beyond bullshit here to the realm of utter fantasy.

He continues, '*My research which began as an attempt to find as much information as possible about the Bermuda Triangle has an unexpected result. After examining all the evidence I have reached the following conclusion: **there is no theory that solves the mystery**. It is no more logical to find a common cause for all the disappearances in the triangle than, for example, to try and find one cause for all automobile accidents in Arizona. By abandoning the search for an overall theory and investigating each incident independently, the mystery began to unravel*'.

'*The legend of the Bermuda Triangle is a manufactured mystery. It began because of careless research and was elaborated upon and perpetuated by writers who either purposely or unknowingly made use of misconceptions, faulty reasoning and sensationalism*'. Take that, believers.

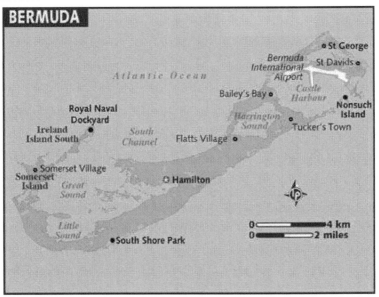

The real Bermuda is shaped like a fish hook. It is a beautiful group of coral islands lying atop a huge undersea volcano. It is completely remote, isolated, the nearest landfall being the coast of North Carolina some 665 miles away. It is not part of the West Indies, though often mistakenly grouped with them though they are twice as far away as for example Florida is to Bermuda. It is subtropical and the most northerly group of coral islands in the world. It achieves this by being bathed in the warm current of the Gulf Stream.

It was Charles Darwin, that brilliant persistent and multitalented scientist, who first gave the correct explanation of how coral islands and atolls form. In brief, a volcanic peak is created. Corals starts to grow surrounding it just below sea level. Gradually erosion brings the volcanic peak to sea level. Corals continue to grow and develop on the dead skeletons of other corals thus forming coral islands and atolls. Bermuda is one of the few coral reef areas in the world that has so far not been affected by coral bleaching, which is a serious worldwide hazard to our biosphere because corals are an important base for the marine food chain. Like climate change, worldwide action is needed on this.

Bermuda was discovered by Juan de Bermudez, a Spaniard in 1505. Hence Bermuda's name. At least it was a legitimate first discovery and not like the 'discovery' of North America whether by Columbus looking for India, or the Vikings who got there earlier. North America was already inhabited by native people whose forebears had actually discovered it many thousands of years earlier.

In the history of maritime exploration and empire building, Portugal was a pre-eminent seafaring nation globally before the British, the Dutch or indeed the Spanish. Henry the Navigator (Prince Henrique of Portugal) was trying to send ships round Africa about a century before the top-heavy Mary Rose was turning turtle in Portsmouth Harbour in 1545. After them, then to pre-eminence came the Spanish, then the Dutch. But the Empires of Portugal, Spain or the Dutch would not prevail against the armed sea power of the first industrial nation on earth. Bermuda, like so many islands and areas around the world, was destined to become a British colony[2]. Fortunately, in this case no indigenous people(s) had to be subjugated or exterminated, or as with the Chagos Islands, removed[3].

In Bermuda's case it was uninhabited. Juan de Bermudez had sailed right on past leaving nothing behind but markings on a sea chart and his name to the islands. The English didn't arrive until over a hundred years later, initially by shipwreck. Bermuda is surrounded by extensive and extremely dangerous reefs which over the years have claimed innumerable victims. Over 300 and counting wrecks have been found so far. It acquired the name of the 'Isle of Devils' from Spanish seafarers. Hurricanes do occasionally hit Bermuda, but they normally lack the force of the major Caribbean hurricanes, Bermuda being so much farther north. Some ships certainly will have been hurled onto the reefs by hurricanes and storms and their crews drowned and ripped to shreds by

---

[2] It's amusing to think that Bermuda, since the handing back of Hong Kong to China, is now Britain's most populous colony with just 60,000 people. When India was handed back to the Indians it had 390 million.

[3] The enforced removal of Chagos islanders from their island homes to facilitate a US base on the largest island Diego Garcia was a bestial act. This is well documented in the book *Island of Shame: The Secret History of the US Military Base on Diego Garcia* by David Vine. It demonstrates Britain's rulers on-going 'lap dog' servility to US imperialism. Update: On 22nd May 19 the UN Assembly voted overwhelmingly for the islands to be handed back within six months. The 6 against were UK, USA, Hungary, Israel, Australia and the Maldives. Insult was added to injury by British complicity in US illegal extraordinary rendition including of British citizens and them being taken to Diego Garcia to face interrogation and torture.

the razor-sharp coral. But the major danger, at least early on, was simply sailing into the extensive and uncharted coral reefs.

However, it was a hurricane that did for the Sea Venture. In 1609 on 28th July Admiral Sir George Somers in his flagship the Sea Venture ran into the reef off the coast of Bermuda. This is beautifully described in Bermuda: *A World Apart* by Roger LeBrucherie.

'After seven uneventful weeks at sea … the Atlantic sailor's worst nightmare, a hurricane, hit the Sea Venture. Mountainous seas and terrifying winds wracked the ship, but there was worse: the ship's seams began to open, and water poured into the hold. For four days and nights every man, woman and child aboard pumped and bailed to exhaustion. Despite their herculean efforts, ten feet of water filled the bottom on the ship, and all appeared to be lost. And then, Sir George at the helm, sighted land on the western horizon and ordered enough sail to be unfurled to drive towards the island. Half a mile from shore the Sea Venture wedged in the reef which held her fast as the storm blew itself out. As the waters calmed, the longboat was lowered and all aboard …including the ship's dog … were ferried ashore'.

Their number included John Rolfe who later married the Native North American Pocahontas. The ship was on route to James Town an English colony in Virginia. They eventually built two new ships and made their way to their intended destination, but two men were left behind. Their names were Robert Walters and Christopher Carter. No Roberts unfortunately. They came later. The arrival of the shipwrecked crew and passengers on the island shore is considered as the start of the permanent habitation of Bermuda - 28th July. It is believed that Shakespeare's play The Tempest written about of year later drew some of its inspiration from the reports of the wreck of the Sea Venture on the 'Isle of Devils'.

The history, culture and nature of Britain's most interesting few remaining imperial outposts, of which Bermuda is the oldest, is charmingly explored by Simon Winchester in his book, *Outposts: Journeys to the Surviving Relics of the British Empire*[4]. The reason for his visit to Bermuda was the shooting dead of the Governor, Sir Richard Sharples, his *Aide De Camp* Captain Sayers and the Governor's dog.

---

[4] I love islands, not surprisingly as I was born on one. Two other excellent books are *Islands: Beyond the Horizon – The Life of Twenty of the World's most Remote Places* by Roger Lovegrove and *Atlas of Remote Islands* by Judith Schalansky.

People back in the UK seemed more upset that the dog had been shot! This was March 1973 and we were to visit the same year in August but by then, as you will see, there was another big story. Winchester wrote of the shootings, *"A state of emergency had been declared. A frigate was dispatched. The well-oiled machinery for dealing with native insurrections was swung into place, on the off chance it might be needed as in Malaya ..... or those dozen other sites of old Imperial trouble"*. He further relates that the two *'young hoodlums'* were later caught and hanged. *"The hangings triggered riots, and, in true Imperial style, soldiers of the Royal Regiment of Fusiliers were sent in to restore order."* The death penalty in the UK had been abolished in 1965. Large numbers of black Bermudians believed that the death penalty had only been imposed as the perpetrators were black and it wouldn't have happened if they were white. I think they were probably right.

For more of the history you'll have to find out for yourself or better still – visit. Bermuda, it's great. No, I don't work for, or receive any payments from the Bermuda tourist board!

My grandfather, William Roberts Snr - there was a William Roberts Jr – my Uncle Billy, of whom more later - was a Bermudian MP or, as it was called, a member of the House of Representatives[5]. Not quite as impressive as it might sound considering that the island then only had a total native population of some 30,000. Even then though it had a high transient tourist population, mostly rich Americans and Brits. He was more like a parish councillor, perhaps, than an MP. Perhaps not. If there is nothing else but your parish within more than 600 miles and you're a 'councillor', I guess you are pretty important. A big (-ish) fish in a (very) small pond. My cousin Gregory has a great memory for life in Bermuda. On a visit from the States recently he told me that Grandpa was chairing the House of Representative's committee on deciding whether ordinary Bermudians would be able to buy private cars. Americans on the US base were needless to say allowed to have them and were driving them around the island causing resentment amongst native Bermudians. He used his casting vote to vote yes and Gregory said he then spent a lifetime regretting it.

My grandmother was an American whose father, I was told, had been a millionaire who had lost it all in the depression. Grandpa owned a

---

[5] Bermuda's Parliament, one of the earliest in the world. It was the first parliament in the western hemisphere founded in1620 called The House of Assembly. William Henry Thomas Joell was the first non-white MP elected in 1883 whereas the first UK's non-white MP was Dadabhai Naoroji in 1892.

grocery store. I can remember that it sold black bottles of rum with no label on. The next time I saw the bottles was in the movie Pirates of the Caribbean. A local alcoholic named Fred Springer - amongst others I'm sure - used to buy them. He used to live, or to us seemed to live, in a patch of rough ground near our house amongst the wild ferns, hibiscus, oleanders and cedar trees. Being kids, we, the local gang, used to mercilessly tease him until Fred chased after us – like in that kids' game where you keep teasing someone by calling out *what's the time Mr Wolf?*". Eventually they shout out *"DINNER TIME"* and chase after you. Like dogs, endless repetition for young children doesn't seem to bore them. As a teacher I say hurrah!

The shop also had one of those stick type of phones. Am I that old or was Bermuda just behind the times? I suspect the answer to both questions is yes. When starting to write this book, Jean said *"you can't say you're a lager lout any more. You'll have to say you're a saga[6] lout"*.

I remember Grandpa was incredibly grumpy, a tradition Jean feels I have upheld admirably. My grandmother was incredibly serving. It was something many if not most women accepted in those days in the colonies of Britain, and indeed in Britain itself, and is still unfortunately the case in much of the world. I was reminded of how bad it was, and in some places still is, by a television programme on Romanian gypsy child brides. In the middle of this horror story, particularly shocking because it was in modern day Europe, a gypsy man was espousing his philosophy of the role of women and opined the role was that of a slave.

How very ancient Greek. Plato would have concurred and many people in many areas and in many times besides. The reality of this and its utter incongruity in modern day Britain was highlighted by the fact that his wife explained that she had to do everything for him. Even put his socks on in the morning! The allegation that someone dresses Prince Charles every morning, including putting on his socks, is apparently a myth. Though there may be a royal toothpaste squeezer, according to some.

We are all, to an extent, creatures of our times and none of us can step entirely outside of them, but my grandparents certainly did in one respect and a pretty crucial one in Bermuda at the time. What was different about them was that they used to let black callers come to the front entrance and not the back. It doesn't sound much but it was pretty

---

[6] For the young, foreign or just plain ignorant, Saga is a company for the over 50s

radical in those times. Bermuda was a deeply 'racist' society. Even in my day they had educational apartheid in Bermuda. I went to a white's only school. Indeed, I know I am white because it says so on my birth certificate!

To set the context. Bermuda was a long-time British colony within the ambit of the slave trade Triangle - no relation of the Bermuda Triangle - and had slavery. I've been told my Bermudian ancestors didn't own slaves, but even if they had, I would accept no responsibility, blame or guilt. Sorry, but I wasn't there, it had nothing to do with me. If you think I owe you something, because my forefathers had been slave owners and yours were slaves, get real. Almost every culture had slaves at some point in history and virtually every human has slaves and slave owners in their gene pool if you go back far enough.

Suffice to point out, so conveniently forgotten or ignored by those who see slavery as solely, or merely a matter of race (actually, physical characteristics primarily skin colour) rather than class, that the first stage of the export of black African slaves in the slave triangle involved, overwhelmingly, their capture by other black Africans. Slavery existed in Africa long before the Americas slave trade Triangle, and Africa had a white slave trade. The coasts of Britain were once raided by Barbary Pirates also called Barbary Corsairs to capture locals to sell them into slavery in Africa and the Middle East. This is excellently covered in the book *White Gold - The Extraordinary Story of Thomas Pellow and North Africa's One Million European Slaves* by Giles Milton. Vikings also raided the British coast to capture natives to be sold into slavery.

A wider and much more detailed account of slavery is in the book *A Brief History of Slavery: A New Global History* by Jeremy Black. Amongst much good information and interesting facts, he points out, '*Historically there was no necessary relationship between slavery and racism. Indeed, enslavement was frequently a punishment for illegal behaviour. There were white slaves of white states, most obviously those who managed the oars of the large number of Christian galleys who contested the Ottoman advance in the Mediterranean. In sub Saharan Africa and Ancient Rome... owners and slaves were often of the same colour'.*

'Native American (American Indian) ownership of slaves in the United States was pervasive until emancipation. Moreover, there was large scale slavery ... in areas usually not associated with a history of slavery and the slave trade, such as India. Thus the history of slavery was a more central and dynamic feature of the history of the world than it is comfortable to acknowledge.' Slavery was fundamentally an economic relationship and not a question of 'race' or ethnic difference'.

Well done grandparents on my father's side; you were liberal (not woolly liberal) and decent and prepared to make a stand to seek to turn the tide. I like to think that perhaps I inherited some of this from you, the standing against the tide that is, not the liberal decency! But it might have been environmental for they looked after me for a while - it seemed like an eternity as a young kid, but it wasn't - after my father died and had been looking after me for some time before that. Or it could be having a parent die when young. That's as good a cause for rebellion against the world as any.

Questions arise. Why were my grandparents looking after me and not my mother? How did I happen to be alone in Bermuda with a father who was dying of cancer? My parents had split up. My mother, myself and two brothers David and Peter had returned to Portsmouth in England where my mother was born. My father had come across to visit us and had a fit in the living room. I vividly remember this with him hitting his head on a heater as he fell to the floor. The cancer had spread to his brain, causing the fit. I believe that my parents had realised then that his operation had not been successful and that they knew he was going to die. I was sent back to Bermuda to be with him in the last remaining months that he had left. I was told much later by my mother that they had intended to get back together, but with airfares being so relatively expensive then, and also the hospital treatment and fares to Canada where he was operated on, there wasn't enough money for everyone to go back at once. So I went first. This sounds a bit bizarre to me, but I'll never get to the bottom of it now. If you want to know things about your parents' past or yours ask them now. Go on; get on and do it before it's too late.

The family doctor, Dr Nash, came in the room and said, "I'm sorry Henry has passed out". My grandparents started crying. In my childish naïveté I thought Dr Nash meant he had become unconscious and I tried to comfort my grandparents, saying it would be all right.

It wouldn't be. What he meant undoubtedly, being a Christian, was that he had passed out of this life into the next. No one realised that I had not comprehended. I guess that even in the inconsolable depth of their own grief at the loss of their son - their third child to die before them - they might have been surprised or impressed by my attempts to console them. How fortunate we are to live in a time and place in which early childhood death is so much less frequent than previously.

The awful, terrible truth that my father would never be returning only dawned slowly. It was irrevocably confirmed when, as was the custom then in Bermudian Catholic families - if not with Bermudians generally - his open coffin was placed in the living room. I draped myself across it and him and begged and pleaded for him to wake up. The depth of denial, despair and gut wrenching, soul destroying grief is something that I wouldn't wish on my worst enemy. Even now as I write about it over 40 years later, as I am on a plane soon to land in Singapore, I weep uncontrollably, embarrassingly. Fortunately, breakfast is served and I compose myself – only to start all over again. I guess it is a bit like post-traumatic stress syndrome[7]. I never had any counselling. I don't think they knew what it was in those days, certainly not in Bermuda.

Though my grandmother in particular did her best to console me, it didn't help and it wouldn't help any 9-year-old losing their dad, that his Mum and his brothers were 3000 miles away on the other side of the Atlantic Ocean.

Philip Larkin's poem *This Be The Verse* starts,
'*They fuck you up, your mum and dad.*
They may not mean to, but they do'.
Dad, you didn't do it deliberately. How could dying of cancer be deliberate, but your death, at such a young age, certainly fucked me up. Your smoking from a very early age at a very minimum certainly didn't help. My Dad was just another statistic for the tobacco companies to ignore as they lied and covered up to make their billions in profits just as so many international giant corporations before them and since. And following in their footsteps, asbestos, the next big human caused

---

[7] I have since learnt that it might be unresolved prolonged grief.

international health hazard, caused by them having no regard for people's health or lives.

I felt a great sense of unfairness and injustice at losing my father so young, both me at nine and him just 30 years young. Because of this, which I suspect, or something else, I have always had a burning sense of injustice. And whether in our country or indeed the world, I've always felt the need to fight it. Like most soldiers returning from war, I dealt with death and tragedy by suppressing it and have been fearful ever since of caring too much about anyone or anything for fear of losing them and not being able to cope with the loss. The fragility of my self-constructed armour is exposed whenever I am forced to confront the depth of others' emotions at funerals, in films, plays or opera and the tears invariably flow.

Years later, in my large inner city comprehensive school, I would see regular notices on the staff notice board about kids that had just lost a parent, and my heart would always go out to them. Name, 7CX mum died recently – Name 8 BD dad died in car accident. The teachers do their best but few, unless they have experienced it, can have any real conception of the desolation this can visit on a young child's life. Our school, Copland, was one of the very few secondaries which had a full-time counsellor, Sue Collins. After she left, she wasn't replaced.

Other than its personally catastrophic ending, Bermuda was a wonderful place to grow up. I know that virtually every place that most children grow up in, appears wonderful, but bear with me – this really was wonderful. I learned to swim when I was three. It would have been hard not to, on an island where nowhere is more than one mile from the sea.

In the Parish of Somerset, where we lived most of the time, it was a stone's throw to the beach. I can remember my father swimming out to sea with me hanging onto his back, my arms around his neck. I can remember my mother hanging conch shells, like giant snails but marine, on the washing line. If you stick a hook in their flesh (foot) and hang them upside down the pull of gravity on the heavy shell will eventually - it takes some days - cause the contents and shell to separate, the shell dropping to the ground and its contents left on the line waiting to be cooked into a lovely conch stew or chowder. The Frogs aren't the only ones who like eating snails.

Like many Bermudians, my father used to have more than one job - if you could properly call them jobs. He did some farming, though on a very small island – it is only 21 square miles in total – the plots were similarly tiny. He grew bananas, potatoes, pawpaws (papayas), loquats, water melons, cantaloupes etc. and had some pigs. He used to give them beer and get them pissed, which he said was good for them – it certainly does the trick for me. Dad went deep sea fishing and I can remember him and the crew returning to the boathouse in Elys Harbour with shark, marlin, barracuda and many other fish.

In the time after my father died, before I returned to Britain, I used to fish in the boathouse for what we call lobsters, actually crayfish. You could catch them by just lowering a line down with a hook and some stale bread stuck on it. The 'lobsters' were so greedy. They would just hang onto it and you could slowly pull them up and out of the water, drop them in a bucket and straight off home to Grandma to cook the poor sod alive. I didn't know at that age that being boiled alive was their fate, but I have to say that at that age, I don't think I'd have much cared. I also caught the occasional unwary fish, which was also cooked and served up by Grandma.

My first return to Bermuda was made after I had just finished being a student and before I started work as a teacher. Jean and I were married (we had got married after our first term at college[8]) and had a baby daughter Kathy who was just six months old. How we managed to afford it, I can't remember or figure out – unless Jean got some money from a rich relative. Our poverty was such that during the Christmas holiday immediately following Kathy's birth in December 1972, my grant had run out. Jean's grant had finished the previous summer when she had completed her teacher training. I was on a one-year postgraduate teacher training course. Penniless, Jean, myself plus baby presented ourselves at the nearest employment office, the Labour exchange, the dole office – whatever it was called then – in Harlesden. I explained that my grant had run out. I had a holiday job in the post office coming up, but it hadn't started and I desperately needed some more money because of the cost associated with having and bringing up a baby. I was willing to work temporarily until the post office job started.

There were no jobs. Would they give me any money then? The answer, to put it bluntly, was no way.

---

[8] We got married on 3rd January 1970 which was the first date you could legally marry without your parents' consent under 21. This was because the age of majority had been lowered from 21 to 18 and became law on 1st January. You had to give notice on 1st to be able to marry on 3rd so this was the earliest date.

I refused to accept it. It was winter, and we were desperate. We refused to leave. Eventually closing time came. We still refused to leave. So a whole load of policemen and a policewoman turned up and asked us to leave. I politely, but insistently, said that we were not going to leave. We've got a young baby to look after, my grant has run out and I need some money or work urgently. They somewhat less politely and even more insistently said that you will leave with us. Realising the chips were down, I made a break for a radiator and clamped myself to it with a death grip. The police led Jean out who, with baby Kathy in tow, was not about to engage in the sort of Custer's last stand tactics I was about to. There then began a tug-of-war between the radiator and the police with myself as the rope. Once they had managed to prise my feet up into the air, the result was inevitable. But I made them work for it.

The next day as the door of the dole office opened, in we went. Back to the same counter, to the same assistant who stared wide-eyed in disbelief. Like some sort of hijacker or kidnapper I reiterated my list of demands – immediate temporary work or money – I would refuse to leave without it. Foreseeing perhaps this continuing with the police having to be called on a regular basis at the end of every day to effect my eviction, or at the start of the day and mounting guard all day to prevent my re-entry, or it ending with my arrest and incarceration (temporarily, for as sure as night followed day on my release I would have been back) – and perhaps taking pity on the baby, he decided to call the manager.

Lo! The problem was both solvable and solved. A cheque appeared forthwith. Now let me say I feel extremely sorry for the counter clerks in such offices who have to put up with abuse every day and who often nowadays because of numerous previous assaults have to serve behind reinforced screens. However, the lesson is clear and almost an iron law of nature. With so much injustice and with so much for so many people to legitimately complain about or take issue with, only those prepared to speak up loudest, to fight hardest or longest or better still, all at once will rise to the top of the queue and be most likely to succeed. The meek shall inherit the earth? Baloney. Or perhaps it can be put as arch-Capitalist John Paul Getty observed "The meek may inherit the earth, but not the mineral rights".

I digress – as you will find I often will. On my first return to Bermuda, family in tow, I was profoundly shocked in getting a cab from the airport to take me to my grandparents who still lived in Somerset at virtually the other end of the Island, to find that the cab driver had known my Dad and knew all about him, the Somerset Roberts and us as Henry's children. I should not have been so surprised as anyone who has been brought up in a village will know. Everyone knows everybody else's, or virtually everybody's, business. We had been living in London where everyone tries hard not to know anyone else's business. Also the fourteen years since my father's death seemed like an eon. Older now it seems like a blink of an eye. Einstein was certainly correct; time is relative. The scientific theory is of course a bit more profound than this.

The huge news when we arrived in Bermuda in August 1973 was that a massive Russian liner, the Baltika[9], had run aground on one of the coral reefs that surrounds the island but fortunately, unlike so many ships before her, had not sunk. Firmly, though temporarily stuck until the next really high tide, or being pulled off by tugs. Uncle Billy and Auntie Barbara were very kind to us and Uncle Billy offered to take me out on his speedboat for the day to sightsee while Jean stayed with Kathy. The grounded liner was a huge event in Bermuda and a sightseeing must. We could also do some fishing.

The liner was sighted and circled and then we settled down to do some fishing. The first bit of excitement of the day, since the grounded liner had been interesting more than exciting, was a bite. I hauled the line up carefully. I was astounded to see there, quite a long way down in the depths of the crystal clear sea, not a fish but a large turtle. Uncle Billy saw it too and urged me to keep pulling the line up slowly and steadily. With a huge combined effort and not a little danger from sharp flailing flippers and beak, we managed to haul the turtle on board and it flopped onto the bottom of the boat on its back. Yes I know, it had turned turtle! The flippers thrashed about as we eyed it. What to do? The thought of turtle soup scuttled crab-like into my mind – to continue the Marine analogies. But wiser counsel prevailed: Uncle Billy pointed out that they were a protected species – his regard for the law was touching in the light of later events. With an equally great effort we managed to evict our new lodger and it slowly swam off none the worse for wear.

After an afternoon's fishing, all edible fish were unhooked and put in a bucket, courtesy of Uncle Billy or the cousins; we set off home as dusk was approaching.

---

[9] I had to look the name up. Baltika had visited Cuba and returning from there in 1973 she ran onto rocks in Bermuda at full speed. All foreign assistance was refused and Soviet freighters stood by, although passengers remained on board. Eventually, a US Navy barge was allowed to remove most of the fuel. She floated free and continued under her own power.

BANG. There was an almighty crash. During the day, the tide had gone out and so had the clearance between the bottom of the boat and the top of the coral below[10]. The powerful outboard was no longer powerful; it was no-go. The boat drifted helplessly. There was one paddle on board but prolonged attempts to make any headway towards the shore a few miles away got nowhere. Darkness descended, lights gleamed from the shore in the distance. The failure of the single paddle to make any impact on propelling us anywhere led Uncle Billy to pronounce that we'd just have to relax and wait for somebody to rescue us. The prospect of drifting off carried by the current into the middle of the Atlantic Ocean and the possibility of not being rescued at all, was not one that filled me with glee.

I had a bright idea. Being a strong swimmer, I suggested they tie the boat's rope around me and I swim to the shore pulling the boat behind me – I think I'd seen too many Rambo type movies. The boat made as much progress as with the paddle i.e. zero. After strenuous but pointless effort I was ignominiously hauled back into the boat.

We waited - and waited - and waited in the pitch dark, my mind morbidly weighing up the chances of being found. Then lo, out of the darkness came forth light – and rescue. We were saved and wouldn't have to die of thirst lost at sea after all. When we hadn't returned, Auntie Barbara had reported us missing. Never mind a Russian liner running aground this was big news too. It made the front page of the *Mid Ocean News* or was it *The Royal Gazette*? – like every good small island, Bermuda had two newspapers[11].

I was to return to Bermuda several times over the years. On one of them I went fishing with my brother Peter who had been living in Bermuda for some time, so by then had gone native. I realised how much I had lost the art. I caught a fish and landed it. Pete told me to kill it. I gingerly and tentatively hit it against the reef rock with minimal impact, the result of which was it still being distinctly alive. Pete grabbed it roughly out of my hand and battered the fucking living daylights out of its head against the rock with the result that by the end of it, it was distinctly dead. A rough diamond Pete; part crocodilian I think – and not just because he has green eyes and deeply lined leathery face as a result of all those years in the sun. I think it's the emotional sensitivity he shares with them.

---

[10] Corals grow up to the low tide level and not further to avoid being desiccated and overheated by the sun.
[11] Now sadly only the Royal Gazette remains.

Twice I went for the summer holidays and worked, once as a tree surgeon and the second time as a furniture remover, having to work to help pay for the flights and costs. During one of these working visits, a curious thing happened. I was invited down to the beach to see my cousin Kirk's boat. When I got there I couldn't believe my eyes. It was huge. F...ing enormous. It was one of those massive power boats that multi-millionaires have to engage in power boat races. I wondered how on earth he, my cousin, who I thought was just an ordinary Bermudian had managed to afford such a beast. I continued to wonder, though at the back of my mind, for years about this; with subsequent events it was to become all too crystal clear.

My Notorious Relatives

I can't believe it. It seems utterly incredible. My Uncle Billy and Auntie Barbara have been arrested in Bermuda for smuggling $1.5 million of cocaine, my brother Pete has just informed me. The shock and feeling of utter disbelief will never leave my memory.

Newspaper accounts told the story. In 1997, Barbara and Billy were sent to prison for 12 years after being convicted of possession, handling and possession with intent to supply of 30 pounds of cocaine. Defence lawyer Richard Hector suggested this resulted out of a police *"vendetta"* against Kirk, their son.

Charges were never filed against cousin Kirk in connection with the cocaine which was found in the refrigerator of Barbara and Billy's West Side Road home. But Mr. Hector, Prosecutor made it clear who he thought was responsible when he told the court that a *"third person"* was involved and *"he has left his parents to face the music"*.

Kirk was later sent to prison for ten years in 2002 when the Supreme Court found that he played a central role in a conspiracy to import 200 pounds of marijuana. Before this he had been on bail for five years as the police could not find enough evidence. In the end a co-conspirator, in return for a lenient sentence, turned Queen's evidence. Is this a case of a super grass, grassing about the grass! Kirk's smuggling activities had seen him using his power boat to evade police. At one point he was Bermuda's champion powerboat racer. Now finally it all made sense. In court he admitted to 20 years of drug smuggling. He was further ordered to pay up nearly $1 million in 2006 in a confiscation order under the Proceeds of Crime Act 1997.

I visited Uncle Billy in prison on one of my visits to Bermuda. I took him the book *The Siege of Stalingrad* written by Anthony Beevor, and said, *"If you think you've got it tough in here just read this. It'll make you feel a whole lot better."* He laughed.

When Uncle Billy (William Edwin Roberts Jrn) died in August 2004 he got a terrific and lengthy obituary in the Bermuda *Royal Gazette* headed 'Bermuda's youngest volunteer'. My father Henry of course was too young to sign up.

The article says that Billy joined the Lincolnshire Regiment in 1943 when he was 18 years and eight months old. *'It was not long before the Bermudians were in action. On October 13 – 15, 1944 they took part in the pivotal battle of Kenrai in Holland. Bill's company led the initial assault on the first morning, but was driven back. Later that day, the full battalion attacked. This time they were successful, but the price was heavy in killed and wounded.*

'A shell exploded near Bill and he was lucky not to be killed. However, he sustained serious wounds.

'Bill was invalided to Glasgow Stobhill hospital field station and then later to Scarborough Rehabilitation centre in Yorkshire.

'Bill joined the second battalion in January 1945 in time for some of the heaviest and coldest fighting in the European campaign. He survived as the Allies drove on into Germany and the official end of the war in Europe at Bremen on May 10th 1945.'

Uncle Billy and his close friend Elliott Aubery had another close shave of a different kind. *'They met two German girls. This practice was frowned upon and forbidden. For young men who had had a constant diet of horror for so long, a chance to return to the real world was too much to resist. One of the girls invited them to her home and a happy afternoon was in progress when someone looked out of the window and saw military police approaching the front door. There was an immediate scramble and the fellows were pushed into a cupboard. One of their caps was left on the table in full view. However, their luck held. The cap remained unnoticed, allowing a happy ending to one of their best wartime stories.'*

After covering some of Billy's post war occupations, towards the conclusion it states. *'Swimming and gardening were Bill's favourite recreations. He learned to love swimming as a boy and kept it up all year round. He specialised in growing vegetables keeping his friends and family well supplied.'*

Billy's time in prison is discreetly and sensitively not mentioned, though the talk of provisioning friends and family might allude to it. When I visited him in prison he said that he was spending a lot of time in the prison gardens which he quite enjoyed. RIP Billy.

A final amusing tale concerning my notorious relatives was when I returned to Bermuda just a few years ago to show a friend the island. When we were in the Museum in St George's, much to my embarrassment my friend divulged to two of the staff that I was born and brought up in Bermuda. Not unreasonably they asked my name and where I had lived. Oh no, I thought but felt I had no option but to say *"Roberts. One of the Somerset Roberts"*. The look of horror on their faces was palpable. Equivalent to me being in London and saying I was related to the Kray twins. I could see by their faces that they were not buying my protestations that I was not involved with drugs or drug smuggling.

Though I didn't realise it as a child, Bermuda for me would definitely have been too small a place to grow up and live in as an adult. Rather than a big fish in a very small pond, I was destined to become a medium fish in a very big pond. Not that I had any choice at the time after my father died. Somehow eventually the money was found for my air ticket and I was put on a plane and picked up the other end by my grandfather on my mother's side Len. A new life was beginning. It was to be different – a masterly example of the British art of understatement!

REBEL WITHOUT A PAUSE

Chapter Three
PORTSMOUTH – A NEW BEGINNING

Portsmouth was, and still is, a city full of yobs, though not as rough as it used to be. An ex-girlfriend Sylvia mailed me from Japan with this little gem.

It was a copy of the colour supplement of one of the Sunday magazines. It had two massively muscular bodybuilders on the front cover; one black, one white. The white one came from Portsmouth. In interviewing them, the interviewer asked the white one if his big size and muscle intimidated people. Not blokes in Portsmouth, he responded, it only encourages them.

The art of eye aversion was a very important art to master if you didn't want to get into a fight every other day, as opposed to the norm of every other week. To look at any fanciable woman or even some not so fanciable, was to incite, "Hey mush[12]. You screwing my bird?" Screwing meant looking at, rather than actually screwing. It was a largely rhetorical question because nine times out of ten, whatever the answer, or even if there was no answer at all, a punch-up followed. But I'm straying into violence which will have a whole chapter of its own. I just wanted to set the scene for young people growing up in Pompey at that time. Perhaps it should suffice to say that when Millwall played Pompey they knew they had a battle royal on their hands. I guess it was only to be expected with Portsmouth being a seaport, the home of the Royal Navy, with Royal Naval barracks, Royal Marine barracks and at one time had 23,000 working in the naval dockyard, not to mention ships with sailors from around the world calling in. When the Yanks were in, prostitutes used to come down from London by the trainload.

I noticed Portsmouth was different. The sea was freezing even in the middle of summer and the beach was stony. The people unfriendly. Mind you compared to London they were your best mates. In Bermuda, I like everyone else, had greeted everyone I met. I soon realised by the mystified looks and the lack of responses that this was not the done thing on the streets of Pompey. My lifestyle also underwent a change. Whilst not exactly living in the lap of luxury in Bermuda, we had been, prior to Henry's death, comfortably off. We had a maid called Margot. My grandparents had a store. When I joined my brothers and single-

---

[12] Commonly used to replace the word "mate". Despite the negative connotations this word has attracted in more recent times, this is historically a general term used in the Portsmouth dialect.

parent mother, I stepped into poverty. Yes, lived in a matchbox, fed on gruel. Monty Python got it right. I can remember mushrooms or some sort of fungus growing in the damp 'spare' room. We three boys lived in one room and my mother lived in the other. I remember us having bread and milk with sugar for breakfast though my mother strenuously denies this.

Memory is both highly selective and liable to distortion. Read some scientific accounts if you don't already know this. Take this as your official government health warning. I have not knowingly made any false statements or exaggeration. I'm willing to stand corrected. However, if you haven't got the videotape, if you are mentioned, aggrieved at not being mentioned, of feel insufficient regard has been paid to your heroism/wittiness/beauty etc. and you feel that I make too much of my own part in everything compared to yours, feel free to sue!

My grandparents on my mother's side were thoroughly, indeed unusually, decent people, decent above and beyond the call of duty. My grandfather Len had worked for the dockyard in Portsmouth and had

then got a job working for the Royal Navy dockyard in Bermuda. He worked on providing the electrical power connections for floating docks. The one he worked on had been towed to Bermuda from Egypt. It was subsequently towed back to England and my grandfather was no longer needed in Bermuda and returned to the Portsmouth dockyard.

He had moved to Bermuda with family in tow including eldest daughter, my mother-to-be, also named Jean. She met my father and got married at 18 and had me at 19. My family bred young.

The Royal Navy dockyard in Bermuda finally closed in 1951. In recognition of the power relationships, the United States base remains on the island to this day. Their 99 year lease for a large part of the island was taken out in 1941.

My maternal grandmother, Dolly, was a saint. She looked after all three[13] of us boys at various times when we were thrown out of home. My grandfather Len was an Assistant District Commissioner in the Boy Scouts. I and my brother Dave only 18 months younger than me, joined his troop, the 51st Hants. Pete seven years younger than me, joined later. One of the joys of this was going camping. Once whilst camping for a week, the troop was in the local church attending Sunday service. We'd been given half a crown for pocket money, a considerable sum at the time, and for some unknown reason my middle brother Dave was made the 'keeper of the coin'. For some even more unknown reason my brother put it in the collection box when it came round. Our entire week's pocket money gone – beyond retrieve!! I was beyond furious. As soon as we got back to the camp and were out of the way of the scoutmasters, I set about my brother. I'd pinned him to the floor in this field and was bashing him demanding an apology.

Being a stubborn bastard, despite the bashing Dave wouldn't apologise, which only made me even more furious. Then one of the older scouts intervened. I turned on him in fury. I had a large sheath knife, the Bowie knife type – my pride and joy. I whipped it out. The older boy took one look and legged it hell for leather in the opposite direction. I shot after him, intent on murder. Not being able to gain on the object of my wrath I hurled the knife with all my force straight at him. I'm grateful to this day that it just missed. The insanity of youthful temper. Unfortunately, or perhaps fortunately, the hurled knife had disappeared into the undergrowth and my strenuous searching failed to discover its whereabouts.

My youthful stupidity in being prepared to inflict death in a fight, or to face it, extended into my twenty's but again that's a story for later. No wonder most violent crime is inflicted by young men. Someone once observed that if the minimum age of conscription was raised to 50, there would be very few wars.

---

[13] I have recently found out that in fact she never looked after David. He lived under South Parade pier on the Portsmouth beach front and then moved to the West Country.

I failed my 11+; the exam which once overwhelmingly dictated the future path of several generations in Britain. Anyone reading this that supports grammar schools[14] I'll have a fifty pence bet that you passed it, or have a kid or kids attending private school and wish you could have got them a good education cheaper. Fifty pence might not sound a lot to you but it's my maximum bet having ended up owing billions of pounds having bet on things I was 100% certain of – wrongly.

Getting back to the bet, another possibility is you have a kid or kids attending grammar school in one of the eleven LEAs that still have them – this being just one illustration of the gutless toadyism of New Labour who failed to turn the few remaining into comprehensives. Thatcher had the sense to carry on with her forerunners policy and most comprehensives were created during her premiership. The only good thing you'll hear me say about her.

Failing the 11+ has self-labelled me, as its self-labelled almost everyone else who failed it, an academic failure. And this at a fairly tender age. Fortunately, I was to have some lucky breaks, but I carried that stamp of failing academically and feeling academically inferior through youth and longer, despite eventually getting to a grammar school in the 6th form and getting a degree.

This has led me to a lifetime of assiduous reading and the pursuit of knowledge in an endeavour to overcome this. Alas, a task like Sisyphus rolling his boulder uphill, never to be successfully completed. I have little time for fiction. It seems to me reality is always so much more interesting, bizarre and exciting than any made up story. Part of the amazement is knowing that the story is true. I think I have always had a problem with imagination, or, with taking things other than literally. Certain categories of jokes I'm unable to get, often even when repeatedly explained – to the amused hilarity of mates. I put it down to mild symptoms of autism[15]. Having read Simon Baron Cohen's book, *The Essential Difference: Men, Women and the Extreme Male Brain* the cap fits so I'll wear it[16].

---

[14] Grammar schools in England: a new analysis of social segregation and academic outcomes. Research paper Durham University published March 2018. Their results show that children who do go to grammar school on average do no better than if they were at comprehensive school. Grammar schools do not boost social mobility and actually harm the life chances of those from disadvantaged backgrounds.
[15] I would say very mild but some who know me well might disagree.
[16] Along with others such as 'Neurotribes – the legacy of Autism and how to think smarter' by Steve Silberman.

My brief time at Southsea secondary modern, where I was sent following my 11+ failure, was unremarkable except for parents evening. My form teacher was a Mr LeHuquet who taught French. I remember him caning one miscreant pupil so hard I swear his feet lifted off the floor. At the parents evening, my mother and Mr LeHuquet shared mutual commiserations on having to deal with a child who was to a large degree out of control ... and getting worse. Never mind the problems of trying to bring up two other kids as well as me on your own. This mutual empathy and shared understanding was obviously quite profound. They were to marry and 40 odd years later still are[17].

My fighting 'career' began at primary school, after coming back to Bermuda when I was at Albert Road Juniors. I had fought my way to the top, but had a one-sided and losing battle with a teacher, Mr Roper. Arriving at Southsea Secondary Modern, though a first year, I promptly took on a second year hard nut and won. In the numbskull world of recognition through personal violence, a good school career loomed at Southsea, but it was not to be. I was soon to be off again.

Two other educational experiences I have reflected on in later life. One was my first (remembered) experience of a teacher at Southsea Modern who could not control their class. Compassion and social responsibility are qualities that most young kids lack in abundance. The teasing, bullying and winding up of Mr Chamberlain - calling him *Charlie chambermaid* or *Charlie chamber pot* - knew no bounds – paper darts, pellets fired by rulers, shouting out insults behind his back. In those days' teachers could use the cane, and he did, but it was not enough to maintain order. Interestingly, on reflection, I had no interest in joining in with this, but on occasions I joined the laughter.

Later in life on becoming a teacher, I realised that a very small number, and I do mean very small, just can't manage it. And I don't mean just occasionally as happens to virtually all teachers especially when learning. These teachers' lives I know are a misery. But they tolerate it for year after miserable year. But what else can be expected from them? They might have a mortgage and kids – and let's face it, exactly what else does having been a teacher easily or naturally qualify you for? Besides, though the pay is poor, especially in relation to the demands and stress, there is a lot worse out there.

---

[17] Sadly, Norman, my much loved step dad, died in May 2014 - and my mother in May 2015.

There are a lot fewer teachers in this category than the despised Ofsted claim and in any event the real purpose of Ofsted was not to weed out incompetent teachers, but to unleash a regime of fear and terror on teachers, the better to control them. To stop or hinder them challenging effectively the schools' regimes or Governments' diktats – or worse, heaven forbid, the state itself.

In truth the teaching profession, or rather the teaching half-profession, for in Britain or rather specifically England it has not yet truly elevated itself to the level of a full profession, has failed in its responsibilities. One of which is that we should assure that the very few who cannot manage are helped to improve, or out. Our collective responsibility to ourselves, to our pupils, the future of our country, outweighs the interests of the few teachers not able to cope.

Of course, it goes without saying that reducing the absurd present high levels of overwork, bureaucracy and stress would massively reduce the already very small number struggling in this category. As it would the waste of the high numbers that train but drop-out. An astonishing and utterly unacceptable number of trained teachers leave the profession. Mary Bousted, General Secretary, told the ATL Annual Conference in 2015 that DfE data showed 40% of teachers left within five years.

Since then things have only got worse – but not elsewhere. Finland for example has a world renowned and respected education system. It has very high standards in its trainee teacher selection procedure and it's an all Master's degree profession. It is such a prestigious job that many more apply than get in.

In addition to Mr Chamberlain, another teacher who was memorable was 'Pops' Marshall, an English teacher at the same school. I remember labouring long and mightily to the absolute limits of my youthful ability to write a story for English homework. It was a true story about a fishing expedition my father had been on in Bermuda when the engine had irreparably broken down far out to sea. They had to start a fire on the boat with oily rags to ensure that the Coast Guard plane searching for them spotted the column of smoke arching into the air and did not miss them. An altogether risky act, I think, but the ocean is a very big place and to be lost in it, especially then, not at all an endearing prospect. I presume necessity was the mother of invention.

Anyhow, and teachers pay attention out there, the source of my strenuous literacy efforts were simple. Money. Yes spondoolicks. Dosh.

Filthy lucre. Pops had a system of giving amounts of money for effort. The maximum up to half a crown, a princely sum then when the cost of a pint was around a shilling. It must have bankrupted him but he had found a method – an essential key – motivation. In education, as in life, motivation is all. Money is not the best and certainly it is sad and deeply warping if it is a person's sole motivation, but whilst money exists in our society it cannot be discounted as a motivator.

But the best motivators are not, or rather should not be, financial. A thirst for knowledge is perhaps the greatest motivator a teacher can instil in a child and I profoundly thank my teachers for their part in this. But an even higher motivation than to instil a desire to acquire knowledge is to seek to serve, to help others. Teachers do this. They change the world – one child at a time.

REBEL WITHOUT A PAUSE

Chapter Four
THE GORDON SCHOOL FOR BOYS – MILITARY BOARDING SCHOOL.

General Charles Gordon, generally – pardon the pun – known as General Gordon of Khartoum or Chinese Gordon, was a good old-fashioned executor of Britain's imperial designs in North Africa and elsewhere. He finally met his end at the hands of the 'Fuzzy-Wuzzies' in Khartoum in present-day Sudan. The Mahdi's followers got this name because 'Fuzzy-Wuzzy' is a poem written by the English author and poet Rudyard Kipling, published in 1892 as part of Barrack Room Ballads. Actually, when Mahdist warriors broke into the governor's palace, Gordon came out in full uniform, and, after not deigning to fight, he was speared to death in defiance of the orders of the Mahdi, who had wanted him captured alive. Well, this is one version. What is certain is that his head was cut off, stuck on a pike, and brought to the Mahdi as a trophy. His body was summarily dumped in the Nile. Interestingly, General Gordon was a hero of the Kray twins. I wonder what he would have made of that. There is a painting of this final moment which I am sure is still hanging at the Gordon School, West End, Woking[18].

The British Empire's imperialist attitude was nicely summed up in a book I happened upon in a second-hand bookshop entitled *General Gordon: The Christian Soldier and Hero* by G. Barnett Smith. In his preface he writes, '*Gordon … went abroad redressing human wrongs, lifting up the unfortunate and the oppressed and commending the love of that Master* (God) *whom he served … Every member of the Anglo-Saxon race, who studies Gordon's life and character, must feel a thrill of pride that he is of the same blood as this immortal Englishman*'. !!

To commemorate one of British imperialism's most glorious servants, funds were raised, led by Queen Victoria and the Royal Family, and the school was set up in 1885 where it began existence as 'Gordon Boys' Home' for 'necessitous boys'. Its aim was to give poor waifs and strays a sound and regimental military education suitably benefiting them to become cannon fodder for our next imperial conquest or adventure. It started in Fareham, Hampshire and then transferred to its permanent site as the Gordon Boys school based in West End, Woking in December 1887 when some 100 Gordon Boys travelled to Brookwood

---

[18] Having checked with the school just before publication, a secretary at the school kindly informed me that the original painting is now held in Leeds Art Gallery. The school has a copy which is now hanging in the Chapel.

Station, and marched to the new school led by their 25 strong, newly formed band.

My mother, who was finding it increasingly difficult with us three boys and in particular me, the eldest, turned to social services for help. This was after she had been chatted up by a recruiting officer at an army event on Southsea common – or perhaps it was her chatting him up – who had suggested that military boarding school was the answer as to how to deal with her difficult eldest child. *That'll put some backbone and discipline into him!* And so, off I was packed.

I was to love it and realise that institutional life would never pose any problem for me, but at the time I felt rejected by a parent for the second time, first by my father and this time by my mother. Like many 'public' schools, which it wasn't by any means in terms of being for posh kids, the Gordon School for Boys had largely changed its nature[19]. Most boys when I went there were the sons of service people stationed abroad and not the waifs and strays of its earlier founding. However, in deference to, or as a relic of its origins, a few waifs and strays or necessitous boys were let in. I was one. I don't know if I was a waif, but I was certainly going astray.

The full dress uniform for the Gordon boys was tartan trews or trousers. The Gordon tartan of course, spit and polished boots so you could see your face reflected in them, a navy-blue tunic with gold epaulettes, brass buttons to be meticulously polished with Brasso, later replaced by staybright buttons – hurrah for the march of technology. Topped off with a Glengarry which, if you don't know what it is, defies easy verbal description except to say that it is Scottish and it goes on your head. Each year in January, Gordon's students still parade through Whitehall following the Pipes and Drums band and take part in a service held behind the Ministry of Defence, where the statue stands to remember the life of Major-General Gordon. They are the only school permitted to march in Whitehall.

---

[19] The 'public' schools like Eton and Harrow etc have this modern-day misnomer, for they are anything but public because of their history. The book *Posh Boys* by Robert Verkaik describes their origin in his prologue. He writes, *'Britain's public schools started life in medieval times as schools for the poor … But they soon became victims of their own success and were hijacked first by the aristocracy and then by the merchant middle classes who had profited so handsomely from the country's industrial revolution'.* Their subsequent functions were not just to provide the rulers of the country but also the rulers and administrators of the British Empire, the largest empire that the world has ever seen and the corollary of this was to be prepared to fight and die leading the troops to preserve this empire.

This was the uniform of Sunday morning parade, marching up and down the square to the music of our military band, *Hearts of Oak* and *Hitler has only got one ball* – you know the sort of stuff. The Commandant – no, I'm not making the title up; you would have thought that they could have thought of something that wouldn't have made it sound like a latter-day Stalag Luft III – took the salute. On one occasion we had a visit from some high-ranking officer. He must have been at least a general because our Commandant was a brigadier, Brigadier Holbrook. The top brass arrived by helicopter. We had been standing for hours on a baking hot summer's day in full dress uniform, plus white gloves for the special occasion with our 303 rifles doing various drills; present arms, shoulder arms …, the timing always being done to mental 1,2,3, 1,2,3. Perfectly coordinated timing learnt from repeatedly barked orders from the drill sergeants that used to come from Sandhurst to take it.

Several boys fainted in the heat and had to be hauled off no doubt to the poor bastards' eternal embarrassment at having 'let the side down'. We presented arms. The General or Field Marshal, whatever he was, took the salute, conducted a racing inspection and was helicoptered off again. Such was one of the great official occasions in military school life.

It was the great unofficial occasions and events that were more interesting. The bullying, as one might expect, was merciless. But being a military school it was pretty regimented and organised. A towel one might think is merely something to dry oneself with. Not so. With juvenile but precocious inventiveness it was fashioned not into one, but a variety of weapons. The simplest was just to tie a knot in the towel. The art was to have the knot as tight as it was humanly possible to get it. This could involve one or more boys on each end heaving, tugging, and pulling with all their might to ensure the tightest and therefore the hardest knot. Another way was to twist a rolled towel round and round as if you would be ringing it dry if wet. Again, having an accomplice or accomplices was helpful.

The final one could be managed perfectly well as a solo effort. One top corner was folded across to be level with the opposite long side. The towel was then tightly rolled to form a sort of whip. When flicked like a whip the tip of the towel could inflict a not inconsiderable degree of pain – which was, after all, the object. All the boys of the dugout - the name for the dormitories - would stand on the ends of their beds with the instruments of torture in hand. Some poor sod having been picked on, would be made to run the gauntlet: up the corridor made by the ends of the beds sticking out from each side of the dormitory as blows rained down on their heads and every other part of their anatomy.

However, in the true martial spirit of fearlessness, in the face of possible pain and injury which such schools are meant to inculcate, some boys, including the oldest and hardest who certainly couldn't have been bullied into it, volunteered for this trial.

Even more 'fun' and an even greater opportunity to show bravery in the face of the enemy were the 'dap' fights. This consisted of turning beds over and making barricades at each end of the dugout. 'Daps' were the name given to plimsolls, a pair of which alongside shoes - worn during lessons - and boots, every inmate was given. The aim was to hurl daps with maximum force to hit the enemy, preferably in the head, behind barricades at the other end of the dormitory.

To successfully hurl your plimsolls, you have to put your head above the parapet as it were and look, and in doing so you provided the preferred target – your face! – for your opponent's daps. True heroism, or madness, was shown by sallying forth dap in hand from behind the protection of your barricade right up to the enemies barricade and see if you could actually deliver your missile over the top and into your opponent's face. Looking back this reminds me of the ritualised combat that used to take place in pre-industrial societies like that of the tribal people of Papua New Guinea. Lord of the Flies had nothing on this[20].

Bravery or stupidity were both keys to success in these endeavours, a combination better still, because any leaving of the protection of the barricade brought forth a hail of missiles and the closer one approached their barricade the more accurate they became. I was good at this. Not so much because my inordinate possession of the key qualities, though I did claim a pretty high rating in the stupidity stakes, but because I possessed a secret weapon.

From an early age I have been very short-sighted. I arrived at military school, a Patrick and left irretrievably a Hank. Instead of the ugly national health specs my mother, with much saving by her and no doubt badgering by me, got me a pair of black horn rimmed glasses made fashionable at the time by Hank B Marvin of The Shadows. As I came in the door, somebody said, "Hey look its Hank B Marvin" and Hank stuck. Why I say this is that in the great dap wars you obviously couldn't wear

---

[20] A bit of an exaggeration. They actually got killed in The Lord of the Flies.

your glasses. Not wearing my glasses has always been a great aid to courage. The blurring and lack of clear detail gives the outside world an air of unreality.

My myopia was a great help in chatting up a girl once when I used to be in the Portsmouth Youth Acting Theatre, and I had broken my glasses. Perhaps it was because I couldn't see her clearly, I thought she couldn't see me. It also helps when bungee jumping. Mind you, I kept them on under the goggles when parachuting to make sure I didn't lose them.

In a fight, not perceiving so accurately the dangers of the outside world is no doubt an advantage in maintaining an inner calm even if outnumbered or outgunned. However, it is sometimes more than outweighed by not being able to see other protagonists clearly. This is essential in being able to read the signs, for example to be able to get to the right distance/place to deliver a punch. You can normally see trouble coming and getting in first and accurately is more than helpful. If there is going to be violence, getting in second is a very bad idea indeed. I never take my glasses off in a fight. What, never? Well hardly ever. It would be an obvious signal of trouble, so you have been warned. But I stray into another chapter.

The Gordon school for boys was surprisingly radical politically. With many military officer fathers, political views often going in families, one might have expected a fairly conservative lot. But the overwhelming view there was strongly supportive of Labour - old Labour as it was then – at the time of Harold Wilson. In the class war that was waged in the outside world we had an instinctive support for the underdog. I don't know if this was a sort of on-going cultural memory from when the school population was the sons of the poor or an external reflection of the internal class war that was on-going within the school. Our aim was to engage in combat with the system and with the rules and the officers that ran it.

You were not allowed to take food out of the cookhouse. One boy in our house – Khartoum – there were four altogether the others being China, Woolwich and Gravesend – had smuggled bread out of the cookhouse and bread smuggling was strictly against the rules. He also smuggled a toaster into school, also not allowed, and was caught making toast after lights out, even more not allowed, by the night Div, short for division. Basically, one bloke whose aim was to stamp out any night-time nefarious culinary or sexual activity. The toast-maker got eleven strokes of the cane for his crimes.

I only managed to get a couple of strokes. You had to kneel over some chairs back to back and got them on the arse. They left a good bruise and sometimes a bloody mark. My crime? We were allowed an occasional pass to wander the local environs at weekends during the day. A boy or some boys had found some dirty photographs that had been dumped or lost on the nearby Cobham common. At least that was their story. It was pretty poor quality porn but wildly exciting to 'locked up', generally girl-free teenage boys. They were distributed at small fees and viewed under the bed covers by torchlight to provide good wanking material – not that adolescent boys need any excuse to masturbate. I remember once managing it eight times in one day.

An offending pupil was caught in possession, grassed up the rest of us, who then owned up and had the salacious material confiscated as well as getting caned of course. I learned a valuable lesson, though not the one they had in mind. If they accuse you of drinking a cup of tea deny it – and keep denying it. I made this mistake once more – my coup de main or coup de grace or whatever you call it which I shall recount shortly.

One other event, or reported event, because there were no witnesses, that vividly stirred the sexual imagery and fantasising of the inmates, should be mentioned. The school had a school nurse. She was young and good-looking. One of the better built and better looking boys had caught a full speed cricket ball in the nuts. Having later experienced this dubious pleasure myself, let me assure you the pain is literally breath-taking. Off this boy went to see the school nurse.

What a wondrous tale he later returned with. The school nurse apparently on inspecting the damaged area had declared his penis needed to be manipulated to make sure everything was still in working order and proceeded to wank him. This may be a recognised medical procedure – nurses reading this, please let me know. But it sounds unlikely to me. As I said he may have been lying, but we believed him utterly and I still do. After all, where else would a female nurse with desires for young boys want to get a job but a boys' boarding school? I know the great pain and psychological damage that can be caused by sexual abuse and this applies by women to boys as well as by men to girls. But the fact of this situation was that the vast majority boys in the school would have given their right arm, or perhaps the left, to have been in his place.

The rebelliousness at the school, which was to contribute to my eventual demise, was evinced by one unusual practice.

"ZONKER!" an anonymous inmate would shout. A strange projectile would arch through the air heavenward like a rocket. No sooner was the word *Zonker* emitted than the whole of the assembled boys sitting down eating a meal in the cookhouse would take up the chant *Zonker, Zonker, Zonker!* This was done under your breath with lips frozen like a ventriloquist to avoid identification. At the same time, we would beat a thunderous tattoo with our hands on the underside of the dining tables in accompaniment. The zonker for those of you who don't know, which I presume will be many, was fashioned out of silver foil, I guess taken from packets of cigarettes which, though contraband, circulated. These were rolled into a hollow tube and the front end of the tube was pinched and twisted still leaving a hollow area at that end which was filled with margarine, nicked naturally from the cookhouse. This gave the projectile sufficient mass, hopefully, when hurled forcefully, to reach the very high ceiling of the cookhouse, yet sufficient viscosity from the margarine tip for it to stay attached to the ceiling. I presume from time to time they must've brought scaffolding in to remove this unwanted ceiling decoration – otherwise given the long history of a school on the site after its move from its previous location, the entire ceiling would have been one zonker Sistine chapel.

The Nazis showed, or rather those fighting them in some of the occupied areas and countries, that if the level of resistance was high enough and – most importantly – collective enough, no level of group punishment was sufficient to quell rebellion. And thus it was. Remember that teacher – don't let it get to that stage or you're finished.

Food had been stolen from the cookhouse and a half eaten sandwich had been posted through the Commandant's letterbox. Luckily they didn't have DNA testing in those days. The regime's guardians were in a heightened state of alert. Then another outrageous act of sacrilege was committed. In the grounds of the school was a life-size bronze statue of General Charles Gordon on a camel. The school had a military band, which used to accompany us during some of our marching parades and drills. They used to have white belts with shiny brass buckles. The belts were kept pristine white by being covered with a white goo, called blanco, that was applied wet and then dried. It also came in a green khaki colour for our Combined Cadet Force uniforms as we were in the army section.

Nameless individuals had decided that the illustrious general and his camel would look a lot more attractive covered in white blanco. Unfortunately for the administration, but not the individuals concerned, the nameless individuals remained nameless. This unspeakable atrocity went unpunished, but a general clampdown ensued. The regime determinedly plotted revenge. The next caught transgressors would face their unbridled wrath.

Step forward 'Hank' Roberts and 'Griff' Griffiths. I don't think I had got into this out of entrepreneurial spirit, something I've have always distinctly lacked, but more out of a sense of danger and excitement and of course rebelliousness, which I've never been short of.

As we walked into the local pub, we realised that chance had dealt us a fateful, even fatal, blow. My mate who entered the pub first was a crack shot with the rifle team. My short sight made me an honorary American – that is more likely to shoot my own side than the enemy, and definitely not a candidate for the school's rifle shooting team. The officer who ran the team recognised Griff instantly and ordered him to report to the Commandant in the morning. We had been engaged in a business enterprise of smuggling booze into the school to be consumed by fellow inmates and adding a small fee for our clearly dangerous efforts. When Griff, in horror, caught the officer's eye as he entered the pub and had stared transfixed like a rabbit before a snake or caught in headlights for what must have been milli-seconds but seemed like an age, I had smartly turned round and bolted back out of the door. As we came in, I too had recognised the officer, but in nanoseconds had reversed my trajectory. Maybe my reactions were quicker than Griff's, maybe because, unlike Griff, I didn't know him very well, nor he me, the horror of discovery was not so great. I was out in a flash. Griff soon joined me.

For Griff the die was cast. He had no option but to report the Commandant next morning as he had been instructed to by the Officer. On the other hand, I hadn't been spoken to. Had he even seen me or seen that someone was with Griff? I figured that probably he had, but would he recognise me? I debated with Griff on the way back and in my head the possibility of not reporting in the morning – or denial. I could temporarily lose my glasses I thought. Perhaps then there was a chance that even if he had seen me he wouldn't recognise me. I didn't think that suddenly going around without glasses when I always wore them might be a bit of a giveaway.

No, I'd do the decent thing. We'd be in the shit together. By lunchtime the next day I was on a non-return train journey back to Portsmouth and Griff on a similar one-way plane ticket to Changi Air Force base in the Far East. Expelled! There's a lesson here as I've said. IF THEY ACCUSE YOU OF DRINKING A CUP OF TEA DENY IT. It was an inmate who thoughtfully wrote to me après le deluge that our expulsions were a devastating blow to Khartoum's chances of winning the cross-country championship. We had both been in the team. This is not irony. It was thoughtful and much appreciated.

Just prior to us being marched into the Commandant's office to receive our marching orders, the housemaster railed at us about our crimes, out of bounds, out after lights out, in a pub, under aged, in civilian clothing - we were not allowed to have these during term time. The latter seemed particularly to enrage him and as a parting gift he gave Griff a belt round the head. He eyed me with clear thoughts of doing the same but then thought better of it. A wise move. In trouble or not, I wouldn't wear it and in the event had mentally prepared for combat. I guess it showed.

I loved the Gordon Boys School, but all good things come to an end. Brigadier Holbrook, I would like to thank you personally for instilling in me that willingness to obey orders, to follow commands and respect for one's superior officers that a military school education brings. If you are still alive and read this, you will see how well it worked for me!!

An interesting post script to this is that I was invited back to the school to speak during my ATL presidential sequence. No, this wasn't to give a motivational speech on how an expellee managed to make good, but to speak in opposition to a proposal for the school to become an academy. My call to arms came to naught. The present staff alas were not as rebellious as the previous inmates. I have a bit of fun though, telling them that I had been expelled from the school, and also caned in a room adjoining the hall where the meeting was taking place.

But my expulsion had come too late. I had already received a good education and learnt some of life's best lessons.

REBEL WITHOUT A PAUSE

Chapter Five
PORTSMOUTH REVISITED

I'd returned to a yobbo hellhole – a spiritual home. But where would I be fitted in? I'd failed my 11+ so couldn't go to the grammar school, but at the Gordon Boys I'd been following a GCE course so consigning me to the preselected factory fodder of the secondary moderns was problematic for them. Fortunately, there was one secondary modern, and only one, in Portsmouth which had a class doing GCEs – Hilsea Secondary Modern. I joined it.

With my mouth, unwillingness to back down and distinct lack of humility it didn't take long to attract the attention of those who saw, as I did, status defined by who can beat up whom. The local alleged school hard nut was waiting outside school to take me on, bravely carrying a hammer. I was willing if he was minus the hammer, but he not so bravely declined to play, nor to simply wade in with the hammer. I was established.

I regularly turned up to school – and the evening classes they ran. Unlike my youngest brother Pete, who famously turned up at school to be told "*Roberts, what are you doing here? You've left!*" He had been an Easter 15-year-old school leaver - before ROSLA - Raising Of the School Leaving Age - and had turned up to school one day during the summer term. He had been bunking school so much and so consistently he didn't even know he'd left! I only bunked off school once as I recall, to go haring around Portsmouth illegally on a mate's borrowed scooter.

At Hilsea Modern I became a prefect. One day I was told that the headmaster wanted to see me because a boy had been put in detention - prefects could do that – but not by a non-prefect. It was, however, written in my detention book. A fifth form – year 11 – friend, 'Kridge' real name Keith Ridge, had asked to borrow my book and written this poor sod's name in it. He apparently had annoyed him. I quickly squared it with him that he would have to say that he took it without my permission, or me knowing that he had written this boy's name in the book. The headteacher Mr Spence bought the lie - you see I had learnt something from the Gordon Boys – or if he didn't, like many married women of suspiciously late or frequently out husbands or visa versa, was not moved to question too closely. He said to me, "As this has been satisfactorily resolved, I have the greatest pleasure in making you deputy head boy". It probably should have been deputy head liar. Later

I would lie for England. Well, not literally. Not that I was a natural never mind compulsive liar, or even that I had any desire to. I have a tendency to say exactly what I think sometimes not even realising, or if I do, not caring that it might be inappropriate or even offensive. I actually dislike lying. I did it as an intellectual exercise to be able to get away with something I wanted to do. Like later going out with as many women as possible at the same time – that I knew I could not do by telling the truth.

Part of their thinking I think in making me deputy head boy was that in a school full of yobbos who better to have as deputy head boy than the leading, but reasonably intelligent, yobbo. It was at Hilsea that my generally left political leanings, though I regard the current so-called left right divide as false, started to become more radical. A fellow pupil Reevo was a self-proclaimed Communist. We talked and shared some views. I began to ponder on the state of the country and indeed the world, what is and what might be.

I left with six O-levels. The teachers at Hilsea, like most teachers at most schools had done a sterling job. I'd mostly stayed out of trouble – in school at least - only being caned once. I was the vice-captain of the school athletics team and had failed to turn up for practice, along with a few others. We were asked what our excuses were. Others dutifully proffered their porkies. I, arrogant as usual, said something like "I haven't got one and I don't need one". I contemptuously held out my hands to be caned. Bloody hurt but be dammed if macho man or rather macho boy was going to show it. Bring back the cane? Sorry, as if that ever stopped anyone, certainly not the ones most likely to offend which was meant to be the object of the exercise. Soon I was off to the Northern Grammar school.

Northern Grammar.

Claim to fame. James Callaghan, Prime Minister was educated there. Second claim to fame. I went there - can't you take a joke? Unfortunately, I failed O-Level English and though I could take A-levels I wouldn't get into any college or many jobs without it. I had to take it again. First time I had failed with the second lowest grade. Second time I triumphed – the lowest grade. This clearly wasn't working. Lateral thinking was needed. Bingo. I applied to take the exam at an external private college, or rather, I persuaded a friend to – using my name – turn up and take the exam for me – successfully. Well, I knew he was good which was why I asked him. Thanks by the way. I couldn't have got to college, progressed at the time to get a degree, or become a teacher without you. I don't suggest this as a career path generally, but I think that it is very important to have a system that does not exclude late developers or people who might be very good at or have great potential in something but can't pass English, or maths at the required grade. Einstein, for example, was a very slow developer.

I could say that I won't name my exam helper to protect you, but in truth, I've forgotten your name[21]. I do remember, however, that your father was a policeman and you told me he had a gun at home. We discussed 'borrowing' it and using it to rob an off-licence. Fortunately, this particular schoolboy fantasy came to naught or my life might have taken a very different turn.

Another turn that might have changed my life was also happening at this time. I starred in a couple of films produced and directed by another pupil at the school. That director was Michael J Murphy who went on to become a film director of over 25 horror fantasy films and is regarded by many as the number one B movie cult director of his time[22]. He died in 2015. The films I was in were *The Legend* and *Theseus and Minotaur*. Michael sent off some rushes of me to some film studio bigwigs as he thought I had some promise. Unfortunately, they responded that I blinked too much. How blinking unfair – I might have become a film legend.

---

[21] I was subsequently reminded of it by my long-term mate Barrie. His surname was Scorey. We nicknamed him Tory Scorey for self-evident reasons but he was a good bloke.
[22] See YouTube for 'Very Rare Interview With Cult Director Michael J Murphy'

Just to update you on my living circumstances over this time. My marching orders came from what might appear a quite trivial matter, indeed in my eyes it was. My stepfather Norman came into the front room to find me on top of my then girlfriend Cathy who I'd met at the Portsmouth Youth Acting Theatre. Now if I had been screwing her, even then I don't think I should have been thrown out, but I wasn't – needless to say a lifelong regret Cathy. I was waiting for her to turn 16. Isn't it typical? For once in your life you do the decent thing and then spend the rest of your life regretting it. Before she reached 16 and before we had sex she'd met someone else with fewer scruples and more charm, and more importantly a car, and that was it. I did at least spend many happy hours fingering you on Portsdown Hill. You might like to know, you most likely still being alive as you were younger than me, that such a fond memory and attraction for the name Cathy was thus established in me, that we named our daughter after you, though a K was substituted for a C[23]. This was with Jean's full knowledge and understanding. Jean your tolerance is without equal – thank goodness.

Anyhow, out I went homeless and penniless. Fortunately, it was just before the summer holidays. I scrounged food off friends and started sleeping in an underground cellar called The Den at the Victoria Road Methodist church where I had been a scout in 51st Hants Troop. You would have to get in and out via a small slit like hole. I think they poured coal down this vent when the church heating was coal fired. It was damp and murky but better than the streets. The woman who ran the Portsmouth Youth Acting Theatre heard about my predicament and said that her husband was a farmer and I could live and work there over the summer.

Welcome to chicken farming and chicken shit. Factory farming, though I didn't recognise it then, is pretty appalling. Now don't get me confused with animal rights extremists and anti-vivisection. If a bit of animal cruelty is necessary to save human lives or to feed a country so be it. I just think the less of it the better. The depth of my concern is shown by the fact I haven't stopped eating anything. I would add, however, that you've got to, or should have, your priorities right. Animals and humans are not equivalent or equal. However, wanton cruelty to sentient creatures is never justified.

---

[23] Jean said that Cathy was the heroine of one of her favourite books, *Wuthering Heights*. She wanted Catherine for this reason, but thought the K was more classy than the C.

To quote from Chopper 3, by Mark Brandon Read, Australia's most notorious criminal and considered by many to be mad, is worthy of serious thought and consideration. Though he is talking about Australia the general point I believe has relevance.

He writes, "*It seems to me that the modern political scene is … at times controlled, by small lobby groups. They are made up of blinkered people convinced that their single interest issue is the most important thing in the world.*

While the greenies are saving our wildlife, forests and waterways our children are dying in the gutters and back alleys of the nation of drug addiction. While the gay lobby is fighting hard for their political rights, and various women's groups are kicking up a storm, children[24] are hocking their bums and fannies' in the brothels, massage parlours and escort services of this country.

No one seems to care about what really matters."

If we set aside the hyperbole, out of the mouths of madness, if he is indeed mad, sometimes comes the germs of essential truths that most, accepting of the class and money driven manufactured consensus fail to see and ignore. This is because it is more difficult to confront fundamental truth and face up to what this requires of us.

Why does the RSPCA get more in donations than the NSPCC? And why is it Royal for animals and not for children? Is it important who owns your county? Does not ownership give control, and is it not important to control your own country?

Are we not pleased that Hitler did not successfully invade Britain establishing de facto ownership and control, or that no foreign power has since 1066? Maybe drug addiction, and the destroyed lives of individuals and families, and the deaths and crime associated with it, or child prostitution should not be the top of our list of concerns, though God knows they should be pretty high. But have we got our priorities right?

Don't get me wrong. Many pressure groups do excellent work on important matters, but it is a question of priorities. Yes, we need a life

---

[24] At least child sex abuse is, somewhat belatedly, being taken seriously in the UK, the establishment, churches and authorities having covered it up for decades.

and having relaxation and enjoyment is right, proper and a necessary part of that. Lager, sex, and table football have certainly been priorities of mine and of the things that you like to do, provided they don't harm other people, I can't see any natural hierarchy. But of the things that you oppose, of the things that you're prepared to act and fight against, surely there should be a hierarchy? Humans and the wrongful and harmful shortening of lives and the lessening of pain and suffering should be at the very top.

Of course we should act to lessen cruel treatment of animals by humans and keeping them in cruel conditions, but our top priority should be our own species. Why? Because you only start from where you are. An animal rights fanatic might be prepared to be tortured and die themselves rather than see it happen to an animal, but it would be odd even for an animal lover to be prepared to sacrifice a father/mother/sister/brother/son/daughter to save an animal. Evolution equipped humans with the highest degree of empathy of any species and it extends outwards from the family to other humans and out from human kind to other animals. This was true even with hunter gatherers who killed to eat.[25]

Cruelty to animals is a behaviour pattern commonly associated with emerging serial killers[26] and serial rapists. Our natural aura of empathy spreads beyond our species and its notable lack on the fringes tends to project back to the core. Psychopaths lack empathy.

So back to the chickens. The chickens were packed in metal cages, barely room to move, each having a space about the size of a page of A4 paper. Wire bars as flooring so that the chicken shit could drop straight through. It was accumulated in vast lagoons. It was spread over fields as manure but there was still too much of it. The stench of acrid ammonia wafted for miles. Parts of the surface had baked rock hard, dried by the sun. Barrie, my mate you will hear about shortly, came to visit me on the farm and cat curious, or perhaps plain unthinking, walked over it. He promptly sank up to his knees in rancid chicken shit. Howling laughter. Good job it wasn't deeper! Drowning in chicken shit. Imagine

---

[25] And it extends back the same way. It is well known that a higher level of sentience and consciousness in animals elicits more human empathy. Even the animal rights fanatics don't put the entire membership of the Animal Kingdom on a par. Harming or killing insects and bacteria is not the same as doing it to say a cat or a dog.

[26] See the book *Psychopaths* by John Clarke and Andy Shea. Part of the so called homicidal triad. Three behaviours commonly observed in childhood of serial killers/rapists. The other 2 being pyromania (obsession with fire) and enuresis (continued bed wetting after 9-10 years).

that on your death certificate. Cause of death – drowned in chicken shit. Not exactly a glorious end.

Pigs are much worse. One pig out craps a human - tenfold. This creates huge waste disposal and pollution problems. Factory pig farming isn't exactly a holiday camp either. They are tied to metal rails so they can barely move and can't turn around. I've seen it first hand when taking kids on field trips to farms including a pig farm. The good news is that pig shit smells like Chanel No 5 compared to chickens.

Through overcrowding, the chickens used to peck each other, sometimes to death. Feathers would be missing and their backside would be a bleeding mess. Sometimes the chicken itself would turn around and peck at its own open wound. You're right, chickens aren't exactly bright. With due respect to Snowball in Animal Farm, all animals are not created equal. Beaks used to be clipped; this, with no comment on the rights or wrongs of this, is said to cut down the harming and self-harming, but that didn't stop it.

There was one curious thing that most people won't know. How many of you have worked on a chicken farm? If you catch a chicken and lay it on its front flat down and turn its head to the side also flat down on the floor, it will stay there. I was and am curious as to the physiology of this. Can someone help?

I was taught to drive a tractor but self-evidently not well enough. I parked it on a slope forgetting to put the hand brake on and dismounted. I stared in mounting horror as it rolled downwards, gathering speed, and demolished half of one of the chicken sheds.

Though not exactly overjoyed, the farmer Mr Cook took it well considering

The summer holiday came to an end. I had to return to school to complete my A Levels. Being a good socialist, Mr Cook paid me the full agricultural union rate for a farm labourer of my age so I had some money, but even at full union rates, agricultural labourers' wages were pitifully low.

Barrie knew someone on his milk round who wanted to let a room so I left the farm – with thanks to them, it was kind - and moved into rented accommodation and off I went to school everyday. This went on for a number of weeks until the money ran out. Then it was back to the church cellar. Food was not a problem, my mates helped but I should say that my main mates, though working mainly, all lived at home. For Barrie, Terry, and Reevo in relatively small houses with no spare room whatsoever, an additional lodger was not a practical possibility.

As those who descend into trampdom know, keeping clean and tidy without money is difficult if not impossible. I'd leave the church cellar early each morning and return late at night. Monday to Friday I'd get a lift into school from Barrie or Terry. I think my gradually more dishevelled look was noticed by my teachers or perhaps they were told by or overheard a 6th former saying *Hank Roberts is living in a church cellar'.*

I moved again. One of the teachers was kind enough to take me in. He lived in Clanfield some way outside of Portsmouth. Mr Connor had a big 750cc Royal Enfield motorbike with sidecar and used to drive me in it each day to and from school. How cool was that. Eventually my parents got to hear about it and contributed to my keep.

As my education progressed so did my political radicalism – and my alternative career as a yob.

Politics first. One holiday while in the sixth form, I intrepidly packed a rucksack and set off relatively aimlessly working my way by hitch hiking westwards. At some stage I walked through Ringwood in Hampshire and someone, a youth, was handing out leaflets entitled 'The Trend'. It talked about how all over the world there was a trend to revolution, to socialism, to communism. At that time, it was true – or appeared so. It said that the world, or rather the capitalist world, was not just. You didn't have to be a genius to work that one out. And that the world including Britain could be organised in a better way. I might have cheated to get GCE English, but I was clever enough or perhaps just youthful enough to not only see the glaring obviousness of this, but willing to try and do something about it. I phoned the YCL (Young Communist League).

I announced my thinking and intention to do this to my parents. Both counselled caution or gave cautious counselling, but to give them credit neither said no. Wisely, as I would undoubtedly have ignored them and then held it against them. I got an address and turned up. "Barrie Jennings", I queried? "Yes mate, come in; would you like a cup of tea?" Now this might seem minor, but to me this was astounding, dumbfounding. Here was somebody who didn't know me from Adam, having not only no idea who I was, but no idea what I wanted, inviting me in and offering me a cup of tea. It was totally characteristic of somebody who is an entirely good bloke and who would do anything for a mate or indeed a stranger. Barrie was a milkman. He later worked his way by sheer dint of effort through Highbury technical college O-levels, then A-levels, did a degree in Russian Studies at Birmingham University, then worked in Russia as a translator. When he returned to England, he worked for the railways and finally qualified as a chartered accountant. To cap it all, he was illegitimate when it still meant something, then carrying a serious social stigma. He was brought up by Kath, his aunt. She was the epitome of kindness and would make any of the waifs and strays Barrie's politics brought into the house, feel welcome and completely at home.

The membership of our small group consisted of Barrie, Reevo, who had gone into the print industry, Jeff Beatty who I had met through the Portsmouth Youth Acting Theatre, and two Jewish girls Lorraine and Carol Shaw. Also, Steve Bonner who was a mechanic, and others more on the periphery who came and went. One was a sailor who had deserted – and his girlfriend who didn't have a political thought in her body – but what a body! An ex-catholic schoolgirl – aren't they just the best when they fall from grace. At least they understand the wickedness of sin enough to really enjoy it.

Apart from meetings, with their discussions and arguments; the Chinese/ Russian split, Czechoslovakia, the nature of the Soviet Union then and under Stalin, activity was pretty unfocused and desultory. Once, a dance was organised by the Southampton branch of the YCL somewhere or other on the West side of Southampton. Our band, The Fiends, were booked to play. We got there well late. Hardly anyone was present; we didn't even bother to set up and play.

Leafleting; especially when Stan Figg, a notable local communist, stood for the Council and inevitably lost. Another local communist was Jim Riordan. He was the step brother of my mate Terry. He was a big cheese in the local Communist Party. Jim had a fascinating life which he recounts in his book, *Comrade Jim: the Spy who Played for Spartak*. When he died in 2012 there was an obituary on Last Words, the BBC Radio 4 programme.

We attended demonstrations in London. There were plenty to choose from – Apartheid in South Africa, Unilateral Declaration of Independence (UDI) in Rhodesia, the Vietnam war etc. I will relate the story of just two of them beginning with the one when I had actually left school and was at Highbury College.

I had worked weekend nights at a well dangerous late-night food and coffee stall right outside the main dockyard gate. I witnessed many a ferocious punch-up. Equal opportunities though; the women, many of whom were prostitutes, were at it almost as much as the men. Mr Bayliss, the man that ran it, kept a large knife handy in case things got completely out of hand. I heard that he once slammed the steel shutter down on some ne'er-do-well's arm which had entered too far inside the kiosk. I can't remember from the story, whether it had entered for the purpose of aggression or theft or a combination of both. The shutter broke the said arm so I heard.

Taking my life in my hands and working nights there, had earned me enough money to buy a Ford van. I couldn't drive of course, but my mates had persuaded me it would be a good laugh and useful and Barrie or someone else with a licence could drive.

We drove up to London in it for a demo. Needless to say we had been completely conned. It drank more oil than petrol, literally. On the way we had to make regular stops at petrol stations to get cans of oil. Dave, my brother, was then an expert shoplifter – he'd been thrown out of home on his 16th birthday with nowhere to live and no visible means of support so had been forced into it as a means to survive. He helpfully nicked a couple of cans of oil. On that demonstration, or perhaps it was another, he got himself nicked.

At a time when it was fashionable for men to have long hair, his hair was cropped short. This was because of recently spending a short time at her majesty's pleasure at Haslar Detention Centre in Gosport – he'd been nicked for stealing 115 pork pies at a rate of one a day. Beefed up from the regular food and exercise and wearing a Mac he looked just like a special branch/plain clothes cop. In the melee between demonstrators and police outside the South African Embassy, believing him to be one of them, they had linked arms with him. The disconcerted rejection of such advances and the struggle to unlink his arms alerted the plods to the chameleon in their midst and he was nicked along with many others. Fortunately, he was later released without charge. What could they say? – 'because you refused to link arms with us' or 'we arrested you because you looked like one of us but weren't!'

I want to say here that like some other wayward youths growing up in a very troubled environment, Dave subsequently became virtually a model citizen and was never on the wrong side of the law again. He also is a great father and grandfather which is more than can be said for me. Which is not to say he leads a boring life. Now he's retired he's out all the time playing gigs with his band Loose Change and I have to say they are really good.

On the journey back, the van eventually and irretrievably died, but fortuitously just on the outskirts of Portsmouth. We pushed it off the main road onto some road works and left it. The police called some considerable time later. Apparently, my van was parked on a newly opened roundabout and was causing an obstruction. We managed to get it back to Copnor where we lived. It stayed parked there for many weeks if not months until the police finally complained again. It had however by then more than earned its keep. Jean, my future wife, was pretending to her parents that she was staying at my parents' house. Instead we were sleeping and shagging in the van.

The other escapade was travelling to another demonstration whilst I was still at Northern Grammar. This launched me into a self-inflicted quagmire. Reevo and I bunked the train and got caught. We were arrested but this time there was no release without charge. The strategy of hiding in the toilet for most of the journey proved to be a less than satisfactory one. The fine I believe was between £11 or £13, not as laughable as it would appear remembering this was the late 60s, but the fine was the least of my problems.

The police turned up at the house and spoke to Mr Connor and his wife. I was confronted. I did what seemed the right thing, as opposed to the decent thing, and lied. It hadn't been me it had been my mate Reevo who gave a false name and address – mine - but he'd owned up to me and would tell the police/court so it would be OK. They believed me and I thought *job done*. Unfortunately, a summons came through the door, which I didn't spot to be able to intercept, and suspicions were raised again.

I continued to protest my innocence with that wide eyed hurt look that is always a good guide to lying to those that can tell. Double or quits. My ever fertile mind for excuses or explanations to weasel out of something hit on a master stroke. My mate Barrie would ring the headmaster at the school pretending to be the police and say that there had been a mix up. Patrick Roberts was innocent and there had been a case of impersonation. When Barrie rang, the Headteacher Mr Hanson sympathised with the 'police officer' and they roundly agreed what a problem I was. However, the case of mistaken identity was a non-runner. A rolling stone gathers no moss. Inevitably I was moving on again. The Connor's finally decided that their altruism was at an end and quite reasonably so. As no-one else would have me – my parents had to take me back.

Chapter Six
VIOLENCE

We humans have an inherent potential for violence. The genetically conveyed predisposition is not equal by sex or within a gender and is accompanied by a hormone testosterone which decreases in intensity as a human being ages. But it is there and undeniable. In every human society ever studied, it has existed. Chimps kill. In the wild they have been filmed killing[27] as well as fighting and bullying. Bonobos (pygmy chimpanzee) do a lot more shagging than fighting, more of the former and less of the latter than us. Oh, for the life of a bonobo! Another relevant fact about them is that after several decades of observation never has rape, infanticide, war or murder been witnessed among Bonobos. Not in the wild. Not in the zoo. Never[28]. Our genetic legacy is somewhere between our two nearest relatives. Our superior intellect has not relegated violence to only a matter of choice. We couldn't all simply choose to be non-violent and have a world of passive individuals. We have not, Spock or Data like, left our emotions entirely behind[29]. Nor is it simply explicable by upbringing.

Rousseau's noble savage[30], living in pre-industrial peace and Robert Owen's model of cooperative societies where good education and upbringing would remove the causes of violence and crime to boot, were an inspiring response to the diabolical conditions workers endured under early capitalism, but alas were Utopian as complete solutions. This did not mean that a better society could not, or should not, have been built; only that its building would lower the level of violence or even abolish state level violence, but it would not end all individual violence. Further, it doesn't benefit a capitalist society to have everyone being non-violent individuals – who would be the cannon fodder?

Having said that, no one should mistake me for one moment as arguing that war is inevitable or caused by human nature. War is the product of the development of a class society and will in the future disappear with it. The abolition of individual violence will require some mechanical or biochemical suppression or alteration of a basic facet of our human

---

[27] Steven Pinker's book *The Bitter Angels of our own Nature* has made the case that per capita meeting a violent death has (despite the carnage of world wars and numerous more local conflicts) been in decline. This is been strongly challenged by Christopher Ryan and Cacilda Jetha in *Sex at Dawn*
[28] Information from *Sex at Dawn*.
[29]Spock in the space adventure Star Trek was a Vulcan who did not have human emotions and in the later series Data was an android with the same lack. I think that not allowing emotions to cloud things that require rational judgement is a very useful ability.
[30] In fact Rousseau never used this phrase.

behaviour before it is eradicated completely. Scientific research of causes will not only enlighten us, but assist with its lessening and, ultimately, eradication. Interestingly I attended a lecture hosted by the Oxford University research group researching violence. A centrepiece of the lecture was research done by a Professor Andrew Larsen of Marquette University in Wisconsin, USA.

Larsen's research uncovered that, between 1209 and 1399, a very high level of violence and homicides occurred in Oxford. The reasons for this included, first the youthfulness of the University students mainly involved. Youth has a direct and high correlation with violent behaviour. Second, the assailants or combatants very often had swords i.e. they were armed. Thirdly, frequently the fighting was between an 'in group' and an 'out group'. Students were divided from each other by 'nation'. In this case northern and southern. Northern being Scotland, Northern England and the Midlands. Southern being Ireland, London and Wales. Fourthly, they were all male. A similar situation applies today with the level and nature of youth gang violence. Then like now alcohol contributed to it greatly. Nowadays there are other contributory factors of course, for example drug taking, 'off rolling' pupils from schools and poverty.

You may want to skip what follows and go onto the next chapter. You have been warned. It is not a pretty picture.

An ignoble start

As befits the eldest brother, my career in violence began with bullying my youngest brother. Again, as befits the eldest brother, the bullying was often done second hand. "*Bash Pete*", I would order Dave and off Dave would reluctantly go to administer the required bashing for fear of getting one himself if he didn't. Yes, I know it was unfair but *so is life*. No Pete really, I'm sorry. I know how much it got to you by the fact that you regularly remind me, and all who will listen to you, of the time when I came home and caught you eating a sandwich. I grabbed it out of your hand and took a bite. "*That's butter*", I said, "*you're not supposed to eat butter*" and I gave you a bash. You were supposed to have the marge which I didn't like. Mind you, you weren't the only one to get it. With our Dad dying young, our Mum had a few 'uncles' before she met 'Uncle' Norman whom she married. One of the 'uncles' had a son who came to live with us for a while when we lived in Albert Grove in Southsea. We nicknamed him *Beatnik,* and as king of the roost I asserted myself in that unfortunate time honoured fashion of bullying him too. If you read this, sorry Beatnik.

At primary school, Albert Road Juniors, I fought with everybody, and, as mentioned earlier, including my teacher Mr Roper on one occasion, and made my way to the top of the greasy pole, or should that be pecking order. My formidable temper, which fighting with a teacher might well hint at, was illustrated in my primary school years by me returning from Southsea Common to my grandmother's house in Inglis Road, Portsmouth and promptly getting the carving knife out of the drawer. My intention at the time was clear and unequivocal. Murder. I intended to return to Southsea Common, where I had had a fight, to finish them off. My grandmother spying this sight enquired as to what I was doing with her carving knife. When I straightforwardly explained what I intended to do she replied as only a grandmother would, *"not with my knife you're not!"*.

Returning from Bermuda to be the oldest male in the family and being the male head of the family in my and my brothers' eyes, if not my Mum's, controlling me and what I did, started to become increasingly hard. I was getting bigger and stronger. My mother resorted to trying to sit on me but it didn't work, certainly not for long. Hitting me also was not much use as, with a true anti ageist and anti-sexist fashion, I hit back. My transfer to secondary school showed every sign of continuing the upwards or rather downwards spiral. Start a new climb up the pecking order - the fight with a leery[31] second year - and a growing disinclination to do anything I was told to by my mother or anyone else for that matter. So it was off to military school. As they say, a problem shared is a problem halved. A problem passed on, is a problem removed.

You can't teach an old dog new tricks they say: well you might be able to but it is much harder to get a dog to stop behaving like a dog. My first fight at the Gordon School for Boys happened no sooner than I'd set foot in the place. Shock, horror; I was not invincible. I lost. At least it was to someone else called Roberts. He was considerably taller than me but lanky. My excuse, manufactured in retrospect, was that he obviously completed his pubescent growth spurt before me. But indisputably I had lost. It was a severe blow to my youthful arrogance. Fortunately, such a humiliation wasn't to occur again in quite the same way. I lost in one of our school boxing matches, but he was a year above me, a trained boxer and in the school boxing team, so it doesn't count. At least, not in

---

[31] Written leery but the ee is pronounced as an *'air'* at least in Portsmouth

my putting the most favourable to myself construction on all events[32]. This is not to say that I haven't had a good battering on occasions but it's been because the opposition has been mob handed. How unfair! Oops … I should remember life's not fair.

I got a good kicking from a couple of marines when I challenged them to a fight in the Indigo Vat nightclub in Hampshire Terrace[33]. We used to bunk in by climbing over a wall and onto the roof to the toilets at the back, dropping in as it were. My mate, who was the drummer in our group The Fiends, was with me but not being a fighter, he took the very wise decision of deciding not to join in.

Another time was when I was doing A Levels at Northern Grammar, a bright young spark, what one would call an entrepreneur, was hiring bands, hiring out venues and making bucks. He also needed to hire bouncers. Being the acknowledged hard man of the 6th form – yes, I know it wasn't exactly difficult - I was asked and as money was offered, I accepted. Now being a bouncer in Portsmouth, especially in those days, you were pretty much guaranteed to earn your money, and it was not something that school boy amateurs should try lightly, especially without backup as I was soon to find out. A gang of Pompey yobs (the best, or perhaps, as I said earlier, equalled by Millwall) perceiving with that rare intellectual prescience that only Pompey yobs can have, that I was 'on the door' though actually inside the dance hall at the time, proceeded to make their view known by hitting me over the head with a chair amongst other things. This necessitated a trip to the hospital for a set of stitches in my head. This has been, shall we say, a not infrequent experience in my life and not the least of potential embarrassments, when with ultimately impending baldness, will be the spaghetti junction landscape that will adorn my naked pate.

During my time at Northern Grammar, I frequented youth clubs - yes they had lots of them then, Government. I remember at one a degree of altercation between me and a local hard nut was stopped by the youth workers. They must have regularly done boxing at the club. I don't think you get this nowadays, but what I do remember is that one of the hard

---

[32] Depressed people have a much more accurate view of themselves/their abilities and how others see them. Having an overly high estimation of one's own abilities, looks, intelligence etc. is an evolutionary adaptive survival mechanism. In a life and death survival situation a realistic appreciation of your abilities and chances of survival if low would not help. Most people in questionnaires say they are above average drivers, have above average looks, intelligence etc.

[33] The last name it had was Scandals. This closed in 2016 and student accommodation has been built on the site. However, the club reopened as Zanzi in Guildhall Walk. Party on!

nut young adult youth worker's suggested that we sorted it out head to head in the club. "*Boxing or wrestling*?" he asked. My opponent who I have to say seemed to fancy himself and his chances more than me wanted wrestling. OK by me. A good stranglehold. Nothing quite like it for me, short of a head butt which is not allowed in an officially refereed wrestling match. Anyhow, he lost which is just a slightly more modest way of saying I won.

On the circuit of Portsmouth nutters, I started to acquire a reputation. This had the consequence that one evening I was in another youth club when somebody came up to me and said, "*Is your name Hank Roberts?*" "*Yes*" I replied where upon he head butted me straight in the face without another word. We started fighting in the club, but the adult youth workers threw us out (no enlightened approach at that club). We started fighting again. I got him in a head lock but the head butt had been a corker right across the bridge of the nose. I was still stunned and didn't have the strength to properly strangle the bastard. We lay there in the street with him unable to get out of the head lock and me feeling too zonked out and weak to properly strangle him into submission or unconsciousness.

After a stalemate of what seemed an age, he suggested I just let him go. "*Fuck off*" I said, realising I was not at my best to start again. But after mutual assurances from each of us that we wouldn't start again we both let go and called it a draw. This would normally be worthless. My brother Dave had a fight with one of a group of bikers over on Hayling Island. He beat him, let the guy get up and the guy promptly smacked him breaking his jaw; remember that lesson!

I guess, my assailant was a bit fucked too, or surprised at the comeback after the nutting. Or perhaps he was just that rare thing honourable and seeing that the fight was going nowhere, was prepared to call it, and honour it, as an honourable draw. Edgar Harrison for that was his name, if you're out there and read this, contact me and let me know which of these it was.

Our paths did meet again briefly. Not having learnt my lesson from the first concert débâcle - a definite slow learner - I agreed to act as a bouncer for another gig. Our budding Peter Stringfellow realised that we needed backup. Who could I suggest better than Edgar Harrison? This time we were given some rubberised piping coshes with which to deal with some of our over excitable clientele. Fortunately, there was no repetition. There was of course a fight - naturally it was Portsmouth - but it was minor. A combination of a stricter entrance policy and reinforcements ensured that only one local hardnut was prepared to ask for business and Edgar dispatched him single handed. Yes, you've guessed it – with a well-placed prize head butt.

My bouncer career was no sooner getting started than it was over. I don't know whether study clipped our event organiser's wings or more professional help was hired, but I was not asked again. Thank God; a young novice's average life expectancy as a bouncer in Portsmouth then was probably shorter than on the Western Front in World War I or a spitfire pilot in the Battle of Britain.

Graduating

Having failed to do well enough in my A Levels to get into university I went to Highbury Technical College in Hilsea to repeat a year. Highlights included getting elected as President of the Students Union, organising a successful canteen boycott and watching Patrick Wall, a very right-wing MP, have a fire extinguisher turned on him by John Molyneux, a radical student leader from Southampton University. I found it hilarious. A photograph appeared on the front page of the Portsmouth Evening News. It showed me watching and laughing as he was sprayed at the meeting at Foresters Hall. As I was the President of the Students Union, the Principal called me in to explain myself. I explained that I hadn't missed any lectures and I didn't spray him. I hadn't known he was going to be sprayed. And in essence it was a free country. The matter was dropped. I left a free man, though no doubt my stepfather who was a lecturer at the college was highly embarrassed by it.

Another was a fight with my mate Dave Middleton who said at some stage he could "*have me*". Well loose talk costs lives. No red-blooded male could take such a claim lying down. Even if they could I wasn't going to. We met on an area of grass like knights of old to do battle. Dave was really fast and quick as lightning, threw a flurry of punches. Alas quick but not hard enough – the punches I mean. He went down, but it was a commendable performance.

This time I managed to get good enough grades at A level to go to college. Listen kids PERSEVERE. Parents/carers be kind enough to let your charges repeat a year. Thanks Mum and Norman.

I went to college, got married at the end of the first term and threw myself into the student movement of the time. This involved amongst other things, drinking copious quantities of alcohol, playing innumerable games of table football – I have to say that study was not the highest priority on my mind – and getting elected to go to NUS Conference. By this time I had left the YCL. This meant putting the true revolutionary line and attacking the revisionists in the CPGB[34], one of the leaders of whom in the student movement then, was one Digby Jacks.

After a skinful one night at the Conference, I was wending my way with a couple of other true believers back to our hotel, singing a song '*Digby Jacks is a pygmy hack*" when what should happen? A mad Scottish psycho got distinctly stroppy – is there anyone out there who knows a Scottish male who isn't a psycho? No, I know this is an unfounded and unfair stereotype. There were certainly some in Camden though. Psycho John, Mad Billy, Scottish Jim – slightly better, slightly, but a very good bloke.

My song had obviously offended his guru and he'd decided to let me know in no uncertain terms. He obviously practised some judo. I fell heavily but managed to grab hold of him as I went down. I pulled him down with me and rolled him over to get on top of him. He was in trouble now. He tried that judo trick of flipping both legs up to catch them round your head to be able to prise you off. No luck, it wasn't working. I'd kept my head low and he was well and truly pinned to the ground.
I manoeuvred myself into the right position to start head butting him. *Digby Jacks was a pygmy hack*. Sorry mate, I won, you lost, end of story you might think.

But life is never quite as simple as that. As I write this on a plane to Thailand my right shoulder, despite physiotherapy, is still giving me some serious pain, but fortunately not the excruciating pain it did. When I was originally thrown, I landed really heavily on my shoulder. After the fight I had it in a sling and it was fucked and painful for weeks. It gets better; but in old age the old injury like an old war wound, is coming back to haunt me. You bloody sweaty sock. It looks like you might have won in the long run[35].

I am generally very against people glassing and bottling people. Never the less it can have its humorous side[36]. A colleague of a friend Jan

---

[34] Communist Party of Great Britain
[35] Sweaty sock is Cockney rhyming slang for Jock – a Scottish person. Finally, with some cortisone shots the 'war wound' cleared up. It did return years later. That'll learn me.
[36] It is a normal and recognised part of a human's sense of humour on occasions to laugh and make jokes about terrible events.

Woolf was put on List 99 and barred from teaching for glassing a colleague – in a staffroom! It's only funny because it is such an unlikely and unusual place for it to happen. Okay, you're right, there is something warped about my sense of humour.

At one of our parties, when we lived in Golders Green with Dave and Jackie Blundell, a prick we didn't know was generally acting in a manner to cause one to take a dislike to him. I mentioned this to Dave Middleton – we were friends again. Dave, ever a man of action, walks backwards across the kitchen area and bumps into him, turns around and says, '*Who you pushing?*' A brief and definitely non friendly exchange took place during which a wine bottle was brandished. Dave politely enquired "*What you going to do with that?*" The response was along the lines "*You'll find out soon enough*". In a move of peerless speed and flow, in one action Dave had pulled the bottle out of his hand and smashed it over his head. Terry came in with a couple of smacks and it was all over apart from Terry getting some glass in his fist. As he was shown the door the interloper was heard to say "*It's alright, I've been bottled before*". Quelle surprise!

My one and only fall from grace was in the Poly Student Union bar. It involved someone obviously tired of living, putting their fingers in my beer and intending to flick it in my face. Again with clarity and symmetry I swear that within the first atto second of the first drop leaving the first finger, I had grabbed a bottle and broken it over his head. It didn't seem to do much damage or even stun him. Fortunately, it was only a beer bottle not a wine bottle.

Anyway he was still up for it. We agreed to not settle our difference in the student bar, very unusual for me. I didn't believe in all that 'let's go outside'. I'll only do it normally if it's somewhere I really don't want to get barred from, or it's a bit too much like shitting on your own doorstep, like work or a works do. In exiting there are only two possible ways. I go first or they go first. Both can have an advantage if you do the essential thing - strike first. If they go first, you can kick them down the stairs if there are any, or leap on their back and get them in a head lock strangle hold. Or alternatively, if exiting first, you can instantly swivel round 180 degrees, starting the punch at the same time as you start the swivel, and punch them in the face. I promptly did the latter which caused his nose to explode with blood and it was all over.

If a person offers you outside, there is not a lot to be said for going to have a fight exactly where he will be expecting it (sorry to write he but it will normally be a bloke). They obviously want a fight. With me, preparedness to fight is not about desire. It's about not being intimidated and not backing down. Quite clearly you want to win. Surprise is one thing that can give you the edge. The SAS mantra is speed, aggression, surprise. Better still say something that indicates that you don't want to know or have backed down, so they drop their guard and talking also engages their mind on something else – and then whack them. The only time you should offer somebody outside is if they are a friend or work colleague and it is inappropriate to whack them straight away or it is not wise, as I said earlier, because of the venue. Their response can also test their seriousness. If they say yes, they are obviously getting leery or fancy their chances. So whack[37] them as soon as possible.

There is a science to fighting to which I shall return. But first let me progress to selected incidents and forays into the field. They are by needs must, selective. Repetitive accounts of simply bashing people; I bashed him and he lost; even if leavened with the occasional, *'they administered a jolly good kicking to moi'*. The books by fighters or those with co-author or ghost-writer that recount blow-by-blow fights in any detail owe more to imagination than recall. An occasional highlight of some will stand out. Just like those that have had many lovers, girlfriends or just plain fucks; most, if not all, details, as well as some, if not many, names and faces are confined to the dustbin of memory loss. And when you remember that fucking is generally more interesting and more pleasurable than fighting, except for very few incidents, detailed recall of fighting would be a Rainman-like achievement, or perhaps more like Shereshesvkii whose feats of memory were recounted by Alexander Luria in his book *'The Man Who Could Not Forget'*.

One of the best examples of strike first was when my brother Pete and I were camping in Brockenhurst in the New Forest. We were drinking in a Hells Angels' pub and we were out the back, playing pool. Pool is not my game. As usual I was f-ing and blinding and losing. The f-ing and blinding wasn't because I was losing, however, I just do it naturally[38]. We were told to watch our language by two older, burly and straight

---

[37] Whack for the US mafia means kill. I, you may be surprised to know, do not use it in that sense.
[38] Some people swear more than others. Some people swear a lot more than others. I am one. More notable is Brian Blessed, the actor and totally amazing all-rounder. Read his autobiography Pandemonium. Whilst not being completely involuntary as those with Tourette's it is not exactly a life style choice. Swearing is dealt with in a special part of the brain. Brain damage can lead to constant swearing or none. Its role in limiting pain or increasing the tolerance of it has been experimentally tested. Unfortunately, the more you habitually swear the less effect it has. That is why people can't help swearing on occasion, and that's why some people can't help swearing all the fucking time. So stop fucking blaming us and making moral judgements!

blokes because they said there were women present. Now why you would take women of a sensitive nature to a Hells Angels pub escapes me. However, whatever they said would have been of no importance because it wouldn't have made a blind bit of difference. Nor did a subsequent remonstrance. Finally, one of the guys grabbed hold of me by the collar and made what I think you would term a physical threat.

My mind immediately recognised what was the necessary response in our little negotiation - mind you not as quickly as normal as I was needless to say completely pissed. However, before I had time to nut him, I suddenly saw his eyes glaze over. They rolled in a moment of utter disorientation. Pete, the ever watchful younger brother, with a war cry of "*I'll fucking kill you!*" had full powered swung his pool cue in a massive arching sweep down vertically on the top of his skull, heavy end first – THWACK. The sound commanded respect and the bar fell into an instant silence. A couple of punches later and it was all over. The Hells Angels who we'd got friendly with - the devil recognises his own - solicitously gathered round and said we'd better beat it before the cops came and helpfully escorted us as we left the pub,

We made our way overland avoiding the main roads, through streams, brambles and stinging nettles. Pete repeatedly saying, rather melodramatically I thought, "*They'll never take me alive.*" He had just recently been released from Haslar Detention Centre. I was the only one who never made it there, more by good luck than judgment. Fortunately, we didn't have a shootout at the OK Corral and managed to get back to the campsite safely.

To digress; this was the campsite where Pete heroically got off with a Hells Angel 'bird' - a notoriously dangerous thing to do - who came over to our tent wanting to borrow a saucepan. Davina was her name and a lovely girl except for the fact that she refused to allow me to make a threesome. This despite the fact that she and another Hells Angel 'bird' had both shacked up with a Hells Angel. How horribly unfair. *Is it because I is ugly?*

I, even more heroically I believe, for surely it is worth more points, managed in a later incident to get thrown off and permanently banned from a campsite in Brockenhurst. Pub bans are two a penny, but campsite bans surely demand respect? Even if they don't, surely the manner of my attempted exit does? After a night (and not the first) of drunken revelry on the campsite, shouting and swearing, that did no doubt keep the happy campers and their kids up all night, we were awakened by camp wardens and police demanding our instantaneous departure[39]. They were exercised about identifying and finding one particularly obnoxious, loud and foul mouthed drunk. Malcolm Hird, one of the group we were there with, came in my tent and said, "*They're after you*". We concocted a master plan. As the others were all taking down and packing away their tents, he would lend Jean and the kids a hand, for they were there too. I would stay inside the tent and get packed up in it. Then they would load me into our van, make our escape and release me from cocoonment down the road.

Unfortunately, their Laurel and Hardyesque struggles to lift me with apparent ease and nonchalance into the van proved abortive. I nobly scuttled out of the collapsed tent truncating the developing farce. "*There he is. There he is. That's the one*", a warden cried frantically. I can't imagine what he had against me except perhaps that when he had come to remonstrate during the night about our noise and language I had 'politely' told him to go fuck himself.

Now being a teacher when confronted by superior authority namely the police I know exactly what to do. Grovel, abase yourself with complete lack of any dignity. Go so low you could get under a closed door with a top hat on.

I proffered my humble, deepest and most sincere apologies. I mitigated my despicable actions by explaining that I never normally behaved like that - after all a teacher wouldn't, would they? - and that it was the influence of the demon drink. I would never, ever, behave in such a fashion again. This apology, and accepting, humbly and meekly, a stern lecture from a policeman about my moral lapse and the error of my ways kept me from getting nicked.

We departed with the fact that we were banned, permanently, from that and all the New Forest campsites, resounding in our ears. Sorry kids, camping in the New Forest was off the menu.

The wisdom of the *Uriah Heap* approach to the fuzz when in difficulty, was only brought home to me again when stumbling homewards one night down Finchley Road, completely pissed out of my head, I espied an ambulance. It was not far from and on the same side what is now the 02 complex. There was no one in it. I presume the driver and other crew

---

[39] Yes I do know this sort of behaviour is out of order and that it warrants punishment. I can only plead the foolishness of relative youth and the psycho active influence of alcohol.

were dealing with some emergency. At least I couldn't see them. The fiendish plan, worthy of Toad of Toad Hall in The Wind in the Willows, of driving myself home in this ambulance then unfolded in my addled mind. I climbed in. In the book of crimes I was about to commit, not the least was that I had no license. I had done some driving lessons but gave up because I could never seem to be at the right place at the right time. However, I had a good idea I could manage. I had also driven Jean's mini around illegally when she had one. Unfortunately, or perhaps fortunately, I had not managed to start the ambulance when I was suddenly and unceremoniously, yanked out of the driving seat. I immediately apprised myself of the situation as one of being in deep shit. I at once went into super grovel mode.

I once acted in a play entitled 'Murder in the Red Barn'. The central villain (why did I always get to play villains), was William Corder. When accused of murder the antihero gives an impassioned plea of innocence as did I - he was of course guilty. My performance was Oscar nomination material then and now. I prostrated myself. I blubbed, yes cried, said that I was a teacher and my career would be finished. That I was drunk - pretty bleedingly obvious - that I never get like this – at which point my nose should have taken on Pinocchioesque proportions, and something about my best friend dying in a tragic accident, untrue of course. I was truly, truly sorry. It was convincing bare faced lying that my super salesman mate Dermot Collins would have been proud of. Now the thing about lying is that virtually all humans do it. Even chimps do it[40]. We developed the ability as a species because it had evolutionary benefits i.e. it works. And it worked!! Instead of collecting my do-not-pass-go, go-straight-to-jail ticket, I won the jackpot and was released a free man to weave my way off into the night. The devil indeed looks after his own.

To weave our way back to the story… on but two occasions has my proclivity to be prepared to mix it, only ever in a just cause of course, earned me the plaudits of members of my family. One occasion was at a party at our flat. This was before Jean finally banned them. I have to say with my acceptance. A Camden Scumbag ripping our toilet seat off and me kicking in our own banisters were the last straws. Kathy came up to me at the aforementioned party and said some yobs were causing

---

[40] In the book *Born Liars* by Ian Leslie, he makes an in depth scientific analysis of the evolutionary advantages of deception and lying. He states, '*The primates*' (which include humans) '*especially the great apes - chimpanzees the gorillas and the orangutans – are practiced, habitual deceivers*'. And recounts numerous studies and accounts of this happening. It also extends further down the evolutionary tree than just primates.

trouble down the other end. I asked a school colleague Leona to hold my glasses. I went up to one of the guys and said, "*Sorry but you've got to leave*". I explained that it was my party; my daughter had said that they were causing trouble and he had to leave. This met with shall we say a response that somewhat lacked clarity. I reiterated my demand with somewhat more forcefulness. This was met with a response that indicated he had no intention of doing as requested.

I can't remember whether I gave him a third chance. I normally believe in them in the right circumstances. I can remember absolutely what came next. It was clear that nothing but force would entice our guest to go. Bang Bang Bang. I head butted him three times in quick succession. Brendan, our son, who had been watching said afterwards it was the quickest head butting he'd ever seen. He said he had thought about one day having a dig at me - no, I don't mean verbally - but after witnessing that he'd decided he didn't want to commit suicide. I was pleased with his approbation. My daughter on the other hand, the one who had instigated the eviction notice, said, "*You didn't have to kill him; I only wanted you to throw them out.*" After I had initiated proceedings a general melee had broken out. I or somebody else had thrown somebody down the stairs.

I do remember kicking them in the face as they tried to come back up the stairs. Byron had jumped over the banister on top of someone. Dermot told me later he'd punched some great big guy who looked like a Hells Angel only to be told, what you doing? I'm on your side. It was actually an ex pupil I'd taught, Tom Droogan, who was a really nice bloke. At some later stage somebody came up to me and said "Are you the one who hit my b…". He did not have time to finish pronouncing the word. BANG, I head butted him. It was pretty obvious that the rest of the word was 'rother', and it was pretty obvious that whether my answer was yes or no, I was sure what the response was going to be. My suggestion is in such a situation don't ask such silly questions.

At the end, Byron was stood outside having a verbal altercation with one of the now homeless gate crashers. I again summed up that the resolution of this argument was a simple one. Bypassing Byron I did a running punch to his head. He staggered back into a van parked in the roadside. Much to my amazement he didn't go down (and out) but came back and carried on arguing with Byron. My conclusion was that either my punch wasn't as good as I thought it was, it seemed a pretty good punch to me, or he was on drugs[41]. It seems a pretty illogical thing to do to return to the argument rather than confront your assailant. Perhaps he was confused or concussed.

I explained to Kathy, as I'll explain to you dear reader, that it is no good telling someone to leave if, when they refuse, you are not going to do anything about it. And if you are going to use force, and what else are you going to do? Try ringing up the police and saying you've got a gate crasher at your party who's refusing to leave and see how long they take to turn up – unless you live in Mayfair or better still Bishops Avenue. The only thing that is important is that you win. As you winning, rather than losing, is what's important, the use of overwhelming force is entirely logical. The thing about losing as I explained to Kathy is not just that you lose but you can get seriously hurt - and surely she wouldn't want that? I'm not sure I entirely convinced her. Kathy informed me that one of them was in hospital for two days; an ambulance had picked him up outside the house after Jean had sat for ages with him to make sure he didn't lose consciousness. Not knowing the gentleman, I didn't visit him in hospital.

On the subject of drugs, myself and Pete and a girlfriend of mine at the time Andrea, got involved in a vicious fight down in a club in Covent Garden called the Rock Garden. The group was called Breaking Glass; which one would have thought might have given me a clue that trouble might lie ahead. I have to say, however, that I do believe that it was Pete's leeriness that started it, though of course it takes two, at least, to tango. At kick off we were well outnumbered. The bouncers were worse than useless and did fuck all. It was a madness free for all. In the early stages I was doing OK, in fact quite well, and punching away like a goodun. Later it got a bit desperate and I thought "*I might end up dead here*". The whole lot were on speed; battering people on speed is often not enough. At one stage I thought of picking up a beer mug - one of those thick ones with a handle - and glassing one of them, but then thought better of it. As, if it all went even more pear shaped, I felt fairly certain that death would follow. At some stage a Mexican standoff was reached: Pete had somebody, probably their leader, on the floor - whilst down there Pete got a good kicking in the ribs. The guy bit him in the leg and was working his way to his bollocks. That's drugs for you. How low can you get!?

---

[41] Some drugs can be helpful in combat situations e.g. angel dust. Gurkhas are renowned for taking drugs before battle. The Viking Berserkers drank before battle. There is dispute on whether this alcohol contained drugs or not and if so, which drugs they were.

Me and Andrea (game as hell) were standing over Pete keeping the gang off. Eventually a truce was reached. We had proved a much bigger mouthful than they had anticipated, drugs or not, in fact downright unpalatable. It was a credible result, though Pete got quite ill later from the rib kicking and developed pleurisy. For my part I have to admit that the reason I thought death might ensue was that the fuckers seemed as if nothing would stop them. For the first and only time in a fight I realised afterwards that I had had a partial evacuation of the bowels. I went to the toilet and discarded my underpants but consoled myself in the indignity of it by knowing that the Roberts' and the heroine Andrea had acquitted ourselves admirably. One of the big muscular bouncers came over at the end of it. *Well done mate, you really earned your money that night*!

Defending family honour

That muscles do not maketh the man was illustrated by a Portsmouth Saga which is the only other time that my fighting has had any family approbation. When my step father Norman's sister Frankie and her husband Sid had died, it had taken a while for him to get matters sorted out. The house had lain empty for quite a period. A next-door neighbour, hereinafter known as 'Neighbour', was a builder, a bully and a yob. When Frankie and Sid had been alive, I had been informed, he had been a right arsehole to them and bullied them mercilessly. As they had departed the mortal coil, he decided to use their garden for storage of his building materials and equipment.

Norman had asked him to move his stuff, but he hadn't. Norman mentioned this to me and explained he couldn't really sell the property until the garden was vacant. He explained what a bullying piece of work this guy was. After discussion, we agreed that he'd put a note through the guy's letter box asking him (politely of course) to have his stuff removed by a certain date. Anticipating trouble - it was Portsmouth after all - I got up a posse to come down from London for a weekend and we would stay at the house. When we arrived the materials had gone and we assumed the problem was sorted, job done.

A sign that all was not entirely amicable and well with Neighbour could perhaps have been gleaned by a knock on our door by the police. Our car had been parked sticking very slightly over onto Neighbour's garage driveway, but by no means blocking access or egress for his car. He had complained to the police. To comply with the fuzz, we duly moved the car. Later that evening – very much later that evening, I, Dermot, John Boucher, Andrew Stone and his girlfriend Julie returned to the gaff. We went straight inside and sat in the front room. Suddenly Julie came in from outside where she had been smoking and said that she'd been punched by Neighbour. We were stunned. It seemed unbelievable, but there was a mark and swelling on her face as clear as day. I looked at Dermot, Dermot looked at me, I looked at John, John looked at me, Dermot looked at John, John look at Dermot and we immediately thought '*you fucking what*'?!

Round we belt to Neighbour's and ring the bell. The door opens. Polite chit chat it was not. Immediate kick off. It looks to me as if Neighbour's got a knife[42]. I am keeping a slight distance for want of avoiding being stabbed and so is Dermot, but we are both kicking at Neighbour for all we are worth. Boucher here does the hero for I believe he thought Neighbour had a knife too. He barged through the middle of myself and Dermot and dived on Neighbour bringing him to the floor. This signalled open hunting season – on Neighbour. Dermot and I leapt into the front entrance of Neighbour's house and proceeded to punch the fuck out of him.

We are determined to do this bastard some real damage. The fact that his missus and his child had come to the top of the stairs and were pleading for us to stop was not about to make us. The leader of the cavalry charge now sounded the retreat. "*Leave him alone he's had enough*", said John. Not by a long chalk thought Dermot and I, but we complied with John's request. The correctness of our prescience over John's humanity was soon shown. No sooner was Neighbour back up and on his feet than he was shouting the odds and offering to drive off somewhere with me - I presume because I had told the toe rag in no uncertain terms a: how out of order he was and b: how lucky he was to still be alive - to finish our altercation.

Irrespective of fairness or unfairness i.e. he was outnumbered, why he imagined I would possibly drive off somewhere, rather than resume the battering I had been giving him then and there, I don't know. I offered to recommence hostilities then and there. Before I had the chance, the police arrived.

No sooner had they arrived and asked a question or two, than a car screeched to a halt. Out rushed Neighbour's brother; the missus must

---

[42] In fact it was retractable metal cosh.

have rung him whilst Dermot and I were playing punch bags with hubby. Ignoring the police and I guess having family and Portsmouth yobbo honour to defend, he launched himself towards us only to be stopped dead by a great straight right from Boucher. The coppers immediately intervened. John equally immediately had the wit to stop. Neighbour's brother, apparently having much the same intellectual level as Neighbour, didn't. The police arrested him and carted him off.

A tricky situation now had to be resolved by the police which for once they did admirably. Neighbour had whacked Julie, but we had whacked Neighbour. Furthermore, we had entered Neighbour's house to administer the whacking to Neighbour. The coppers felt that this was a pretty even-Stevens situation where the arrest of everybody that was concerned, apart from Neighbour's brother already nicked, would not do a lot of good and make for a great deal of late night paperwork.

I was particularly concerned that Neighbour, being an obvious nutter and probably deeply unhappy at not exactly having come out the best of the situation, might want to burn the house down with us in it. I enunciated this concern to the police in front of him; he sincerely assured us – his sincerity struck me as utterly bizarre at the time – and the police that he would not burn our house down, whereupon the police departed.

We returned to the house. Andrew Stone, Julie's boyfriend, the muscle man who could probably bench press more than the rest of us put together - I exaggerate but certainly far more than any one of us - hadn't moved. Hadn't stirred a muscle! Was he a coward? It sure as fuck looked like it, but I don't know what went through his mind. I certainly think he wasn't a fighter - after all it was his girlfriend. Anyway, they soon stopped going out and I went out with her for a while.

Norman was proud of my Neighbour battering and I was proud that Norman was proud. Neighbour, if you or your brother or any other or all of your Pompey mates don't like the verdict or want a rematch, you know where to find me. Neighbour, hopefully you've learnt to stop being a bully by now. All of us can learn. If I can, you can too.

Camden Madness

The Hawley Arms and the Marathon[43] 'Restaurant' in Camden are two of the loves of my life. The Hawley Arms became famous when Amy Winehouse was drinking there. She was drinking in the Hawley long before she became famous and I had been drinking there way before that, first starting when I was at college.

Me at the football table in the Hawley Arms

It had a completely eclectic mix of Camden lowlife including me and my mates, and a table football machine on which I spent a serious portion of my life.

Apart from being linked by geography and madness, The Hawley and the Marathon are linked in another way.

To my knowledge I have only battered one person twice and I have to say, sorry but you deserved it. I first noticed Sonny's proclivity for aggression whilst just chatting to some mates, regular Hawleyites - then a charming low life rock and roll type pub. This person who was standing next to me was starting to make statements that appeared distinctly leery. I said to Joby - also known as Wolfman because of his hirsuteness - "*I think the person next to me is getting leery*". Not slow in coming forward, Joby immediately turned round and said "*Here, you're getting cheeky with my mate? I'll fucking kill you now*". Sonny, the would be aggressor, as they say shut the fuck up.

---

[43] Sadly the Marathon nowadays is hardly even a shadow of its former self. My understanding is because of the regular trouble there the police decided to crack down and get their late licence removed. Either that or the new owner stopped paying off the police (or maybe both). We had a meeting of a group of regulars who wanted to help preserve it as the oasis of madness that it was. I advocated a full on campaign. The new owner went for a family connected solicitor. I nicknamed it the Stavros solution. I said wrong solution. If you try the Stavros legal route you will need at least a barrister from the Inns of Court and even that will probably fail. It lost its late licence and is now a relative oasis of peace and calm. Hence almost no one goes there now.

He was a really nice bloke Joby. He drove me up to see Dave Leavers when he was in the nick and was a hilarious barrack room philosopher the whole way. He tragically died young, many believing he had been murdered. Joby was involved with people who were not exactly on the side of the law. He was famous for having faced trial five times and having got off for the fifth time, turned to the prosecution and said, "*Joby five, coppers nil*".

But this was not to be a permanent Omarta by Sonny. I was drinking at the Hawley one day with Lynsey. Our relationship was not one of peace and light. Strong feelings breed strong emotion - is that a tautology? Sonny interfered, deliberately in my view which culminated in my advising him to stay out of it. The advice was ignored and the conversation as it continued led me inexorably to the fact that Sonny, though smaller than me, not only rated his chances, but was prepared to bet on himself. I should mention that there were two Sonny's at the Hawley – white Sonny and black Sonny, the latter a perfectly good bloke.

Having arrived at this juncture in the Hawley, there was no question of my facing bardom by battering him inside. It had to be outside for which I have to say he showed a puppy-like enthusiasm. Gypsy background I later learned. I'm not prejudiced at all but fighting is as integral a part of gypsy culture as caravans. How much do you know about caravans? Precisely; don't have a fight with a gypsy unless you have to.

Remember who goes first? I did. As he came out the door, I swivelled and nutted him. The distance wasn't right for a punch. I may seem like Woody the Woodpecker but the forehead part of the skull is the thickest and strongest part of the skeleton[44]. I then went on to break his leg. He claimed I had fractured his nose as well. I know that when he came back subsequently seeking witnesses from the Hawley, nobody, including the landlord Alan, saw anything - your honour. Sonny went, quite reasonably, to try and get criminal injuries compensation. I heard later that he had concocted a spurious claim that the solicitor representing him had turned up pissed and fucked it up. He didn't get any compensation.

---

[44] There seems to be a debate over whether the lower jaw bone or the forehead is the strongest bone. Can someone help?

The result of this fight was clearly, in Sonny's mind, unfair. Mind you, *when has a gypsy fought fair?* I have to ask. By this I mean Queensbury rules. By their own rules, of course, it is fair.

I was up the Marathon. Sonny was on full blast about the unfairness of the previous verdict. Was he clearly wanting a rerun? – yes. A rerun by Queensbury rules. You must be fucking joking. Nut – I head butted him again. We grappled and fell to the floor of the Marathon. I can still remember the shocked look on the Marathon's gatekeepers face, not knowing that school teachers behaved like this. The previous incumbent owner, Tony, knew what I was like. Sonny was bundled out. Always know the owners or the managers. I carried on drinking inside.

Sonny was once described to me as a terrier. And so he proved to be. He was waiting outside the Marathon when I left later and launched a spirited attack on me. After a few minutes' tussle, I got him in the inevitable headlock (stranglehold). Submission followed but only after the fashion of the bikers of Hayling Island i.e. after they've ostensibly given up, launch a sneak attack. He sounded off again and was ready to carry on.

Excuse me, call me old fashioned, but it you have surrendered don't try and get all heroic. Fortunately for him the assembled throng – including Pete who had advised me to let him go and not continue my vigorous strangling[45] – stopped the re-enactment. Round two. Fortunately, I believe, Sonny finally learnt a lesson. But if not Sonny round three? Sonny, if I can learn so can you.

For all of you who want to learn I very briefly summarise my experience. Strike first if possible - and appropriate of course! Use deception saying or doing something that leads them to think that you are not going to kick off first. Practice, either in a controlled situation like boxing etc., or real life. Being able to take punishment and carry on is ultimately even more important than the ability to dish it out. Take care to avoid a check mate move i.e. being knocked out or a hold that you cannot escape from. Better still, if you can do it avoid it completely.

---

[45] Pete had always contested my inclination to strangling rather than punching – but once you've got a good stranglehold the end is almost inevitable whereas a good punch, unless it's a knockout, leaves the outcome far from certain.

Pompey

I conclude this saga of macho nonsense/madness tales with the epitome of idiocy. What? you're thinking. Can it get worse? Yes it can. We're in Portsmouth in the Kings Head, opposite the Kings Theatre. Pete, drunk, is having a heated argument with his wife Christine. He gives her a slap. It's completely unacceptable and out of order, to put it mildly. I'm there with a gang down from London including our wives and girlfriends. We all disapprove but I am in the van, as brother, and elder brother to boot. My remonstration is severe to put it mildly.

Pompey yobo interferes. I explain that I know it's out of order, but its family and we will deal with it. It almost kicks off in the pub but calms down.

We spilled outside. I don't think it was closing time but it could have been. I think it was the continuation of the domestic that led to our following out. Thwack. I was hit on the hip by the main protagonist inside the pub who had been waiting outside with a car jack.

Two groups were in the street fighting. Pete grabbed the car jack off my assailant after a struggle and hit him over the head with it. A full blown conflagration broke out. I was rolling around in the street with another assailant. I'd managed to get the better of him when I felt a glass being broken over my head. The police turned up. They took one look. The police left. The mass brawl eventually petered out as they have a habit of doing. Humans can't fight forever – either all the opposition are dead, or we are, or the battle peters out – no pun intended. This concluded with the police turning up mob handed – strategically at the petering out stage, and me and my car jack assailant making an arrangement to meet the next day to do battle.

Later round at Pete's we reviewed our war wounds. It was then I discovered the bits of glass in my head had been delivered by Lyndon, my mate. He explained to the assembled throng how he had poured out his pint on exiting the pub and whacked it over the nearest enemy's head. It was only the fact of the glass in my head that enabled us to deduce that he had glassed me! He was instantly forgiven for it being in the most noble of causes.

The challenge laid down by the car jack assailant, i.e. meet outside the pub at noon, could not be brooked without the eternal *j'accuse,* if only by oneself, of cowardice. Only maturity would comprehend its stupidity.

At Pete's next day I selected my arsenal. An axe[46] and another weapon I cannot recall. As I waited outside the pub, the overwhelming worry was that he might not turn up with similar accoutrements, but with a sawn off shotgun. How deeply unfair and cowardly that would be. I waited axe in hand plus the other offensive weapon. Should he have turned up, I would have without doubt sallied forth to his death or mine. The inestimable stupidity of which I now realise. I tell it like it was, but I also recognise looking back that nearly all of this behaviour is nothing to be proud of.

The criminal justice system needs to realise the stupidity of youth and not incarcerate them long term to reinforce the natural absurdity of post pubescence. Many things can and should be done to capture or trammel youthful rebellion or hormonal rage. I know but for the grace of good luck I could have murdered somebody – or visa versa – to not one bit of benefit of humankind, never mind myself or my kids. But – the worst thing, as I said, I ever faced was Jean. Even a knife is not as bad as a flying Hellman's mayonnaise jar!

---

[46] Pete subsequently reminded me that one was a billhook and he actually produced the other one, a roof axe

Chapter Seven
THE POLY – INTO THE FRAY

To get back to my education. I'd applied for college. I did it on the basis of which student bodies seemed to be having the most student activism and causing trouble at the time. They were LSE, Hull University and Regents St Polytechnic. I probably, naively, was too open about my political leanings and activities as well as telling them that I had been President of the Students Union at Highbury in my applications. I got turned down by both LSE and Hull. So, it was off to Regents Street.

It was the Freshers Fair. It's a day when new students can see all the clubs and societies that the students' union have to offer. I sauntered around and found one entitled Soc. Soc. This was the Socialist Society. I looked at their wares and realised that is was pro-China from the literature on the stall. At that time there was a dispute in the international world of socialist countries between those that supported China and those that supported the Soviet Union. A tall and heavily built student obviously manning the stall came over to engage me in conversation. My opening remark was "*All you Maoists believe that the sun shines out of Mao's arsehole*". It was my introduction to Dave Blundell who was to become a lifelong friend and comrade. As there was no rival, I joined the Soc. Soc. Although pro-China, it wasn't a Maoist organisation.

I found that they were doing good and useful work on some of the key student issues. I also found out how you were supposed to behave as a student. That is copious drinking and playing table football, going on numerous demonstrations, breaking up meetings, handing out leaflets and attending the occasional lecture. At one stage a news stand had been thrown through a South African embassy window on an anti-apartheid demo. Somebody climbed through the window to try and set fire to the embassy. A student at the Poly called Ed Davaron was charged with this. He was being tried at the Old Bailey. I and others from the Soc. Soc. and student union turned up to protest outside. A group of us were arrested and taken into the Old Bailey to appear before the Judge. He warned us that we were in contempt of court and that he could send us to prison. But luckily instead he gave us a stern warning. Do this again under any circumstances and you will be sent to prison. M'Lud did not have to repeat himself. Thus did I get the street cred of being able to say that I have been up before a judge at the Old Bailey.

The students' union, and much of society at that time, was a hotbed of political debate. It was the time of the Vietnam war. I went on the protests as did many thousands of others. I remember being on the front line alongside Tariq Ali and 'Danny the Red' (Rudi Dutschke) outside the American embassy in Grosvenor square. We linked arms and charged into the serried ranks of police defending the embassy. Good job we didn't get in as we were later informed that they had marines with submachine guns with orders of shoot to kill if anyone got inside.

Another memorable demonstration was one against racism. It was memorable for two reasons. First because it was a joint one with The Black Panthers. Second because we had a huge banner made out of an old movie screen. We had painstakingly painted in huge letters Smash Racism on it. The smash in red and the racism in black. Beautiful. The only problem was we had used Gestetner printing ink which took a very long time to dry. It hadn't dried by the time we went on the demonstration. It was a very windy day and the screen ripped. The banner was now a giant flag pole. Flapping in the wind it covered many of us in red and black ink!

The students' union at the time had control of their funds. We could use our money as we liked. Always pushing boundaries, we passed a motion to send money to the ANC (African National Congress) specifying that it had to be used to buy arms to support them in their fight against apartheid. Over the three years there were many other battles we got involved in. Student finances were always difficult for the mass of ordinary students. So we were in economic as well as political battles. Taking action to try and keep down halls of residence fees, to increase student grants and also trying to cut the profiteering that went on in student canteens.

We organised a boycott of the canteen with the aim of forcing them to drop their prices. We bought all the food and provisions and intended to set up our stalls in the large foyer outside the canteen in the New Cavendish St building. I decided that we would simply take some of the tables from the canteen and move them to the foyer to set up our alternative food provision. No sooner had we started moving the tables than a security guard was called and started furiously wrestling with the table trying to stop me moving it. I just said to the others carry on moving the tables out which they did. The security guard realised he didn't have the numbers to stop us and gave up. The boycott was a success. One day is all it took. There was a review of the prices and they were reduced.

The lesson from this is that there is strength in numbers and superior force. The Poly like other places such as Sussex and Bristol universities amongst others, were like fast breeder reactors for student rebel leaders, many of whom carried this through to their adult life. At the Poly with me were Fawzi Ibrahim, author, who became a lecturer and went on to become NATFHE National Treasurer. Geoff Woolf who went on to become NATFHE General Secretary. Bill Greenshields who went on to become NUT National President. John Carty who was the first Soc. Soc. member to be elected to the Student Union Presidency. Many others went on to play a leading role in their unions and workplaces including Phil Katz, designer, and Dave Blundell mentioned earlier. Dave also was the champion whisky drinker!

REBEL WITHOUT A PAUSE

Chapter Eight
SLADEBROOK – A SCHOOL LIKE NO OTHER

Part One

All schools are unique. Even those that attempt to be clones of the French schools, where it was said that at a certain time of day, the Education Minister could tell exactly what was being taught in every school in the land.

And of course, all schools differ over time. In many ways Copland, my second and final school bar a week, was unique in its own exceptionality, but times were different too. The early 70's was a world away from the 90's.

I believe to a large degree you make your own environment, through your activity, individual and collective, or lack of it. Your individual and collective control of your environment is not total. But your action can make things better and your inaction allows things to be made much worse for you by others. To paraphrase Karl Marx[47], we make our own history but within constraints.

The anthropologist Margaret Mead made the point, "Never doubt that a small group of thoughtful, committed citizens can change world. Indeed, it is the only thing that ever has".

Sladebrook was like that. It summed up the essence of the 1970s and early 80s where the organised strength of teachers was at its height despite the separate unions. If only they had been united then they would have been even stronger. This organised strength was mirrored across the Britain's workforce in the mines, in print, in engineering and other areas[48].

I turned up for work at Sladebrook at the start of the autumn term 1973. I remember I had a lightweight lime green suit which I had bought when

---

[47] 'Men make their own history, but they do not make it as they please'. Karl Marx 18th Brumaire of Louis Bonaparte 1852
[48] Read *Working at Masseys. The rise and fall of Massey Ferguson* by Ken Tyrell. His book starts, '*In 1965 unions controlled to a very large degree factory recruitment ...*' Many factories were closed shops and to get a job you had to get the agreement from the union first. Wages and improvement in conditions steadily occurred. Unofficial strikes were legal and frequent and in many instances, though they were not legal, occupations of work places also took place. People nowadays who have not seen and lived through this would find it hard if not impossible to realise what power the workers had in and through their unions at this time.

we, myself, Jean and our baby Kathy spent the summer in Bermuda after I'd finished at teacher training college. I hadn't had time, or perhaps I just hadn't bothered, to try and find a job beforehand. So I applied in Brent the area we were living in – a single room with me, Jean, Kathy, plus 2 kittens, Topcat and Dibble. They were found in Milton Park, Portsmouth where I worked for a college summer job – they were left in the plastic bag hanging on the park entrance gate. How could we not adopt them, such beautiful tortoiseshell fluffballs? Our room was one of multiple rooms let above a grocer's shop in Chamberlain Road, Kensal Rise, North West London. Our numerous cohabitees were UCL students from the chemistry department. They were certainly in the right department as they were consuming every illicit chemical and substance going, including opium – which I thought would have been pretty rare in Britain in those days. Perhaps they had done the hippy route to Kathmandu, Afghanistan. They even managed to get one of our cats stoned once, causing it to fall down into the garden below, fortunately none the worse for wear. We could never use the living room because it was always full of stoned UCL students.

Brent was desperately short of teachers at this time. I later realised this was a phenomenon that occurred with the overall predictability and regularity that locusts swarm. I might have deduced the seriousness of the shortage from my job interview. They had a vacancy – at Sladebrook, unbeknown to me at the time the 'toughest' school in the Borough, in the most deprived catchment area. In fact, it was the 8th most deprived catchment area in the country. At the interview I was told, *"We've got a vacancy for someone to teach RE and geography."* I remember I said *"Well my degree is in economics, specialising in economic history. My teacher training was in history. I've got an A level in geography so I suppose I could teach that, but as far as teaching RE is concerned, I'm an atheist"*. *"That's good"*, the Headteacher Mr Fitt said, *"You should be able to teach all the religions completely impartially. I have pleasure in offering you the post."* And thus I started teaching geography and RE! A travesty really, but with a serious shortage of staff, which was subsequently only to get worse; quality control was there almost none. We used to joke that if a three legged dog had wandered in off the streets, it would probably have been given a job.

During the first term I not only became the school NUT rep, but we had our first strike. The situation in the country, in London and in Sladebrook was ever more terrible in descending order. What to do? We pretty quickly followed Margaret Mead's mantra and formed a small group of highly motivated people to set about seeing what could be done and trying to do it.

Our merry band of men, and it was just men at the very start, comprised of myself, Pete Whaley, a chemist, but not of the kind that we'd had to share the flat with, and Robin Pumphrey, St Paul's, Oxford. Pete was a bit of an anarchist, clever, indeed seriously sharp and the last person in the world unquestionably to take shit off anyone or about anything. Robin, who was my head of Department when I worked in the integrated studies department, was without doubt the cleverest person I have worked with, or possibly ever known. As those that know me will realise, I'm not used to deferring intellectually[49], but in this case needs must.

Robin had suffered previously with some mental health problems and suffered later in life. But when at Sladebrook he was at the top of his game. He was an analytic genius and barrack room lawyer beyond belief. Actually to call him a barrack room lawyer doesn't do it justice. He was up there with the best of the best professionals. Eat your heart out, Clarence Darrow.

Our band expanded to include Patrick Underhill, another fine mind, would be barrister, with a superb command of language who represented us at one of the hearings - the union one - after we occupied the headteacher's office. A performance worthy of Rumpole. Moving outward in the circle of involvement; Eileen Gilmore, later Patrick's wife. Janet Leigh who typed most of the numerous documents we produced. Remember, this was before the days of laptops and males' general incompetence in secretarial skills was taken for granted. She later married Pete Whaley and became a well-respected headteacher in Ealing. Jenny Gardiner, head of geography, whose involvement in our antics was a long way from her strict Protestant upbringing in Northern Ireland. She and Robin became partners. Is there perchance of pattern building up here? Martin Withington and Helen Sigall also later married. I was best man at their wedding. Raj Ray[50], one of the inner circle and a forthright and stalwart campaigner for racial equality and against discrimination; always with us in the forefront of the struggle.

---

[49] That said, when you've attended as many lectures at the Ri as I have you realise that there are people out there well cleverer than you. It's just that I and most people don't have them in their circle of friends or associates. This is not to say that I don't have friends or associates as clever as I am. I do. It's just that I don't have any outstandingly cleverer. That's as modest as it gets in this area. Of course many are better human beings than me (not hard, Jean).
[50] Raj sadly died after a period of illness in 2015.

John Willoughby another stalwart; determined, a champion athlete, brave and resilient, not just in the occupation but during his two-year suspension. PE teacher – and handsome. How the girls swooned!

And special mention must be made of one of the later arrivals at the school, Lesley Thompson (now Gouldbourne). I first met Lesley at the NUTs training centre on a reps' course. She immediately caught my attention by wearing a T-shirt with a big Cuban cigar on it, accompanied by big, bold wording 'I was rolled in Havana'. Now I may be mildly autistic and not very good at dealing with verbal communication of this nature, but I can read! I understood of course immediately. She was political!

A job came up at Sladebrook for a senior teacher post. I told Lesley and she applied and was successful. She was the most senior teacher in the occupation of the head's office. Sandy Davies, the head who experienced 20 staff occupying his office for a day, could not believe that someone who was a senior teacher and whom he had appointed could be so disloyal. C'est la vie baby. When the battle for Sladebrook, educational Stalingrad that it was, ended, Lesley followed me to Copland, as did Margaret May and Ann Humphreys, only to face educational Stalingrad part 2. Through all, Lesley has been an incomparable friend and comrade. We have had a few ups and downs, but that is because she is so bad tempered and bossy, unlike me!

During these years I used to walk to school which took about twenty minutes. Or rather I'd bounce. My nickname among the pupils then was Bouncer because I walked with a 'spring in my stride'. To help prepare for the battle of the day ahead I had a Sony Walkman, the latest technology at the time for listening to music, especially my favourite band of the time. This describes the band I listened to.

The gig was finished almost as soon as it started. It was the Rainbow theatre in Finsbury Park. A hundred or so strong gang of neo-Nazi skinheads were charging round in a circle Sieg Heiling. We looked on disgusted. We'd have liked to have had a go, but it would have been suicide. The band Sham 69. As I said earlier it was over almost before it started.

A blogger writes a description of one of their gigs at the LSE in Holborn. *'Although Sham 69 classed themselves as a left wing band many of the bands followers were not. Many of the lads … were British Movement who seemed to take great delight in watching the LSE which was then a hot bed of Left Wing thought and politics getting smashed to bits. The bar was looted and the till stolen. All over the place the students were getting bashed. Sham were brilliant that night. Think the police let the gig go on as there would have been more trouble if the thing had been called off'.*

We also saw Sham 69 at the Roxy cinema near my school in Harlesden. I saw one skinhead fan, a boy from my school, being held by his legs over the edge of the balcony. Good job they didn't drop him. His head would have made a nasty dent in the concrete floor below! This time Sham 69 completed the gig only for it to be followed by many of the fans breaking up and utterly destroying all of the seats. The Roxy closed soon after.

I loved and still love the band. Yes, they are still going and just as good as they ever were. I still go to their brilliant live gigs but its less dangerous than it used to be! Their songs are hard-core working-class rebel songs, to a massively fast thrash beat. The lyrics are shouted rather than sung by the fans who know them all. The mosh pit goes bonkers and is positively dangerous. There is a palpable visceral hate of the system. Them. The other corporeal body - the rich. It's an adrenaline frenzy. No wonder the odd fight breaks out. Jimmy Pursey, the front man lead singer, has the charisma of some of the best royal Shakespeare company actors I've seen like Mark Rylance and Kenneth Branagh. And a Jagger like work rate but his movement is less flowery and more brutalist.

Their music is what I listen to now before I go down to Camden to listen to *Metalworks*. Their songs include *Hersham Boys, Borstal Break Out, Rip Off,* and *If the Kid's are United.* My personal favourite when going out is *'Come on, come on, Hurry up Harry, come on, We're going down the pub, We're going down the pub'.*

Occupy

The beauty of an occupation as opposed to a strike is that you can do it anywhere. You can have the element of surprise and if quick about it, i.e. don't stay there too long, you can get away with no action being taken by the boys and girls in blue. I have generally found that the police are not keen to be arresting teachers. We are, after all, both public servants and they are aware that we, like them - and all other public servants - are being shafted by Government.

I woke up. I thought *"what the fuck have I done"*. I am suspended from school along with 19 of my schoolteacher colleagues and we are facing disciplinary action for gross misconduct and, especially likely in my case but probably for all, the prospect of never working in teaching again. The idea of occupying a headteacher's office seemed a great idea at the time and indeed it does in retrospect, but only because we got away with it – i.e. it worked. But I'm ahead of myself.

They were closing in. We were facing compulsory redeployment. The then headteacher Sandy Davis, instead of standing up for his school and his staff, had been suborned. He was going along with the Authority's plan to get us. Big mistake. I have the bright idea. *Let's occupy his office to protest at what's going on. To show we won't take it and see if we can back him/them down.* I tell people, by word of mouth, that we are going to speak to the head to protest about this tomorrow morning. The utterly reliable hard-core of the hard-core knew that the intention is to occupy the Head's office if he won't talk to us. This is information on a need-to-know basis. We can't afford a security leak.

If we are all in his office, I can foresee a problem of communication with the outside world and if we do this we want the outside world to know – via the media and press. I ask my long-term mate and ally, Barrie, to have the day off and station himself outside the front of the school below the head's office. We gather outside the head's office well before school starts. A goodly crowd of us gather with myself, Robin and other brave hearts at the front. We knock. Sandy comes to the door. We say we want to speak to him about compulsory redeployment proposals. Sandy point blank refuses to meet us. Another big mistake. We think, *you are going to meet us, whether you like it or not*. He's standing in the doorway clearly not intending to allow us in. We push past him and suddenly we are all in the office. We reiterate the demand to talk about the proposed compulsory redundancies. He point blank refuses and shortly exits his office, leaving us all there. We settle in.

Time passes. School clearly cannot function with 20 of its teachers sitting in the head's office. Not our problem. All he's got to do is talk to us. Surely he will?

Quite some time later, I can remember I was sitting on the head's chair with my feet on the desk – no, I've never wanted to be a head - when the phone rang. I answered it. It was Fred Jarvis, General Secretary of the NUT, ordering us to vacate the office. By this time NUT rule 8 had been instituted and it was against the rules of the union to be taking unauthorised action – such as occupying a headteacher's office. Well fancy that. I calmly explained that we would leave when the headteacher agreed to talk to us about threatened compulsory redeployment and would not otherwise. He said that we would be suspended from the union. I responded, "*You better go ahead and suspend us then*".

I threw a message out of the window to Barrie asking him to contact the TV. He went away and did this and then came back to await further instructions. He was approached by the school caretaker, Arthur Titmus, who told him he'd have to leave the premises or the police would be called. Good old Barrie, steady under fire. "*Go ahead and call the police*" he responded.

We are there all day. Towards the end of the day we are all given letters saying we are suspended. We go to leave the school and the BBC is waiting outside. I'm interviewed. It is the first item on 6 o'clock news (27.6.84). We all agree to meet around my flat the next morning. I hadn't expected this to happen and I feel a massive weight of responsibility. The one thing I know for sure is that stasis will be death. We have to mobilise support as quickly, as widely and as strongly as possible. Everyone is on board. There are no recriminations. And we agree an action plan with everyone having a role and doing their bit. A demonstration outside the school is organised with large numbers of staff coming out with placards and banners to support us. We ask schools across the borough to show support which they do, sending delegates and getting colleagues to cover for them.

One school, Cardinal Hinsley, led by the NUT Rep Tony Corrish, even organised an unofficial strike to support us. Magnificent mate! Who could ask for more? Messages of support flood in from across the country.

A hearing before the governing body is arranged. It lasts all evening and goes on into early morning. The governors' blood sugar level is low. Everyone reiterates their commitment to the school, their concern for their colleagues, and most importantly how wrong and uncaring it was of the headteacher, not to at least have agreed to speak to his staff about this very important matter. As indeed it was. The governors are won over. They agree to reinstate us all – and without penalty. It's 3am in the morning, or thereabouts. We agreed to return to school to resume normal duties later that morning. It's a tough call, but everyone manages it.

An amazing postscript is that one of the teachers Anne McDevitt[51], later Anne O'Brien, comes in late. She knows nothing of what was planned and what's gone on. She asked about what's happening. It's explained to her. Unhesitatingly she immediately decides to join the occupation. Anne, you were and are, priceless.

On the day of the occupation Sandy Davis came round for a pre-arranged interview with Jean as a prospective parent. Brendan was looking for a secondary school. Jean asked him how he had found time to come round considering the problems at the school that day. He sidestepped the issue!

Apart from a few who left before the occupation, or arrived after, the pretty hard-core was composed of the 20 of us who participated in the first and only occupation of a headteacher's office for a whole day in UK history. Believe me, you have to be pretty hard-core to do that. I recount the circumstances later, but I give the roll call of honour here.

Anne McDevitt	Chris Campbell	Dave Muldown	Kate Curruthers
Eileen Gilmore	Hank Roberts	Jenny Gardiner	Martin Withington
John Willoughby	Karen Boyd	Lesley Thompson	Bill Beginsky
Margaret May	Mary Ekumah	Jenny Pamplin	Mary Harriman
Raj Ray	Robin Pumphrey	Suzanne Levy	Mary Herrity

In no way do I denounce those who did not partake. It was pretty insane in one way, but we had got away with, or perhaps I should say achieved so much together, that we thought we could get away with almost anything and win, which we did.

All are not equally good at fighting just as all are not equally good at anything. Humans are different - even identical twins. Again, Karl Marx said from each according to their ability, to each according to their needs, with neither ability nor needs ever identical from one person to the next. Contrary to what many think he did not say all are equal or all should have equal shares.

---

[51] Sadly, Anne passed away in 2016. She had bravely battled a serious lung disease for some years.

Most of those that did not join the occupation, gave unstinting support to those that did when we were suspended and faced the threat of dismissal and possibly never being able to get a job in teaching again. I thank you all; as I'm sure all who were suspended do too. Group cohesion of those suspended was crucial to our success, but so was the support we had within and outside the school.

Ours was a very strong, extreme action, but even if it was not taken by the majority, it had majority support and there was strength in that unity of support. Unity is, or rather, gives strength as always.

Sladebrook - what was it like? What did we do? Why did we do it?

What was Sladebrook like? I could start with some statistics, but I won't. I'll start with some stories, all true, that sets the context of being a teacher at the school and indeed a pupil. I have taught murderers, rapists and armed robbers. I also taught some of the nicest people on earth. If you teach all of your life or most of it, you're bound to teach a wide spectrum of humanity from worst to best. But the truth is Sladebrook was a school serving the Stonebridge estate, a very deprived catchment area; the eighth most deprived in the country. We were national headline news in the Daily Express for two days running.

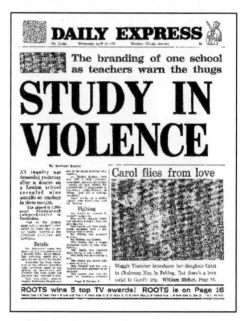

It is a fact of life, a statistically proven correlation, that of the most horrendous and degrading crimes, more of them occur per head in poor areas than in better off ones.

It is also a fact that, the more unequal citizens - or subjects! - are within a country, the more horrendous and degrading crimes per head will occur. There is less crime in more equal societies. Privilege can fuck people up, but poverty, especially severe poverty on average, fucks up people even more.

Ergo in the Sladebrook context. I taught Michael White. He robbed a jeweller's shop in Wembley and forced, under threat of death, a brother to have sex with his sister who was also working in the shop. I taught another who murdered his cousin because he borrowed his crocodile skin shoes without his permission.

And I taught another, Paul Ramsey, who I met at a party in Harlesden. He told me he'd just got out of prison after doing eight years for armed robbery. He then went on to say, intending, I think, to start to get a bit facety and aggressive, what a bastard I had been as a teacher. I responded, "*Well, you were clearly a very nice boy*", the irony of which, fortunately, was not wasted on him and he thought it amusing, kick-off being thus avoided. I could go on… And on.

The way to lessen the incidence of such actions and causation of human misery is simplicity itself. Make society more equal and **make schools more equal**.

We successfully resisted one attempt at school closure by bringing a legal challenge. As well as a possible plan to turn it into a church school, there was also a plan led by Ambrosine Neal, a Brent councillor, to turn it into a black only school. Hadn't she/they heard about apartheid and didn't they think that South Africa's apartheid segregation was wrong? If it was wrong there, how could it possibly be right in Britain? Yes, I know it sounds unbelievable, but it's true.

Every time they sought to reduce our staffing, we fought it. Our aim was not just to seek a better deal for ourselves and our students. Mind you, if it's good enough for Eton and its privileged parents and pupils, why would it not be good enough for some of the most deprived pupils in the country?

A team of us – me, Robin Pumphrey, Pete Whaley, Brian Elias, Paul Millar, Helen Grey, John Willoughby, Martin Withington, Peter Harris and others including even Robinson - produced an analysis of the data in a document which encapsulated the situation the school faced and calling for a balanced reduction in schools rolls. Known as *'Falling Rolls'* as the actual title was so long, it was very well argued and based on sound reasoning. We said, as there was a fall in the number of pupils on roll, but differentially in different schools, if we evened out the numbers, all schools and pupils could benefit. Furthermore, schools would still be there when rolls began to rise, which we predicted they would – and they did.

One of the things that often amazes teachers today is that our kids were on part- time education for a year and a half. This was due to a drastic shortage of teachers. In fact, at one point we were twenty teachers short. The academic year of 73/4 had a massive 66% turnover of staff. This was at root a funding problem. They weren't putting enough money into education of which the major cost is staffing. The pay of London teachers had not kept pace with the cost of living. Their solution to the problem as always was just to increase class size. Unlike today we stuck to the union's class size guidance. We taught full time but the pupils came in on a rota basis with most of the school doing a three day week for most of this time. Exam classes were protected.

We are facing the situation of serious staff shortage and lack of funding today. At present this is being partially covered by unqualified and inadequately qualified teachers for their subjects and also by increasing class sizes. The same attitude should be taken today. Insist on properly qualified staff. Insist on no oversized classes. If there is a gap in provision, make it show by putting the school on part-time education for the pupils. This is not anti-education, it is pro education because it puts pressure on the authorities and government to properly sort it out. Without that pressure it will only continue and get worse.

A further document produced by the Brent Teachers Association for the Education Committee, called *Falling Rolls – The Positive Option*, or *Falling Rolls 2* for short, shows how frustrated the education committee had become at the strength of our resistance to their attempt to run down and eventually close the school. Again, we produce very clear and straightforward data and arguments showing that classes of 20 as there were at Sladebrook did bring educational benefits.

Not following this elementary, obvious and sound economic as well as educational advice, some schools were run down, eventually to close. Four in south Brent and one in the north, Neasden, bordering the North circular that divides Brent into two - the poorer South and the more prosperous North. The South suffered 80% of the secondary school closures compared with the North's 20%. The reason for this was claimed to be the lower levels of educational achievement in the south compared to the North. They chose to ignore the fact that educational attainment is directly related to levels of poverty and social class background.

Why did they want to run down and close Sladebrook? The truth is it was for political reasons. The same reason they wanted to destroy the miners' union, though we were on an infinitely smaller scale. If you challenge 'them' at whatever level, they will seek to crush or eliminate you, and the better you are at it, the more resources and force they will use. Look at the miners. It wasn't economics that drove Thatcher and her allies to seek to destroy coalmining and the miners. We still import huge amounts of coal; we're even importing American wood for one power station. Does that make economic sense? Of course not. The action was to weaken the NUM, as is made clear in the book *The Enemy Within* by Seumas Milne, and the film Still The Enemy Within co-written with Penny Green. Destroy the NUM, weaken the working class and strengthen the ruling class.

We led the fight in Brent against the massive decline in our real pay having a three-day unofficial strike over it in April 1974. At that time, the NUT did not have any rule (Rule 8) preventing members from taking action if they wanted to and we were prepared to lose our pay to do so. Oh heavenly days.

Another Brent school then called John Kelly Boys where Ron Anderson worked - later to be a Brent Labour Council Chair of Education and nicknamed 'Red Ron' also took action. This action worked and a substantial pay increase arose from this and other battles. Brent, though in outer London, was also given the higher Inner London allowance. Struggle pays.

Further, our school was the only school where the school pupils had a mass walkout and lengthy demonstration to the town hall to protest at staff shortages causing part-time

education. The fact that Margarita Doyle, the pupil who led this demonstration, was our babysitter at the time is entirely coincidental … entirely.

In the battle between the more radical wing of the Sladebrook governors and those just going along with the attacks by the Headteacher and LA, an emergency governors meeting was called – in a Harlesden car park. This meant that the pupil governor Peter Hillman could briefly leave his Saturday job for 'us' to have a majority. The meeting duly constituted passed a suitably supportive motion. Anyone know of a more bizarre place to have a school governors meeting? Let me know.

In *Stepping on White Corns*, Jim Moher, a local councillor at the time, writes, '*The BTA* (Brent Teachers Association), *led by the tail of its militant wing … had blocked three attempts to rationalise secondary schools in the face of plummeting rolls in some of the most unpopular southern comprehensives*'.

The provision of reasoned and logical argument about how to make the best educational use of falling rolls only aroused more fury and determination to lance the boil i.e. get rid of us and close the school. This was best epitomised by the then Tory Chair of Education Arthur Steel saying publicly, and having it reported in the press, that Sladebrook teachers should be "*burnt out*" of the school! Roz Rayburn, at the time a teacher in another Brent school in the south of the borough and a political colleague, gave me a gift for us all of a rather charming cartoon depiction. (Photo of Brent Council chamber occupation below.)

We called for an investigation into this outrageous - if not faintly ludicrous - remark. We were not fanatical Japanese fighting to the death holed up in Iwo Jima and Councillor Steel was certainly not leading armed forces employing flamethrowers to overcome fascist tyranny.

I will mention here our Deputy Head of Lower school, John Wilkins who was an excellent teacher and good trade unionist. Every so often though he would be roused to anger and would react like an erupting volcano. John had been a Japanese prisoner of war during WW2 and had been forced to work in a Japanese coal mine among other things. Not surprisingly he still had absolute hatred of all Japanese. John told me he'd been bombed twice by his own side whilst being transported as prisoners of war in Japanese ships. He described how in one case he had not panicked as the ship was hit as others had when they were crammed in the hold. Many had been killed in the crush to get out. He had had to climb over their dead bodies. After the war the impact of the horrific deprivations and inhuman treatment of those imprisoned and forced to work including in Burma left its mark on many for life. There was no recognition of post-traumatic stress syndrome as there is today. John campaigned long and hard for compensation for Japanese prisoners of war which was finally agreed in 2000.

Robin's victory over Thug Lizard

Why would you give anyone the nickname Thug Lizard?? Nevertheless, that's the nickname Robin gave to Robinson the headteacher that followed Ken Fitt. I wouldn't say he was a thug - though reasonably burly - nor did he look like a lizard but Robin must have seen some resemblance and the nickname amongst staff stuck. Mind you some people must have found him attractive, as it was rumoured he had an affair with a local headteacher. Nothing wrong with that except that it was alleged they both went off to the Channel Islands for a liaison in school time.

Anyway, Robinson promised Robin that if he gave up his Head of Department job as Head of Integrated Studies job, he would promote him to another departmental headship. Unusually for Robin he made a mistake in trusting the Lizard and giving up his job without having already formally got the promotion. However, there was one bigger mistake than that. It was Robinson trying to shaft Robin.

Robin, as I said, had a razor sharp legal mind. He studied his law books and decided that Thug Lizard was guilty of deceit and negligence, a pretty rare and arcane tort, and brought legal action against him. He found out all the procedures that you have to go through and got through every hoop and then represented himself in court.
I accompanied him as his McKenzie friend[52], but the conduct of the case, the mastery of the law and legal procedure was all his own.
The judge tried his damnedest to let Robinson off and to stop Robin's questioning, but Robin would not be silenced or cowed. It was a masterclass in determination and skill making your case and having it heard despite all obstacles. The case was adjourned to have the summing up the next day. We stayed up the entire night working on it. A lot of the time spent howling with laughter at what had transpired, the delight at having got our Headteacher into court, of talking a judge down, and the sheer Kafkaesque nature of the whole thing.

My contribution was a small one, but key. *"Robin,"* I said *"He is a head teacher and you are only a teacher. Why should he find for you, and don't give me the law? You have to show them that you are really one of them. Slip it into the summing up that you went to St Paul's and Oxford".*
He did.Guilty came the verdict and Robinson was ordered to pay a fine of £500. Not huge but no small sum in those days and anyhow the real victory was in winning the legal case against Thug Lizard. School was in uproar at the result. People were crying with laughter down the pub at the blow by blow recounting. Robinson's credibility and authority was further shot to pieces and the inmates were confirmed as running the asylum.

---

[52] Person who can support a defendant but not address the court

I remember a famous occasion where Pete Whaley told Robinson off in a staff meeting saying, "*Staff meetings are not supposed to be a monologue by the headteacher*". Once Robinson walked out on his own staff meeting to be accompanied by Patrick Underhill saying in his powerful senatorial voice, "*There he goes, there he goes.*" And he did. Sladebrook had won.

Part Two
Asbestos

Adding asbestos makes this a long chapter, but it is a crucial aspect of my time at Sladebrook. The start of my life as an asbestos nerd and inveterate troublemaker and campaigner against the dangers of this hazardous killer being in our schools started in 1984. If you are not as asbestos or H&S nerd, you might want to skim read some of this. They make the point that absolute unabated persistence is necessary to deal with important issues. It is chronicled by no less than six investigative reports I completed as Sladebrook's Health and Safety Rep, particularly covering the secrecy, negligence and cover ups. Robin gave invaluable assistance. What follows are extracts from the reports interspersed with explanations of how we got the information.

ASBESTOS: THE SECRET REMOVAL OF ASBESTOS (INCLUDING BLUE ASBESTOS) FROM THE SLADEBROOK SCHOOL SITE AND THE ATTEMPTED AUTHORITY COVER UP. (Later known as Asbestos I)

'*Suddenly, when heating was turned on the first time this term, smoke was seen in the bottom corridors of Sladebrook's D block. The Fire Brigade was called and two fire engines arrived. They discovered that the smoke was coming from paint on a boiler in the boiler house. The caretaker then informed staff who were present that the boiler had been painted after asbestos had been removed during the summer'.*

'*A visit was made to the Borough Health and Safety office to inspect the central asbestos register'.*

'*On two separate occasions (May 1984 and August 1984) suspected asbestos was discovered, samples taken, samples analysed, asbestos confirmed and asbestos removed. All in total secrecy from the health and safety rep, staff and governors.*'

'From 17 April to the beginning of May the boiler insulated with the blue asbestos (in an extremely friable and dangerous condition) was allowed to continue to ventilate into the school playground ... The sole safety precaution, so we are told, was that the boiler room was locked'. The fibres continuing to ventilate into the playground meant they were breathed in by pupils in the playground.

The then headteacher Sandy Davies – the Headteacher who had replaced Robinson - lied about his knowledge of events. The authority backed up his deceit or indeed instructed it in the first place. They refused to answer my questions about it though they had a legal obligation to. I ended the document, *'As school health and safety rep I require that:*

> *'In the light of the proved untrustworthiness of the Borough in respect of asbestos at Sladebrook an independent asbestos survey be conducted.'*

As a stop press, we reveal that a third secret asbestos removal had taken place. This creates **Asbestos II Pupils at Risk: the authority cover up continues**. We include photographic evidence. Into 1985 and still cover up and denial. So we produce **Asbestos III: asbestos scandal at Sladebrook: The enquiry into the authority cover up**. On the front cover it says,

'Inside on page 6: **'SPACEMEN AT SLADEBROOK'**
ASBESTOS REMOVAL DURING SCHOOL TIME WHILE CHILDREN WERE ON THE PREMISES.
EYEWITNESS ACCOUNTS'

All very dramatic.

In Asbestos III we cover a meeting of Brent Council's Education Committee held on 29 January 1985 where under an item called The Removal of Asbestos from Sladebrook High school it was resolved:
' (i) that this item be referred for a full investigation of what happened to the Asbestos Executive Committee to meet within one month;
(ii) that all the children and members of staff that could have been exposed to asbestos be placed on the Register currently being compiled for tenants that may have been exposed to asbestos, and that this provision be available to all;
(iii) that Officers be asked to conduct a survey of all Educational Establishments with a view to ascertaining the extent of asbestos use and that the survey be carried out within the next few months.
It was also recommended:

(iv) that a trust fund be set up with children and members of staff at schools that may be affected by problems of ill-health related to asbestos in the next thirty to forty years.'

We also reveal the reality of these resolutions;
'One Brent Councillor confidentially indicated to the school Health and Safety Rep that they believed that the Brent Asbestos Executive would never meet, or if they did they would avoid the real questions. They stated that too many important people were involved in the cover-up and further, that the removal of asbestos is such an expensive business that it cannot be allowed to be brought to the Brent's public's attention in an openly revealed scandal'.

Despite the resolution of the 29th January there was no meeting of the Asbestos Executive. Though the Education Committee which had seen the evidence felt there should be an inquiry, 'the Chair of the Asbestos Committee felt that there was *"no business to discuss"*! A date, however, was finally set. The rest of the document contains a series of massively awkward questions and direct evidence of the cover up.

We accuse them. *'Any avoidance of these questions by the Brent Asbestos Executive would be a dishonest and shameful continuation of the cover up. There must be no whitewash. The Brent Asbestos Executive must meet in public session, take evidence publicly and publish its detailed findings. The Director of Education said: "The Council take its duties in respect of asbestos very seriously".'* (21/12/84)

We handed these out at a full council meeting and watched proceedings from the gallery. I can still remember watching the Director of Education Adrian Parsons reading it in the meeting. The allegations were true. If they hadn't been myself and Robin not only would have been sacked but no doubt done for libel.

The saga continued. By fortuitous accident one day when I just happened to walk past the main school building boiler house. I noticed not just some external evidence of asbestos work having been done in the boiler house but the door of the boiler house was unlocked! There were no iPhones then to take photos. Robin lived near to the school and after I told him, he shot home to get his camera. When he got back, putting my job on the line I entered the boiler house to take photos. If I'd got caught, I am certain I would have been summarily dismissed on the spot. As the Chinese saying goes, courage is not the absence of fear or despair but the strength to conquer them.

The result was the production of **Asbestos IV Cause for Concern** and the photographs contained on pages one and two. The best bit is the quality of allegations on the front cover.

**PUPILS ON MEDICAL DANGER LIST
ASBESTOS FACT DELIBERATELY CONCEALED FROM PARENTS BY HEADTEACHER WHOSE LIES TO SCHOOL GOVERNORS AND DIRECTOR OF EDUCATION MISLED COUNCIL
THE COVER-UP CONTINUES BOTH INSIDE SCHOOL AND AT AUTHORITY LEVEL
BRENT AUTHORITY FALSIFIES EVIDENCE: CONSERVATIVE COUNCILLORS GUILTY OF CRIMINAL NEGLIGENCE
BRENT MP AND EDUCATION COMMITTEE DEMAND ANALYSIS OF ASBESTOS IN SLADEBROOK HIGH SCHOOL'S BOILERHOUSE C.
ANALYSIS FORBIDDEN BY BRENT CONSERVATIVES**

Aren't they just brilliant? I have never lost my compulsion to explain everything in long dramatic headlines! But this was all true. The stop press at the end of Asbestos IV was that myself and Robin were facing dismissal hearings after complaints from the headteacher – me '*of blackmail*' and Robin of '*refusal to reply when spoken to*'. You couldn't make it up.

We first heard about my alleged 'blackmail' of Sandy Davies regarding the asbestos cover up by having a letter from the Director of Education read out to us. I replied that blackmail was a criminal charge. If they tried to do that, I would take legal action and I was certain that the union would back me. They wouldn't give us a copy. Robin and myself were told that we needed to collect the letter so we went to the office of the Deputy Director of Education Gordon Mott, at Brent Education's Department HQ in Chesterfield House.

At the education office Mott came out into the corridor with the letter. Robin asked to see it to read it. When he had, he accused Mott. "*You've changed the letter. This wasn't the one read out to us previously*". Mott tried to take the letter back, but Robin held onto it. They physically tussled with it in the corridor and eventually it ripped in half.

I knew Robin was in trouble. You can't have virtually a fight with a Deputy Director of Education and get away with it. Robin very soon received his letter of suspension. During his suspension we made a mannikin of Robin which 'appeared' every day sitting in his chair in the staffroom. Up yours.

The disciplinary hearing before the governing body was set. I hadn't been suspended. After all, I was not the one fighting with the Deputy Director so I could be Robin's representative. How could anything but a guilty verdict be found? David Sassoon from the education office conducted the prosecution. Mott gave his evidence recounting how Robin had fought with him – true – also adding a choice selection of swear words that Robin had abused him with - untrue. I questioned him carefully and repeatedly over whether there could be any doubt whatsoever about the words Robin uttered. There was no doubt whatsoever about the words. He had written them down straight away after the event. Fortuitously, suspiciously fortuitously, a witness was found. A secretary happened to be working in her office and her door was open onto the corridor where the confrontation was taking place.

I questioned her relentlessly about whether there was any distraction or noise – an open window with traffic noise, a fan on, another person in the office talking to them, a radio on, any telephone interruptions. As I went on and on and on and her repeatedly stating ever more forcefully that she had heard everything clearly, they became increasingly angry. My questioning included if she had written it down straight away. Could it not have been some time later? I continue my interminable questioning to ever greater anger.

Finally I say, "*That's very interesting. Your evidence is that there was and could be no doubt whatsoever about the words said*". I then produced with a theatrical flourish a small pocket tape recorder and announced that I had taped the whole incident. There was no swearing whatsoever. Your evidence is false. Robin acquitted. Education office humiliated. How could I have had the prescience to take a pocket tape recorder when we simply went to collect a letter. The answer is paranoia. But just because you are paranoid it doesn't mean they aren't out to get you. **Remember that**.

But we didn't stop there. We were relentless – something that has remained with me in all our campaigns. **Asbestos 5** (for some reason we didn't use V) was produced and again I will just give you the headlines from the front cover as they give the flavour of the contents.
THE COVER-UP CONTINUES.
HEADTEACHER'S BLACKMAIL ALLEGATION AGAINST SCHOOL HEALTH AND SAFETY REP. UNANIMOUSLY REJECTED BY GOVERNORS.

EWO'S[53] ORDERED TO PARTICIPATE IN ASBESTOS COVER UP. BRENT EDUCATION AUTHORITY CONTINUES TO REFUSE TO OFFICIALLY INFORM PARENTS IF THEIR CHILDREN'S NAMES ARE ON AN EXPOSURE TO ASBESTOS HAZARD LIST. ASBESTOS AT SLADEBROOK – FAILURE TO TEST OR TENDER FOR BOILER HOUSE 'C' – THE GROSSEST OF INCOMPETENCE OR CORRUPTION?

As one might expect there never was any Local Authority investigation and formal report. A lid was put on it when the Head Sandy Davies adroitly exited. An astonishing sequel was that the next Head Colin Ravden engaged in precisely the same covering up over asbestos work at the school during 1987. And yes - you've guessed it. We produced **ASBESTOS 6**. The headlines were as forceful as ever.

HEADTEACHER DELIBERATELY FLOUTS AUTHORITY ASBESTOS SAFETY CODE
DIRECTOR'S INSTRUCTIONS DEFIED
ASBESTOS SURVEY AND SAMPLING CONCEALED

All six asbestos reports are available in full on my website. To cut a long story short Ravden too had to go, and he did. Part of his woes, that had been added to by the election of Jean as Chair of Governors, was the Governing body voting to send him on a management training course! Who says recidivism amongst those in authority isn't what it used to be?

Wrongdoers in authority are seldom sacked outright – or jailed. If they have served authority well they are normally just moved on, an ever present and prevalent disgrace.

Health and Safety brings its own rewards

After a big fight, fuss, hoo-ha things normally improve as it did with health and safety. My health and safety expertise grew through attending training and learning from casework, and I became Chair of the Brent Schools H&S Committee. Also, I alternated as Chair and Vice Chair on the Corporate H&S Committee. With persistence I managed to get Brent to organise three very successful H&S Conferences – Brent Town Hall in 2004, Wembley Conference Centre in 2006 and finally in 2010 at the Atrium Conference suite at Wembley Stadium itself (see poster).

---

[53] Education Welfare Officers

One other notable event was when ITN did a programme that explained how asbestos had been found in Hay Lane Special school in Brent. They had been allowed in to the school to film and the resulting programme showed clearly how dangerous asbestos fibres could be unwittingly released into the air. Many staff refused to enter the school at the beginning of the Spring term in 2008 as they considered it dangerous. We demanded that they be redirected to a safe place. In the end everyone gathered in what was called the Oriental City (now demolished). After spending the day negotiating with the Authority, myself, Gill Reed and Jenny Cooper had successfully got a list of agreed actions. Brent tried to blame the ITN crew for exposing the asbestos!

It was front page news in the local paper. The Health and Safety Executive however were probing Brent instead.

This action and consequent H&S work on the dangers of the asbestos led to Hay Lane and Grove Park, its sister special school, being demolished and a £29 million new school The Village being built with state-of-the-art facilities for the pupils who have complex special needs.

What happened at Sladebrook, Hay Lane and to a Brent pupil who developed mesothelioma through exposure to asbestos in Brent primary schools, is covered in the hard-hitting document **Asbestos Management in Brent schools: Local and National Implications**. My aim in suggesting this piece of work was to further the continuing struggle against asbestos in schools and other educational establishments. The Report was co-authored by Gill Reed, who did so much of the research and collection of data, and Jenny Cooper. It was launched at the 2016 NUT conference and received national press coverage. It's on the JUAC website.

JUAC is the Joint Unions Asbestos Committee which has and is, doing lifesaving work to highlight the dangers of asbestos in schools. This body came about through me putting a motion to the ATL, NUT and NASUWT conferences demanding that such a cross union body was set up. At the 2009 NASUWT conference Carole Hagedorn seconded the motion speaking about her having contracted mesothelioma, a fatal disease, through being exposed to asbestos in schools where she worked. She bravely continued to speak out, undergoing pioneering treatment in the US which gave her a few extra years and was a

fantastic campaigner until her tragic and untimely death in 2014.

My fight to get asbestos removed from schools was also the reason I won the Alan award in 2009. You can understand why this one of my most treasured awards by the description of why it is awarded, as well as the brilliant 'two fingers' trophy! *'The Alan Award, in memory of Alan JP Dalton, who died in December 2003, is awarded to the Hazards Troublemaker of the year who has been most Alan-like. In other words, someone who has been most effective in stirring up trouble for criminal employers and complacent governments in order to make workplaces safer and healthier for workers and environments healthier for communities.'*

Doru Athinodoro, who at the time was the Health and Safety Officer in ATL - now a very hard-working regional official, nominated me. As well as feeling honoured, I also found this embarrassing at the time as I felt it should go to Michael Lees. However, he won it the next year. Extracts from my nomination form explain why he so richly deserved it.

'Michael Lees, since the untimely and terrible death of his wife Gina from mesothelioma, has dedicated his life to ensuring that schools and other educational establishments are safe from asbestos. Gina was a primary school teacher and the most likely cause of her being exposed was putting drawing pins unknowingly into asbestos containing boards when putting up displays'.

'He is an indefatigable campaigner for the removal of asbestos from all educational establishments. The ATL and NUT are currently making this a major focus of their campaigning, in no small part due to Michael's work'.

As part of the campaign group Asbestos in Schools (AiS) I write; *'Michael is always the first to respond or suggest the next step on this work. He looks at everything in great detail and responds in detail, producing the research, evidence and papers that we all use as ammunition. Michael does this in a totally unpaid capacity, and much of the activity and the success of this campaign is down to his hard work'.*

I end with, *'Michael is an inspiration to us all in the selfless manner he has taken on this cause, and through his work, if we succeed in dealing with the asbestos threat properly, he will be the saviour of many lives'.*

Michael received an MBE for his commitment and determination to raise awareness on asbestos in schools in 2014. He is now enjoying a well-earned retirement. Michael is truly an inspiration.

Chapter Nine
SCIENCE APPLIES TO EVERYTHING

Politics, like so much else, is destined to be further enlightened, even replaced, by science. At present views on how we should run and organise our society are totally based on 'political' judgements and rarely if at all does science enter into it. But it should – and will. Or to put it more accurately, it is accepted that science is the path to the right, or at least best possible solution(s). Yes, there can be more than one solution.

Science has shone a rational and explanatory light on many subjects believed in previous times to be beyond its bounds. Take love and art for example. Without going into depth and pursuing hares as I am wont to do, let me take them in turn.

Love

Overwhelmingly love is an evolved emotion to secure bonding in particular in the 'higher' animals whose offspring have prolonged periods of helplessness and require looking after. It can on occasions apply to both parents but more often it is just or more potentially the mother. This is an adaptation to secure survival of the young and the species. See the mother bear for example defending her young in the face a much bigger and more powerful male, intent on infanticide. This is to bring the female more quickly into reproductive readiness with the chance of extending his gene pool.

Love is transmitted by the biochemical oxytocin. It is normally biologically programmed to ensure humans love their offspring at birth, mainly in women but also sometimes with men. It is also bio programmed to occur on reaching sexual maturity to promote reproductive coupling in humans at their biological optimum age. This usually lasts round seven years which is why so many divorces take place around that time.

Art

With art it has often been claimed that there are no rules, no science. It is just arbitrary individual choice. The saying is *there is no accounting for taste*. Oh, but there is. A scientific approach led to the 'discovery' of certain colours being complimentary and other not, and why.

Some aspects of the science of art, allied of course to the science of human perception, has been known for a long time. For example, humans love of symmetry, perhaps the best-known example being Islamic art and its repeated geometric motifs and designs. The insanely inventive experimental neuroscientist VS Ramachandran, and a colleague William Hirstein, have written a brilliant paper entitled *The Science of Art – A Neurological Theory of Aesthetic Experience*. In it they propose '*eight laws of artistic experience*'. In addition to symmetry they propose seven others. One is a psychological phenomenon called Peak Shift effect. This works even at the level of a rat. If a rat is rewarded for discriminating a rectangle from a square it will respond even more favourably to an elongated rectangle. This is referred to as 'supernormal stimuli'. A sketch of a female – or male – nude selectively exaggerating their sexual differences of form will be seen to be more attractive.

A second is grouping. A third is binding, a fourth is contrast. A fifth is perceptual problem solving, a sixth is an abhorrence of unique advantage points. A seventh is visual puns or metaphors and the eight is the afore mentioned symmetry. They likened this to the Buddhist eightfold Path. I summarise but I really do recommend you read the article in full available on the Internet. Not an easy read, but well worthwhile.

Like the good scientists they are, they advocate experiment to substantiate evidence and recognise that there is more to discover or uncover. This does not obviate the fact that all humans are not the same. This is not to deny culture has an impact of course. Or that individual responses can vary.

Music and poetry

With music it is the same. I went to see an excellent lecture at the Royal Institution recently by a Dr Lewney on the scientific basis of music and human appreciation of music – which also has long evolutionary roots. The lecture entitled *Experience: The Science of Music*. Dr Lewney is a fantastic rock guitarist and he peppered his talk with a variety of brilliant rifts. Unfortunately, this was not one of the Ri lectures that was recorded. You can see him deliver a similar talk on YouTube in 2011. You can also find out more in the book *Physics and Music: The Science of Musical Sound* by Harvey White.

Science even illuminates that most esoteric of human expression – poetry. There was a good article in The New Statesmen entitled *The Love Affair Between Science and Poetry*. It argues these two subjects are not as different as we might think and covers the science of what happens in the brain when we read poetry. It can be used also to convey political messages. Shelley was a master at this. My favourite is to put some stanzas together from two of Shelley best poem.

Song to the Men of England and *Masque of Anarchy*

Men of England, wherefore plough
For the lords who lay ye low?
Wherefore weave with toil and care
The rich robes your tyrants wear?
Sow seed, but let no tyrant reap;
Find wealth, let no impostor heap;
Weave robes, let not the idle wear;
Forge arms, in your defence to bear.

Rise like Lions after slumber
In unvanquishable number--
Shake your chains to earth like dew
Which in sleep had fallen on you-
Ye are many -- they are few.

Most poetry of course speaks to aspects of the human condition which existed a long time before class. John Cooper Clarke is another one of my favourite poets. When I was a punk, he was the punk's poet

I even had a go at poetry myself for my Mum's 80th birthday. Here it is on the right. John is my step brother, Norman's son from his first marriage. Apart from being brainy – he went to Cambridge – he's witty. A trait he shared with his Dad alongside their great command of language.

A POEM FOR MUMS 80th

109

I used to love doing the following poem in my classroom with me going round the room with a metre rule to act out the drama. The kids loved it too when I let them have a go at playing the lead role. Here it is.

The Lesson: By Roger McGough

Chaos ruled OK in the classroom
as bravely the teacher walked in
the nooligans ignored him
his voice was lost in the din

The theme for today is violence
and homework will be set
I'm going to teach you a lesson
one that you'll never forget"

He picked on a boy who was
shouting
and throttled him then and there
then garrotted the girl behind him
(the one with grotty hair)

Then sword in hand he hacked his
way
between the chattering rows
"First come, first severed" he
declared
"fingers, feet or toes"

He threw the sword at a latecomer
it struck with deadly aim
then pulling out a shotgun
he continued with his game

The first blast cleared the backrow
(where those who skive hang out)
they collapsed like rubber dinghies
when the plug's pulled out

"Please may I leave the room sir?"
a trembling vandal enquired
"Of course you may" said teacher
put the gun to his temple and fired

The Head popped a head round
the doorway
to see why a din was being made
nodded understandingly
then tossed in a grenade

And when the ammo was well
spent
with blood on every chair
Silence shuffled forward
with its hands up in the air

The teacher surveyed the carnage
the dying and the dead
He waggled a finger severely
"Now let that be a lesson" he said.

With all the problems of youth violence in our society nowadays regrettably you might not get away with doing this today in your classroom.

Sex

Why have a section on sex? My son Brendan when I asked him how I should write the book, said, "*Tell it like it is*" so I will. Sex has been a major part of my life and has been a major part of your life. Even if you are a virgin, sex has been a major part of your life. Without it you and in fact everyone else in the world would not be here. Okay there are now babies born by invitro fertilisation but still there is a need for an egg and a sperm.

In fact, we now know that the constructs of you don't just come from your mother and father, and, not only are they affected by environmental factors, but also fetal cells received from older siblings.

When I was eyeball to eyeball with a Komodo dragon - this story is told in Chapter Twenty - little did I realise that behind its yellow ringed steely and threatening gaze was a deep secret. It was this. They can reproduce both sexually and by parthenogenesis. Asexual method of reproduction, or parthenogenesis, is rare among vertebrates: only about 70 backboned species can do it (that's about 0.1 per cent of all vertebrates). Biologists have long known that some lizards can engage in parthenogenesis. But scientists were amazed to discover that

through parthenogenesis, female Komodo dragons can produce male offspring.

As an article from *Scientific American* explains, '*The ability to reproduce both sexually and parthenogenetically probably resulted from the Komodo dragon's isolated natural habitat, living as it does on islands in the Indonesian archipelago. ... The ability, researchers speculate, may have enabled the dragons to establish new colonies if females had found themselves washed up alone on neighbouring shores, as might happen during a storm*'.

In *The Sex Imperative. An Evolutionary Tale of Sexual Survival* by Dr Kenneth Maxwell he says, '*After the primordial earth produced the 'miracle' of life, a remarkable and strange 'accident' soon came to pass. This accident was sex – a new creation that would irrevocably alter the course of life on our planet. This magnificent event would engender the multitude of life forms that have come to walk, swim, and fly upon this earth'.*

In the development of life on earth there was not ever a smooth and uniform transition of an ascending ladder. Some organisms did not need to climb any ladder being well adapted to their environment and the challenges of it. With others adaptation occurred and with some repeatedly and through this species diverged.

As sexual reproduction evolved an ever-greater number and different methods of reproduction were adopted. This led to the radiation and multiplication of species. There are some very strange methods of reproduction. Here are but two. Antechinus is a tiny, mouselike marsupial of Australia. During their brief mating season, the males copulate with as many females as possible over a one to three week period. Coupling can last for up to 14 hours straight. This strips their bodies of vital proteins in the process and dismantles their own immune systems. The exhausted males drop dead. Fuck yourself to death; way to go.

The Anglerfish spends its time in the bottom of the ocean and finding a mate is difficult, but the species has solved this evolutionary challenge. The male anglerfish is tiny compared to the female. There are different species, but the biggest difference between the male and the female of an anglerfish species, I calculate, is the female being over 3000 percent more than the mass of the male. The male uses his 'nose', which is a disproportionately large part of his body, to seek out the female who produces a strong-smelling pheromone which aids location. When a male finds a mate, it bites into her with his razor sharp teeth. Enzymes then start to break down his face fusing him with the female. The body slowly atrophies becoming a sperm-filled parasite. Biologists call this sexual parasitism; the male receives protection and precious nutrients from the female's circulatory system, and in return the female has a steady supply of sperm for when she's ready to reproduce. There are many other even stranger methods.

How come blokes claim to have slept with more women, than women claim to have slept with men. The answer is men lie and exaggerate and women do the opposite. In *Sex by Numbers: What Statistics Can Tell Us About Sexual Behaviour* by Professor Spiegelhalter he quotes this,

'Can we trust people's replies? 30 per cent: the increase in the number of sexual partners reported by US female students who thought they were attached to a lie detector'. Everyone knows men exaggerate.

It was a huge advance to have self-replicating molecules. It was followed by self-replicating organisms. But cloning only gets you so far. Sexual reproduction is necessary for the advance of the variety of species and the development of their capabilities. Organisms developed the ability to move around under their own steam in exploring their environment, searching for a more suitable environment, searching for food, and escaping predators. If there was going to be sexual reproduction between the different sexes, with the ability to cover ever greater areas in time and space, a reason to benefit in getting back together with a mate had to evolve. The more you had of this reason, the more likely you were to have offspring. So, as you go up the scale of ability to separate time and space, the reward for getting together - sex - gets greater. Whoopee for us. For humans, the biggest travellers in time and space, the reward is orgasm. An evolved trait for obvious reproduction of the species purposes. But also some species engage in sex for purposes of social cohesion as do Bonobos and Japanese macaques.

If total national happiness is the correct measure for a nation's approach, as it is for, correctly I think, Bhutan, then finding vaccines or similar preventative measures for sexually transmitted diseases should be a national priority for any sensibly and properly organised society. On balance, the more sex the happier a society will be. It is after all the most, or at least one of the most pleasurable activities adult humans can engage in. Ergo the more of it the happier on average people will be.

What is happening in Britain today? Do you think that the advent of dating apps like Tinder and Grinder which make it easier for people to connect with sex in mind is leading to greater sexual activity in our society? The answer surprisingly overall is no. In the book mentioned earlier, Professor Spiegelhalter gives good statistical evidence from surveys done over three decades in 1990, 2000 and 2010 that sexual activity is slowly but consistently going down in the UK. He speculates as to the reasons but says that there is strong evidence that we are so busy and over connected with too many competing demands on our time to fit in or want to have sex. I have no doubt that it is societal reasons of stress and exhaustion from over work causing this and that most people's societal experience in our society has been getting worse over time.

Sex is good for our mental and physical health. It lowers the heart rate and blood pressure. It boosts the immune system to protect against infections and certainly lowers stress. Sex helps with sleep. Half of women in response to researchers said they would prefer to have sex more often as did two thirds of men. Discussing fantasies improves sex life. Only about half of couples do this.

I once believed that the problems surrounding prostitution would be best dealt with by legalising it. The evidential base has proved that this is not the best way. The best way to minimise the problems associated with prostitution is to legalise it for women and make it illegal for men. Such a law has been in existence in Sweden since 1999. Evidence indicates that the Swedish approach has countered the growth of organised crime and human trafficking and set up effective programs to help women exit prostitution. It has also successfully shrunk the size of the Swedish sex industry and increased the social stigma against the purchase of sex.

This Nordic model as it is called has been adopted in several countries including Northern Ireland. Julie Bindel writing in The Guardian in 2017 supports such a law here. *'What those who oppose us fail to realise is that decriminalisation, as it is most commonly used and understood, also means allowing pimping, sex-buying and brothel-owning. And this is not the way forward – unless we want to make it easier for the men who run the global sex trade to make more money out of women's bodies.'*

Shock, horror. I like porn. This is in common with most other men. And yes women too. In July this year I read an article in the Independent with the headline *All genders watch porn, get over it* written by Franki Cookney. She writes, *'Women are just as likely to be aroused by porn as men… In 2015 a poll of more than 3000 women found that more than a third watch it once a week'.* So what's wrong with it? She goes onto say, *'We hand over decisions about what is normal or desirable to the algorithm; we let capitalism* (i.e. the profit motive) *control the narrative about sex'. 'When we start from the assumption that … all genders watch porn because they like it – and that liking it is normal – we can focus instead on offering people choice, on fostering an honest critique of what we see'.*

Fabian Thylmann who set up PornHub simply pirated virtually all of the worlds pornography and put it on his site on the world wide web. This has considerably worsened the already great exploitation of sex workers in the porn industry. They are now expected to do even more and often worse for less money. Moving away from the direct impact of free porn, Jon Ronson in his podcasts *The Butterfly Effect* shows that young people are being sexually educated by porn, and as a result of porn addiction are having less sex as a consequence. Erectile dysfunction is increasing among young men, and people with mental health issues are being taught confusing lessons by the likes of Pornhub. The young as always need to be protected.

Some years after the children were born, Jean and I discussed the situation as to whether we were interested in having sex with other people. We agreed we'd give it a go. It was still the time of sex, drugs and rock and roll, though we never got into the drugs. I got into it much more and for far longer than Jean. I have slept with between one hundred and two hundred women – yes, I'm prepared to take a lie detector test. Most were one-night stands, and some became girlfriends. It was a wild ride but did have a cross to bear as you'll read about later. I have engaged in group sex mostly with people or friends I knew, but occasionally through sex clubs. One thing about sex clubs that most people won't know is that mostly the only sex going on is between partners or groups who know each other and have gone there specifically to have sex. Humans, especially women, generally like to know at least to some degree whom they are having sex with.

Where do humans stand? Somewhere between bonobos and chimps by nature. Bonobos are totally promiscuous. Having sex for them is not just about reproduction but also, and importantly, for social bonding. Chimpanzees are by no means monogamous. Far from it. Humans also are not monogamous by nature. We might be able to work this out by various clues. In our society in the UK heading towards half of all marriages end in divorce. Extra marital sex is widespread.

Our natural state is well explained in the book *Sex At Dawn: How We Mate, Why We Stray and What it Means for Modern Relationships* by Christopher Ryan and Cacilda Jetha. In the earliest hunter gatherer societies women naturally would have sex with more than one man. One reason was to prevent jealousy on whose child was who's so strengthening the social cohesion of the group. Everyone looked after each other as a group to ensure survival. It was also believed that the sperm built up the baby bit by bit so having sex with a number of partners made for healthier, stronger offspring. To quote from the book, *'This approach to sexuality probably persisted until the rise of agriculture and private property no more than ten thousand years ago. In addition to voluminous scientific evidence, many explorers, missionaries, and anthropologists support this view, having penned accounts rich with tales of orgiastic rituals, unflinching mate sharing, and an open sexuality unencumbered by guilt or shame'.*

The book also explains why women vocalise louder than men during copulation. *'The Kama Sutra contains ancient advice on female copulatory vocalisation in terms of erotic technique.' 'British primatologist Stuart Semple found that, "In a wide variety of species, females vocalise just before, during or immediately after they mate. These vocalisations," Semple says, "are particularly common among the primates and evidence is now accumulating that by calling, a female incites males in her group." Precisely. There's a good reason the sound of a woman enjoying a sexual encounter entices a heterosexual man. Her 'copulation call' is a potential invitation to come hither, thus provoking sperm competition.'*

In a recent wonderfully titled book *Why Women have Better Sex Under Socialism: and Other Arguments for Economic Independence* by Professor Kirsten Ghodsee, she very ably marshals the evidence for the assertion in her book title.

She examines what is called the sexual exchange or sexual economics theory where women decide whether to offer sex and men 'buy' it with non-sexual resources. *'Sexual economics theory assumes an underlying capitalist economy in which women have an asset (sex) they can choose to sell or give away either as sex workers or in less overt, but no less transactional ways, as sugar babies, girlfriends, or wives.'* And in the Soviet Union, *'Because some urban Soviet women felt secure in their economic position, sexuality lost its exchange value and became something to be shared.' 'The reintroduction of free markets in Russia coincided with a return of the commodification of women, particularly when compared with the late Soviet past.'*

She then goes on to look at East Germany quoting Ingrid Sharp's research. *'Divorce in the GDR was relatively simple and had few financial or social consequences for either partner'.* *'Unlike in the West, women were not forced by economic dependence to remain in marriages they no longer enjoyed.'* Ghodsee quotes from research on self-reported sexual experiences in East and West German female students carried out Kurt Starke and Ulrich Clement in 1988. They found that *'East German women said they enjoyed sex more and reported a higher rate of orgasm than their Western counterparts'.* It is pretty logical that if you are in an inferior or dependent position, sex would be generally not as enjoyable as it would be if you were in a more equal, or even equal, position. My attitude to women in general is that of course they are equal. No one would accuse me of being a male chauvinist!

Science and Politics

Many if not most times science does not give a single definitive answer or solution, but a range of options with different probabilities. However, it does give some definitive answers with global warming. Is it happening? Is it a problem? And is that problem human caused? The answer to all three questions is a definite yes. Global warming is denied by Trump and our domestic fellow traveller Nigel Lawson amongst others. They are not idiots. They have an ideological position that is impervious to evidence or alternatively they accept the evidence but just don't care because they believe that their immense wealth will enable them to protect their and their families' individual futures. In the meantime, they want to rip off the world's people and resources without let or hindrance.

Overwhelmingly scientists view is that global warming can be stopped. It will though require a much higher level of protest and militant activism to achieve this in the face of such powerful vested interest. The school kids taking strike action is great start to this. The importance of an individual and individual responsibility is well illustrated by Greta Thunberg. She was not seeking celebrity. She acted alone and out of inner principle. She could not have foreseen the extent and rapidity of the impact of her actions any more than Rosa Parkes could when she sat in the whites only section of the bus and refused to move. Individual stances do count and occasionally can be the spark that starts a prairie fire. Read Greta's book *No One is too Small to make a Difference.*

Next. Take equality. Scientific evidence[54] shows that extensive inequality is bad for the general happiness of a society. It also shows that it is bad for the level of production and output. The fight for greater equality in our increasingly un-egalitarian society is not one of misplaced emotion, of jealousy or resentment of those not at the top of the pile. It is based on a rational scientific approach of how a society is organised to the best benefit of not just the majority, but all.

The Equality Effect - Improving Life for Everyone by Danny Dorling, contains irrefutable evidence that even the rich have a better life in a more equal society. In the foreword by Owen Jones he states, '... *The case for greater equality – as this book wonderfully shows - is hard headed. Greater equality is good for all of us. Societies with greater equality tend to do better on a whole range of metrics: from their educational performance to their well-being, from levels of crime to financial stability. Higher levels of inequality breed mistrust, segregation and division. They are bad for aspiration...*'

Of course, the facts are that knowing how something should be best or even just better done, or even proving it to be so, does not make it happen. We live in a class-based society where control and power are exercised by a minority, and in the crucial sense i.e. those that really control, as opposed to those that merely serve and do their bidding - consciously or unconsciously - in areas like philosophy, economics, government etc. are a tiny, tiny minority. Not the 1%, more like the 0.001%. It is a sad fact that today in Britain, and to a large extent around the world, inequality is increasing.

The arguments made by authors such as the late Hans Rosling in his book *Factfulness: Ten Reasons We Are Wrong About the World and Why Things Are Better Than You Think*, and also Steven Pinker in his book *Enlightenment Now: The Case For Reason, Science, Humanism and Progress*, in essence that absolute poverty across the world has decreased, average lifespan, education levels, and other measures we associate with human progress have gone up, which are correct (read Rosling's quiz 'Test Yourself' on pages 3 to 5) does not detract from the increase in inequality. Pinker admits for example that '*Economic*

---

[54] Read Richard Wilkinson and Kate Pickett's book, '*The Spirit Level; why equality is better for everyone*' and their latest book, *The Inner Level: How More Equal Societies Reduce Stress, Restore Sanity and Improve Everyone's*. Richard Layard is another. There are many, many more looking at the impact of growing inequality.

inequality has increased in most western countries since its low point around 1980, particularly in the United States and other English-speaking countries, and especially in the contrast between the very richest and everyone else'. Of course, it has increased in Eastern countries too. Just to take the two biggest ones. for example, India and China. He argues, however, that there is nothing wrong with any level of inequality per se so long as those at the bottom are ok.

As we know from our own experience, from what we see every day around us in Britain, everybody is not ok, particularly the poorest. Widely, one could almost say wildly, differing levels of incomes and lifestyles are a source of human resentment and this in and of itself is bad for humans mental and physical health. In Britain for example most of us know that we are better off than our grandparents. Many now are becoming economically worse off than their parents. Also, many more are beginning to fear that they may become worse off than their grandparents. They are but a cut or liquidation of their pension, another possibly even bigger and worse recession, a cut or loss of a social security benefit, continuing reduction in real pay or loss of job from a serious problem if not destitution.

Humans are an innately and fiercely egalitarian species and it extends into our evolutionary past. Frans de Waal's book, *Mama's Last Hug: Animal Emotions and What They Teach Us about Ourselves*, ably gives evidence for this. In a lecture I attended by him at the Ri, as well as showing an extremely moving video of the chimpanzee named Mama in her last hug with her former long term keeper who had known her for 40 years, he also showed the video of the Capuchin monkeys reaction to being unfairly rewarded for completely the same task. Search for YouTube *Two Monkeys Were Paid Unequally: Excerpt from Frans de Waal's TED Talk.* Humans attitudes on this matter have long evolutionary roots for us as a social species.

REBEL WITHOUT A PAUSE

Chapter Ten
INDEPENDENCE OR NOT

I watch the television with steadily mounting disbelief. Incredulity doesn't do it. Gobsmacked. The all-night newscaster eventually announces near the end, but before all the votes have been counted: Leave have it. It's Brexit, well the vote is. I said to Jean, *'Just watch the powers that be try and weasel out of this'*.

Let me straight away put my cards on the table. I voted Brexit. As did many Labour voters particularly in the north. Don't get me wrong. I think the EU is an undemocratic corrupt neoliberal multinational corporate attempt to set up a neoliberal super state. Both its attempted single currency the Euro, and itself as a political entity, are bound to fail. Our country's vote was symptomatic of this, as is the horrendous situation in Greece and increasing problems in Italy, Spain etc. To think that you supposedly have to be right wing, racist and xenophobic and or thick to think or say this is pretty infantile.

Two of the greatest socialists of my generation Tony Benn and Bob Crow were anti EU. As were/are a number of left-wing groups and parties and individuals. I will say this; if we keep the same free market neoliberal policies, our spiral of decline will continue irrespective of whether we are in or out of the EU. The Labour Party used to be against the EU but its position changed, as did much else in the move to New Labour. When Margaret Thatcher was asked what she thought was her greatest legacy, she replied "*Tony Blair*".

Similarly, the trade union movement. Its number halved. Its strength and militancy a shadow of its former self came to adopt a general position that it is the EU that is the originator and protector of our workers' rights. Did the EU stop the recent anti-union legislation or any of the anti-union legislation since we joined the Common Market in 1973? Has the EU stopped the massive growth of zero-hour contracts? Is it stopping privatisation moving into the NHS and education? Did it stop any of the other numerous privatisations? Has the EU stopped the teachers' pay alongside most other workers suffering a decline in real pay of around 20%, leading to the growth of food banks and homelessness? It didn't stop the terrible lapses in health and safety that led, for example, to the Grenfell fire. Protecting us? I don't think so. It has happened because we have not combated neoliberalism strongly enough.

It was also within the EU that our economy collapsed, and we had to bailout the bankers, speculators and assorted superrich. The EU did not and will not ride to our rescue. Nor is there any other shortcut, or easy way out. Rely on the EU to improve things? Don't hold your breath.

Two left wing authors Larry Elliot and Dan Atkinson, who write normally for the Guardian wrote a thorough demolition of the history and nature of the EU; some heavy going but well worth a read. Its title is *Europe Isn't Working*.

One day I believe there will be worldwide governance. This is necessary to effectively deal with world issues such as climate change and the pollution of our oceans. Hopefully it won't be by a tiny handful of multibillionaires or their representatives, and it will have some grass roots democracy, bottom up not just top down and with proper accountability. Not the present system and certainly not some kind of expanded EU system.

I wrote two articles for the magazine *Education For Tomorrow* which are included next, with some minor updates.

Can a socialist support Brexit?

The short answer is yes. The late Tony Benn and Bob Crow were two who notably did so. In doing so though, one can receive a response from many, who would place themselves on the left, ranging from incredulity to allegations of racism, xenophobia, Little Englander and of supporting right-wing Tories who want to take away our rights. The retorts are simply name-calling and (not normally accompanied by any depth of analysis). Right-wing Tories do not need Brexit to be busily fighting, and unfortunately achieving to a considerable degree, the removal of our rights and the worsening of our pay and conditions. All of this has happened while we were, as we still are, within the EU. How so many trade unionists can say that being in the EU is the source of our rights and the EU has, and will, protect them, I find bemusing. For example, hasn't the massive increase in zero hours contracts occurred on the EU watch? Haven't our working hours lengthened whilst our pay and conditions have declined, whilst those of the rich and superrich have gone through the roof? What we have won or defended, we have done through our struggle. Teachers' strike action, especially joint action, mitigated the worst of our pensions cut – not the EU.

However, we need to go deeper in our analysis in looking at the facts and look at what the real purpose of the establishment of the EU and its precursors actually was. Some argue it was to stop war in Europe. There has been war in Europe – Yugoslavia and Cyprus. The EU is now seeking to establish its own nuclear enabled army. If it wanted to seek to ensure peace in Europe it would declare neutrality as Switzerland did which kept their country out of the World Wars. Another good idea would be the abolishing our paltry nuclear force (paltry compared to the US and Russia's[55]) which only serves to make us a Russian target in the event of war between the US and Russia or the US against Russia and China.

But I digress and my above comments or contentions are not the crux of the Brexit issue. What were and are the main purposes of the EU? From its inception in 1973 as the common market, the EEC, now EU, it is to have,
1) free movement of capital
2) free movement of labour within its borders
3) free movement of goods and services within its borders.
It is termed a free market. What it is, is a customs union.
In addition, on its journey it has sought to abolish borders between countries; the Schengen Agreement, to adopt a common currency, the Euro, and to aim for full union, not just economic union, but also political union.

Let's look first at the free movement of capital. Margaret Thatcher abolished exchange controls in 1979. The effect of this was to make the export of capital far easier, and there was a massively increased exodus. In 'Re-examining The Removal Of Exchange Control by the Thatcher Government in 1979' Daisuke Ikemoto writes, '*The abolition of exchange controls reduced the role of the state in economic management and increased competitive pressures for business.*' '*Exchange controls abolition also changed the balance of power between labour and capital. Due to liberalisation of international capital movements, companies' management teams came under increasing pressure to make bigger profits and not to concede generous pay*

---

[55] 97% of the world's nuclear missiles are held by Russia and the USA. *Global nuclear weapons inventories, 1945–2013* by Hans M. Kristensen & Robert S. Norris

settlements to trade unions. At the same time, they also obtained the option of moving their business out of the UK if the companies' wage costs were judged too high. For Trade Minister John Nott, the dismantling of exchange control was an essential part of the Government's economic strategy to reduce the state intervention in the economy and break the power of the trade unions.'

Right from the start, the plan of those at the top was to create an economic and political entity that did not just support free movement of capital within that entity, but globally.

Europe Isn't Working, a book written by journalists Larry Elliott and Dan Atkinson contains many enlightening quotes as well as much relevant information.

They write, *'However, as Rawi Abdelal of the Harvard Business School notes, Germany was not interested in solely removing barriers to capital movements inside the Community – which would have made good logical sense as an aspect of the Common Market – but with everyone else as well, the so-called erga omnes (towards everyone) principle. 'The result was profoundly important, for the European Union ended up with the most liberal rules imaginable. Europe's rules oblige members to liberate all capital flows, no matter the source or direction.' Germany, he writes, was determined that there would be no 'fortress Europe' in capital market terms and that financial globalisation would be embraced more or less unconditionally.'*

Elliott and Atkinson continue, *'It is a mark of how far Delors had moved in a few short years that he devoted an early part of his first presidency of the European Commission (1985-88) to an attempt to remove all barriers to the free movement of capital. Abdelal notes that in the early part of 1986, the Commission President was working on plans to oblige member states to liberalise capital movements among themselves and with the outside world. What would once have been a hugely controversial subject was agreed in two years, and in the June1988 capital movement directive mandated that there be no obstacles to transfers or transactions of any kind.'*

They add, *'If the left's heady romance with monetary union had required the sacrifice of exchange controls and most protectionist trade measures, the third demand would have proved a deal-breaker: a de facto prohibition on the creation of a new state-owned enterprises, other than in an emergency, and strict rules on how existing publicly owned entities were to be financed.*

And continuing,' *Henceforth, nationalisation would be permissible only if the entity in question were treated on an arms-length commercial basis, and public investment would have to meet the same criteria as private investment. If it were inconceivable that a private-sector investor would have put in the money, then the state was barred from doing so. Furthermore, any advantage derived from state assistance of any kind would have to be 'given back' further down the road'.* The impact of the unrestricted movement of finance capital i.e. not just within the EU but a global requirement of EU membership has been well documented in numerous books and studies.

Of capital coming into the UK a good book is *Private Island - Why Britain Now Belongs To Someone Else* by James Meek. His book analyses it from looking at all the privatisations first and there is a long list. '*When Margaret Thatcher's Conservatives came to power in Britain in 1979, much of the economy, and almost all of its infrastructure, was in state hands. ... How much of the economy? A third of all homes were rented from the state. The health service, most schools, the Armed Forces, prisons, roads, bridges and streets, water, sewers, the national grid, power stations, the phone and postal systems, gas supply, coal mines, the railways, refuse collection, the airports, many of the ports, local and long-distance buses, freight lorries, nuclear fuel reprocessing, air traffic control, much of the car, ships and aircraft building industry, most of the steel factories, British Airways, oil companies, Cable & Wireless, the aircraft engine makers Rolls-Royce, the arms makers Royal Ordnance, the ferry company Sealink, the Trustee Savings Bank, Girobank bank, technology companies Ferranti and Inmos, medical technology firm Amersham International and many others.*

In the past 30 years, this commonly owned economy, this people's portion of the island, has to a greater or lesser degree become private. Millions of council houses have been sold to their owners or to housing associations. Most roads and streets are still under public control, but privatisation has reached deep into the NHS, state schools, the prison service and the military. The remainder was privatised by Thatcher and her successors. By the time she left office, she boasted, 60 per cent of

*the old state industries had private owners – and that was before the
railways and the electricity system went under the hammer.'*

All of this has been done and the process is still continuing, in particular
in education under the academies programme under/within the EU.
They have not, and are not, saving us or protecting us.

Meek then analyses what happened after these huge swathes of state
assets were handed over to the privateers. He looked specifically at six
areas – privatised mail, privatised railways, privatised water, privatised
electricity, privatised health and privatised homes. His analysis of the
degree of foreign ownership is what leads to the subtitle of his book
Why Britain Now Belongs To Someone Else. Does foreign ownership
matter? Ownership gives control and foreign ownership means foreign
control. The history of Britain and its empires well illustrates the
implications of foreign ownership of countries and territories.

At one time the British Empire was the biggest empire in history. It was
one on which the sun never set and as John Newsinger writes in his
excellent *People's History Of The British Empire: The Blood Never
Dried.*

Our ownership and domination of the world through the unrestricted
export of capital and goods, and the destruction of indigenous foreign
industries[56] by force of arms as necessary, led to millions being
exploited, starved, enslaved and slaughtered. It also led to wars with up
and coming rivals, and eventually, to campaigns and wars of national
liberation of subjected peoples.

Despite pretentions, Britain is no longer a world power. As Johan Van
Overtveldt writes in *The End Of The Euro: The Uneasy Future Of The
European Union,* '*As the twenty-first century advances, the United
States and China are the only viable contenders for the top position,
distantly followed by India, Japan, Brazil, Russia and Germany.
France's place is in the third tier with Indonesia, Mexico, Iran, Saudi
Arabia, South Korea and the united Kingdom*'. The UK is being de-
industrialised as rapidly as its remaining industry and other capital
assets e.g. hotels, shopping complexes and housing are brought up by

---

[56] For example, the Indian cloth exporting industry. This is best described in *Inglorious Empire: What
the British Did to India* by Shashi Tharoor.

foreign superrich individuals and companies and profits made exiting the country.

China is the latest country buying up swathes of Britain and much else around the world. How the tables have turned since the British Empire used armed force to force China to take opium imports. Theresa May raised national security questions over the part-Chinese, alongside the French, ownership of Britain's biggest nuclear power station, Hinkley Point. A brief but firm response from China that they would not take such a response kindly and the implication for Britain of China using its enormous economic clout in its response, meant May caved with alacrity. In principle, she had a point. A foreign power owning, or even part owning, your biggest nuclear power plant is a potential security risk especially with any potential for armed conflict. As John Pilger's seminal documentary *The Coming War With China* showed, US imperialism is busy encircling China with bases, troops ships, submarines and aircraft in an alliance with other far Eastern countries, in particular an ever more belligerent Japan. Serious territorial disputes exist between China and Japan. Britain as the US's poodle will be expected to follow the US's lead as with Iraq, Afghanistan and Libya, with only a massive public outcry that pressurises many MPs into voting against full-on armed intervention on the ground into Syria.

There has, nonetheless, been covert intervention and overt bombing with the aim, looking increasingly unlikely, of achieving yet another regime change, irrespective of the consequences to country and people.

The fact that many companies or individuals have global reach – Trump for example has over 100 companies doing business is in Russia, – does not change the problems regarding the import or export of capital, the loss of independence for a country, the loss of its industrial base, the outflow of capital, the outflow of profits not to be reinvested in the country.

A part of this outflow of capital is known as outsourcing. In relation to the United States the reasons for this and its consequences are extremely well explained and documented in the book *How The Economy Was Lost – the War Of The Worlds* by Paul Craig Roberts. He explains, '*Corporations offshore their production, because they can more cheaply produce abroad what they sell to Americans.*'(and the rest of the world of course). '*A country that offshores its own production is unable to balance its trade'. The US is on a path to economic Armageddon. Shorn of industry, dependent on offshore manufactured goods and services… The US will become a Third World country'.* The UK is on a similar trajectory with the same policies. This has again been well documented by Elliott and Atkinson's previous book.

For Britain, the EU and its euro has accelerated this globalising and outsourcing of UK industry. Luckily, as most who previously advocated it now admit, we did not adopt the euro and take that crucial step towards full political and economic union of a single Superstate.

Roberts continues, *'The advent of offshoring has made it possible for US firms using First World capital and technology to produce goods and services for the US market with foreign labour. The result is to separate Americans' incomes from the production of the goods and services that they consume'.*

'This new development, often called globalisation, allows cheap foreign labour to work with the same capital, technology and business know-how as US workers. The foreign workers are now as productive as Americans with the difference being that the large excess supply of labour that overhang labour markets in China and India keeps wages in these countries low. Labour that is equally productive but paid a fraction of the wage is a magnet for Western capital and technology.' Further offshore outsourcing, starting with call centres, is now rapidly spreading and moving up the value chain to any work that can be done electronically. India has its increasingly large supply of well-qualified people with a good command of English. Bangalore, a high tech research centre now rivalling Silicon Valley, is now one of the New York cities of Asia, massively developed on the basis of capital export and outsourcing.

Having touched on some of the adverse effects of the unrestricted free movement of capital in and out of a country, now let me turn to the vexed issue of immigration, or rather migration, for one country's immigrant is another country's emigrant.

Massive propaganda, advertising etc. has changed many people's understanding and beliefs in Britain about the expectation or indeed the right to be able to live in any other country not simply other EU countries as is the situation at present.

In growing up in Britain as a teenager I became aware, as did everyone else at the time, that Australia was keen to have immigrants from the UK and there was a system where you could do this for just £10. Even then there was no freedom for all to do so. There were numerous barriers, including a controversial one of no blacks, regarding education, health and job qualification. I am Bermudian. I was born there and my father was Bermudian. Even so, I am not simply allowed to return as I like, to live and work there. I would have to apply for a work permit, and to live there permanently, for residency. To get a job in Bermuda a Bermudian employer has to show that there is not a suitable Bermudian resident who can do it and is able to take the job. This makes and keeps Bermuda a high wage economy and a low unemployment economy. Unrestricted immigration for Bermuda would be both disastrous for the Bermudian economy and practically ridiculous if not impossible. It is only 21 square miles in size.

The US, despite its size, does not have an unrestricted policy regarding immigration. Indeed, it is quite strict whilst still being a country with a present policy that encourages immigrants and makes use of it, or rather employers make use of it, to employ skilled and highly skilled labour at wages and salaries that are below indigenous and naturalised American citizens present or past wage levels. Its leaky borders allow large numbers to enter the country and labour market illegally enabling employers to exploit them by paying low wages and having worse conditions. This happens also in Britain, but to a lesser extent.

Regarding labour, i.e. workers, we have to remember workers are human capital. Say someone studies and is trained by a country to the highest level of oncology surgeon. Is it right that they can individually, and those similarly qualified, simply up stakes and go to the US where salaries are considerably higher? Is it right that they should get this highly qualified human capital, to the cost of which they have contributed nothing, and others, us in Britain, have borne a collective cost? Is it right that developed countries, asset strip developing countries? This became a problem with teachers in the UK, particularly London, when large numbers were being poached by recruiters going to Caribbean countries to entice them to come and work as teachers in the UK - a similar process went on wholesale with nurses. Steve Sinnott, a previous NUT General Secretary who tragically died early at the age of 56, was very concerned at this asset-stripping of the valuable human capital of poorer countries. In his obituary in the Guardian April 2008, Fred van Leeuwen, the Education International General Secretary at the time, drew attention to the key part Steve played in drawing up a protocol about teacher recruitment designed to prevent Britain from asset-stripping Commonwealth countries of their teachers.

The situation regarding large-scale immigration into Britain and its effect is not a new one, and the conclusion of its undoubted ability to hold down or even lower wages, and also cause divisions within the workforce the better to divide and rule, is not new either.

Engels wrote, '*Irish immigration to England is getting more alarming each day. It is estimated that an average of 50,000 Irish arrive each year, the number this year (1847) is already over 220,000. In September 345 were arriving daily and in October this figure increased to 511. This means the competition between workers will become stronger*'. Further, '*it has been calculated that more than 1 million have already migrated*'.

Engels quotes Thomas Carlyle, '*... the condition of the lower multitude of English labourers approximates more and more to that of the Irish, competing with them in all the markets: that whosoever labour,... will be done not at the English price but at an approximation of the Irish price; at a price superior as yet to the Irish, that is, superior to scarcity of potatoes for thirty weeks yearly; superior, yet hourly, with the arrival of every new Steamboat, sinking nearer to an equality with that*'. Engels continues, '*Nothing else is therefore possible than that, as Carlyle says, the wages of the English working man should be forced down further and further in every branch in which the Irish compete with him. And these branches are many*'.

'*It is easy to understand how the degrading position of the English workers, engendered by our modern history and its immediate consequences, has been still more degraded by the presence of Irish competition*'[57]. He explains that this is because the Irish immigrants were prepared to tolerate worse and more overcrowded housing, cheaper and worse food – overwhelmingly just potatoes – poorer clothing and generally a worse standard of living. This is the case today with many immigrants tolerating being forced economically into

---

[57] Sources. 1) Frederick Engels writing in Le Reforme. The Commercial Crisis in England – the Chartist Movement – Ireland. 2) Frederick Engels Conditions of the Working Class in England 1845

inadequate and grossly overcrowded accommodation and an altogether grossly lower standard of living.

In *The First International And After*, Karl Marx writes, '*In dragging down the working class in England still further by forced immigration of poor Irish people, the English bourgeoisie has not merely exploited Irish poverty. It has also divided the proletariat into two hostile camps... In fact in all the major industrial centres of England there is a profound antagonism between the Irish and the English proletarians. The ordinary English worker hates the Irish worker as a competitor who brings down his wages and standards of living.*'

Employers and our Government like and indeed often foment this division as a divide and rule strategy of clear economic benefit to our rulers, but also of political benefit in misidentifying the main enemy as immigrants, rather than those who are running our increasingly corrupt and defunct system. In talking about immigrants, I make a distinction about asylum seekers. Lenin was a temporary one, and Marx, in his later years, a permanent one. Of course, if someone's life is seriously in danger we ought to, alongside other countries, give them refuge. However, there needs to be far more focus and concentration on stopping the origin of so many being caused by wars. It is insufficient to analyse the whole situation as one of '*they need our help, let them in, they are welcome*'. That is there will be no solution until we discuss, consider, understand and up our game in opposing more forcefully imperialist aggression in foreign countries which is creating ever more forced emigration – this immigration – and refugees.

At present there is a growing shortage of teachers. One way Government is hoping to deal with this is by removing the need for teachers to be qualified, but another way they are hoping to deal with this is by importing EU nationals. In the Observer 1.01.17 Daniel Boffey writes, '*During a time when the Government has repeatedly failed to meet its teacher recruitment targets, data suggests foreign nationals have increasingly been drafted in to fill in gaps. Department of Education figures show close to 5000 teachers from EU countries qualified to teach last year, up from just over 2000 in 2010. The largest numbers coming from Spain, Greece, Poland and Romania. The number coming from Greece has shot up more than six fold ...*' I wonder why!? '*Yet despite the influx the DfE has failed to hit necessary recruitment levels for the fifth year in a row it was revealed last week.*'

'Shadow Schools Minister Mike Kane said he feared that the Government's policy on EU nationals could further jeopardise schools' ability to fill shortages.' No. It is the government's policy of failing to train enough UK nationals that is the problem. And this is the result of lowering teachers' pay and worsening their conditions.

The article continues, *'Professor John Howson, a Government Advisor on teacher recruitment, said that in recent years, with pressures on funding, headteachers had looked to teachers from Eastern Europe, in particular to ease staff shortages. He said: 'I suspect that quite a lot of recruitment agencies have been operating particularly in places like Romania and Bulgaria where the standards in teaching maths are probably quite high.'* But, their living standards are lower and therefore their preparedness to work for less. As to the standards for maths 'probably' being quite high, the standards of teaching in Finland are definitely high in all areas. We won't be getting them from there though, even though they are in the EU. Their pay and conditions are infinitely better than here.

Re the EU's Single European Market (SEM). First, it should be pointed out that the EU is a customs union. It imposes custom tariffs on many, many goods from countries outside the EU i.e. it is in itself protectionist. The biggest - but by no means the only - protectionist area is agriculture and the Common Agricultural Policy (CAP). In the book *The Great Deception; Can the European Union Survive?*, the authors Booker and North write, *"By far the most expensive object in the budget, the CAP had become a byword for inefficiency, fraud and excess. Its subsidy system was creating huge surpluses: the beef and butter 'mountains', the milk and wine 'lakes', much of which were then dumped on third (world) countries, undercutting their markets and causing them immense damage."*

They then came up with a brilliant wheeze to lessen the embarrassing massive surpluses being produced at huge cost to the taxpayer. The ultimate absurdity of capitalism - pay them to produce nothing! 'Set-aside'. *"As a result of grants offered to fruit growers to cut back their production, hundreds of British apple orchards were rooted up."*

On the continent the overproduction caused by the huge subsidies was met by the simple destruction of surpluses. In one year alone *"this would result in the destruction of 77% of the French apple crop and 73% of*

Italian pears. Greek farmers were paid millions to 'bulldoze 657,000 tons of peaches into the ground. The net result of compulsory set-aside was that in the first four years 'alone!' the scheme cost ... Taxpayers £4 billion". After giving many other examples Booker and North conclude *"The single market had far from succeeded in dismantling all protectionist barriers. All too often the promised 'level playing field' was a mirage."*

They demonstrate and comment on one in particular of the intrinsic flaws in 'free' open markets both within the EU, and the wider world scale. It is the example of what happened to the British fishing industry.

Fish in our territorial waters were opened up to be caught by other EU countries. Britain has gone from Europe's largest fishing nation to being allocated just *"13% by value of the catch. When the fishermen hauled in their nets, they often caught a range of species for which they had no quota. Since it would be a criminal offence to land these, the only alternative was to return their illegal catch to the sea, by which time the fish would be dead. This practice was to lead within a few years to an ecological disaster as fishermen were forced to 'discard' billions of fish every year".* We are told the environmental 'discard' has been ended. Fishermen must now bring all their catch back to land. But only so that millions of fish can be discarded to landfill instead. When a country has full control of their waters as Iceland has, they can conserve their fish. Iceland's fisheries flourish. Well done Iceland for winning the Cod Wars – a lesson for others.

What has happened and is happening in Greece? This is what I said in my ATL Presidential speech in September 2012. "If we think that the effects of the austerity policy on education in the UK are bad now, and they are, look at the effects in Greece. A June TES article 'Teaching in a climate of despair', paints a bleak picture. *"How would you feel if your salary had already been halved in the past two years? Where some teachers struggle to afford to feed their own children, pupils have fainted from hunger? Schools shut for days because no one can afford the heating? More than 1,000 schools closed? This is not some fictional nightmare, a disaster in the developing world, nor a grim vision from history. This is Greece in 2012".* This is spreading. Italy, Spain, Portugal, Ireland – where next?" Since then things have only got worse in particular for the Greeks.

Protectionism

Before looking at wider issues concerning free trade itself, I would like to look at the hypocrisy of the advanced industrial nations that denounce any protectionist policies of developing countries. In the book *The Bad Samaritans; the Guilty Secret of Rich Nations and the Threat to Global Prosperity*, the author Ha-Joon Chang writes *"Practically all of today's developed countries including Britain and the US, the supposed homes of the free market and free trade, have become rich on the basis of policy recipes that go against neo-liberal economics."*

"Today's rich countries use protection and subsidies, whilst discriminating against foreign investors". However, for third world countries, *"WTO* (World Trade Organisation) *agreements act strongly to prevent this and it is proscribed by aid donors… notably the IMF and World Bank."*

"People in the rich countries" he continues, *"preach free markets and free trade to poor countries in order to capture larger shares of the latter's market and to pre-empt the emergence of possible competitors. They are saying 'do as we say not as we did' and act as Bad Samaritans taking advantage of others who are in trouble"*.

"Britain and the US are not the homes of free trade, in fact for a long time they were the most protectionist countries in the world".

"For developing countries, free trade has rarely been a matter of choice, it was often an imposition from outside, sometimes even through military power". He gives the example of the opium War. *"This was a particularly shameful episode even by the standards of 19th-century imperialism. The growing British taste for tea had created a huge trade deficit with China. In a desperate attempt to plug the gap, Britain started exporting opium produced in India to China. The mere detail that selling opium in China was illegal could not possibly be allowed to obstruct the noble cause of balancing the books"*. When China resisted war ensued and China was heavily defeated. One of the colonial 'unequal treaties' was signed in the Treaty of Nanking 1842. China was forced to lease Hong Kong and give up the right to set up its own tariffs.

The author continues, *"So there it was – the self-proclaimed leader of the 'liberal' (free trade) world declaring war on another country because the latter was getting in the way of its illegal trade in narcotics. The truth is that the movement of goods, people and money that developed under British hegemony between 1870 and 1913 – the first episode of globalisation – was made possible in large part by military might rather than market forces".*

Concluding my quotes from what is a detailed and excellent book which I highly recommend, Ha-Joon Chang says, *"There was a brief period during the 1860s and the 1870s when something approaching free trade did exist in Europe especially with zero tariffs in Britain. However this proved short lived. From the 1880s most European countries raised protective barriers again, partly to protect their farmers from cheap food imported from the New World and partly to promote their newly emerging 'heavy' industries such as steel, chemicals. Finally even Britain ... abandoned free trade and introduced tariffs in 1932. The official history describes this event as 'succumbing to the temptation of protectionism'. It fails to mention that this was due to the decline in British economic supremacy, which was the result of the success of protectionism on the part of competitor countries, especially the USA in developing their own industries."*

I also recommend an Australian book, *The Great Multi-National Tax Rort*[58]. *How we are all being robbed* by Martin Feil. He recounts and documents the hollowing out of the Australian economy by 'free trade' policies. The multi-nationals destroying national industries and he describes transfer pricing strategies and methods whereby multi nationals avoid tax.

The simplicity of the situation is clear, indeed stark. If you are the top dog and produce products the most efficiently and cheaply, you do not want any barriers to getting your goods into other countries to be sold. An advantage of this is that it will undermine the development of competitor goods because they will be unable to price match yours.

Free trade in this context fosters and breeds underdevelopment.

Trade is War

In his book *Trade Is War: the West's War Against the World*, Yash Tandon writes in his introduction, *'The WTO is a veritable war machine. If small and middle sized countries do not 'follow the rules' as dictated*

---

[58] Australian/NZ slang for a fraudulent or dishonest act or practice, "a tax rort"

by the powers that effectively control the WTO then they are collectively and individually subject to sanctions'. He continues, *'It is not a war in the ordinary sense of the term – war with bombs and drones – but trade in the capitalist Imperial era is as lethal, and as much a 'weapon of mass destruction' as bombs. Trade kills people. It drives people to poverty. It creates a wealth at one end and poverty at the other; it enriches the powerful food corporations at the cost of marginalising poor peasants who then become economic refugees in their own countries or who (those that are able-bodied) attempt to leave their countries to look for employment in the development countries of the West – across the Mediterranean from Africa to Europe'* (for example).

He touches on the example of India. *'In the 17th and early 18th centuries, English trade with India ended up with England colonising India. The East India Company, chartered as a company of merchants of London trading in the East Indies initially came to trade in commodities such as cotton, silk, dye, salt, tea and* (of course) *opium. Over time by skilfully playing the game of divide and conquer, the company created its own administration and military force to rule over India. The natives revolted in 1857, which the British called 'rebellion'; it was brutally crushed and in 1858 the British Crown assumed direct control of a vast country approximately 13.5 times the size of England.'*

In *De-industrialisation in India: Process Causes and Effects*, Pratik Sharma writes, *'....By the standards of the 17th and 18th centuries i.e. before the advent of the Europeans in India, India was the industrial workshop of the World.' 'Britain experienced 'industrialisation' in the mid-18th-century and India experienced 'de-industrialisation' at the same time. The process of de-industrialisation of India began with the gradual disappearance of cotton manufacturers from the list of India's exports and the remarkable growth of cotton manufacturers in the list of her imports mainly from Britain.'*

It was the usual colonial imperialist policy. One way free trade. A policy of protection through the imposition of import duties. But for India we preached free trade! And enforced it by economic and military power as required. Trade was war. India's indigenous cotton textile industry was destroyed; Britain ruled the world.

In another book *The Case Against the Global Economy* edited by Goldsmith and Mander, in the introduction Mander prophetically writes, *'It is new that the world's democratic countries voted to suppress their own democratically enacted laws in order to conform to the rules of the new central global bureaucracy. Also new is the elimination of most regulatory control over global corporate activity and the liberation of currency from national control, which lead, in turn to what Richard Barnett and John Kavanagh described as the 'Casino economy' ruled by currency speculators'.'*

As always if nothing is done it only gets worse, but could even they have envisaged the likes of TTIP (Transatlantic Trade and Investment Partnership) and its burgeoning family. Bilateral Investment Treaties (BITs) and Free Trade Agreements (FTAs) are binding agreements between two or more countries. Investment protection provisions contained in these agreements called Investor-to-State Dispute Settlements (ISDS) allow private companies to sue governments for any government action that has limited or interfered with their profits or potential profit. The cases are heard in secret by unelected unaccountable international tribunals. ISDS cases can be brought to compensate investors for damages resulting from legislation in areas like environmental protection, data protection, privacy, financial markets, food standards, health, labour, social security, energy and media. Judgements, of which there have already been 767 by 2017, have cost millions even billions (2014 Yukos Universal registered for tax purposes in the Isle of Man!) was awarded US$50 billion against Russia.

In a series of broadsheets entitled Trade and Brexit Briefing, supported by War on Want, Friends of the Earth, Global Justice Now, Trade Justice Movement and UNISON, Briefing 4 states, *'The UK decision to leave the European Union (EU) means that for the first time in 40 years, trade policy will return to UK government competence ... With the UK government's ability to negotiate its own trade deals, comes a huge opportunity to achieve a truly progressive trade agenda in Southern countries.'* (And indeed I would argue for Northern too.)

I conclude with an extract from Larry Elliott and Dan Atkinson's book, *Europe Isn't Working.* In writing about socialists' opposition to the EU it states, *'As a general rule, they tended to be the sort of leftist who had never bought into the reinvention of Britain's Labour Party and its fellow movements in European... countries as enthusiasts of free markets. John Pilger* (the veteran campaign journalist) *is a case in point. He issued a scorching blast in 1998 at the notion that the single currency would have much to do with the joys of European togetherness or with European notions of democracy and prosperity for all... Pilger ripped*

*into Europe as a cartel run by Germany's 'conservative elite' and the
Bundesbank, which wanted to bring all the other countries to heel with
stringent economic conditions ...* (Pilger says) *'As governments strive to
meet these conditions by cost-cutting on jobs, health, welfare, education
and transport, economic and social disaster beckons throughout the
European Union, especially in the poorer countries'.*

Prescient I believe. His view has not changed. So, in answer to this
article's title, Can a socialist support Brexit? if Tony Benn and Bob Crow
could and John Pilger can, I believe the answer is yes

Brexit update

It is now three years since our country voted by a majority to leave the
EU i.e. for Brexit. Brexit has not happened. Who would have foreseen
this? Well at least I had a serious doubt immediately it had occurred. As
I wrote earlier at the time, *just watch the powers that be try and weasel
out of it.* Millions and millions of pounds have been spent on trying to get
out of this decision. Even if the people's decision was 'wrong' as it
certainly was when they voted Thatcher in, the way that democracy
works is that is if there is a majority vote in favour that is what happens.
If there ceases to be a democratic way of deciding things the other
alternative is by force of arms.

As the historian David Starkey[59] wrote in his article in The Mail on
Sunday on 17 March 2019, *'In holding a mediaeval king accountable to
his subjects – or some of them, at least – Magna Carta was a
revolutionary step and is rightly celebrated'.* He continues, *'All is not well
with Britain or our politics… Is it silly to think there is a touch of 1215 – a
whiff of revolution – in the air?'* Continuing, *'The referendum was a very
British revolution and it has been followed by a very British counter-
revolution which shows every sign of succeeding.' 'Don't be deceived by
the lack of violence or the comparative good manners of those now
seizing control. This is a coup, and what is at stake is the nature and
legitimacy of Parliament itself.' 'Ruled by comfortable, smug elites,
Parliament is choosing to ignore the ordinary British people as they
attempt to hold Parliament to account.' 'It is no exaggeration to say that
British democracy, which stands in direct line with Magna Carta, is now
unravelling before us.'*

---

[59] Yes I know that Starkey is right wing but the issues of democracy, self determination and nationhood
transcend party and previous categorisations of 'left wing' or 'right wing'.

'*The people voted 52 to 48 per cent to leave, an estimated 74 per cent of MPs voted to remain. No representative assembly can sustain such a gulf. Either people or Parliament must give way*'.

He quotes the great German poet and playwright Bertolt Brecht:
Wouldn't it
Be simpler in that case if the government
Dissolved the people and
Elected another?
He ends, '*And where will it end? In another very British revolution? Or something nastier? I don't want to prophesize, good historian that I am, but I fear the worst.*' My line is that they shall reap as they shall sow.

Since the original vote I got hold a copy of the document opposite, which further shows, whether it is liked or not, what the mood of the people was contrasting to those in Parliament in this democratic exercise.

In parliamentary elections or council elections or trade union elections, a single vote can make a majority. Regarding the leave vote it was a small majority percentage in favour, but actually a large number (1.3 million) but we are

EU Referendum Results 2016

By Votes
17.4m Leave | 16.1m Remain

By Constituency
406 Leave | 242 Remain

Constituency By Party
Lab: 148 Leave | 84 Remain
Con: 247 Leave | 80 Remain

By Region
9 Leave | 3 Remain

By MP
160 Leave | 486 Remain

Brexit isn't the problem. It's our MP's who are the problem.

looking at a principle here. It has been clearly documented that there was misinformation on both sides of the campaign. Welcome to elections and especially politicians! Overturning of a democratic decision of this nature, size and purpose is more than just asking for trouble. Have I got this wrong? If so, how?

Will Podmore in his meticulous and solidly researched book *Brexit: The Road to Freedom* clearly clarifies these results compared with general elections. *'Some said the majority was not big enough to be decisive. But leave voters outvoted stay voters by a majority of 3.8 per cent. This was a bigger margin of victory than in nine of the 20 postwar general elections: 1950, 1951, 1955, 1964, 1970, February 974, October 1974, 2005 and 2017. Were those nine elections not decisive? In a democracy, the majority gets its way.'* *'Some said the turnout was not high enough for the result to be valid. But the turnout, 72.2 per cent of the electorate, was higher than in seven postwar general elections – 1970, 1997, 2001, 2005, 2010, 215 and 2017 ... Were those seven elections not valid?'*

Are We the Cause of Our Downfall?

But isn't our downfall primarily caused by internal forces? Haven't people, institutions and Parliament in the UK been destroying Britain either actively or through inactivity? If they get control through Brexit of an independent Britain, won't they just carry on doing this?

Internal forces have indeed been a major factor in our massive decline.

Tony Benn well characterizes the early changes in British society as a change from the power of the wallet to the power of the ballot. He also characterised the history of the last thirty years up to his death as being a reversal with the transfer of power i.e. being from the ballot to the wallet. This is not to limit the working class in making some progress in developing more power in some constitutional realms or indeed unconstitutional. Civil disorder and riot i.e. physical protest and rebellion have always played a great part in Britain, and around the world, in halting our rulers' excesses. Witness Britain's most recent clear example[60], the Poll Tax Riots, which led to a climb-down and the rapid withdrawal of the poll tax policy and led to Thatcher's demise within months.

Power has and is being taken from the ballot and aggrandized to the wallet. This process is very well documented in Paul Foot's book *The*

---

[60] The Poll tax riots happened in 1990. There has subsequently been extensive rioting in many areas of the country in August 2011. We were on holiday on Easter Island and gasped in amazement when we saw television news footage of London in flames.

Vote. How it Was Won and How It Was Undermined. Since he wrote that it has only got worse.

Before this, the distribution of social production going to the workers had never been so high. In one sense MacMillan's phrase *'We had never had it so good'* was true. The effort of the fighters for social justice as a product of the war and war years and a new generation of students and young workers, 'children of the 60s', of whom I was lucky and privileged to be one, pushed our power and our treatment to a new high.

The 1970's was the time of the greatest equality in the distribution of wealth in Britain. Danny Dorling, one of the much-published experts in this field, writes in his book *Inequality and the 1%* that there was *'growing equality between 1918 and 1978... since the 1970's however wealth inequalities have grown again ... The 1970's, the era of maximum redistribution - are often pilloried. However, the 1970's were the best decade in which to be normal, not a bad decade in which to be poor, but a terrible decade in which to be rich .... No wonder there is now an attempt to rewrite history and describe those times to be terrible, when for most they were so good. The rewriting of history has worked and the media today presents a persistent gloomy assessment of the 1970's'.*

In *Poverty, Wealth and Place in Britain, 1968 to 2005*, a detailed study by the Joseph Rountree Foundation, it says, *'The trends indicate that during the 1970s, levels of poverty and core poverty dropped at fairly similar rates, both declining by around a third over the decade. During the 1980s, both poverty and core poverty increased substantially, effectively reversing the improvements seen in the previous decade'.*

And as a third, in the *Cost of Inequality – why Economic Equality is Essential for Recovery,* Stuart Lansley writes, *'The 1970's was to prove the high point of equality ... From that decade the level of inequality headed relentlessly in one direction, back towards the much wider gaps of the 1930's'.*

In his TV series on the history of post-war UK, Andrew Marr points out that from the time of Thatcher's election in 1979, *'Two Britains emerged in the 1980s. The rich got richer but the bottom 10% saw their incomes fall by about 17%. A lot of people fell through the cracks. Once Britain had prided itself on not seeing people sleeping on the streets or begging. Not anymore'.*

One eternally true overriding law of nature is that change is inevitable; nothing stands still forever. If you don't finish off your opponent, they will come back - and with the aim of finishing you off. Thatcher was chosen for the task - as was Hitler in Germany which is not to say that they were moral equivalents, though time and place maketh the man, or in her case, woman. In truth the old tweedledum and tweedledee in which Labour and Tory in office were not that different[61], was to be replaced by a new tweedledee and tweedledee in which they were virtually identical. Blair and Brown, and the various A N other(s) that will follow[62], have not only simply followed Thatcher but taken the whole process further.

Everything that has not been privatised - and God knows that list is extensive enough[63] - will be. Next up are education and health – in fact we are part the way through. These, of course, are the heartlands of social provision. Areas of public space and public provision carved out at huge effort and sacrifice by our forebears to ensure that all, especially the poorest and most vulnerable, got a reasonable education and reasonable health provision. Guaranteed - and provided - by the state because private provision for profit and/or charity did not, and could not, provide it for all. Neither in any case were they the best methods to provide it for the common people or indeed the nation as a whole.

We are by nature egalitarian - but not equalitarian - and it is about time that we acted to bring our society into harmony with our nature. This does require an end to passivity. Independent thought is thinking beyond the dross pumped out by most of the media. It does require collective action and participation. Nothing liberates the human spirit more - our essence as social animals - than participation in collective effort or struggle, except success and the achievement of victory.

---

[61] There were differences but all the main political parties operated in a very different consensus of social democracy accepting high levels of taxation of the rich, nationalisation etc, etc.

[62] Written before Corbyn's election to Labour Party leader. He is certainly not A N Other or business as usual. That said, he will face immense difficulties in being able to make any real change in the status quo. The push for real change must come from the actions of those below.

[63] List of 165 industries privatised: see website

Chapter Eleven
COPLAND – A NEW ERA

Sladebrook was a school like no other. But it is no use living in the attics of history as my friend and colleague Brian Williams would say. Our task as humans is to try and make our environment better suit our collective needs, and personal needs and wants. This includes you working by individual example, and collectively with your colleagues, to change your working and living environment. As I pen these words, I am in Tibet looking some of the time out of the windows of the high-altitude pressurised train to Lhasa. It is a desert landscape. I see areas of land divided up into thousands of little rock squares, with stones sticking up out of the ground. I ask our guide what they are. He says it's very windy up here and this is done to get grass to be able to grow and take root in land that otherwise would be bare. People changing their environment. It is the human condition. Our destiny, collectively as a whole so long as we shall continue to exist, but also individually. The study of science has shown us that nothing is inevitable though some things may be massively more likely – or unlikely – than others. The important point is, as it said in the Small Faces song, "*Whatcha gonna do about it*".

Under a deal with the Local Authority I agreed to move from Sladebrook to Copland. That got Brent off the hook of possibly losing a High Court case for victimising me on the grounds of trade union activity. It got me off the hook of possibly losing my job and never being able to work in teaching again. I set about organising at Copland. First though, I had to prove myself as a good teacher. I'm given the worst class in the school. Probable the reason Alan Davies accepted me when every other secondary Head in the Borough refused. I set about re-educating them, helped greatly by my control freak nature.

Easier said than done. One particular little bastard, sorry challenging pupil, I made stay in and work from my stock room for a month. The Deputy Head of Year said that I couldn't do that. I said words to the effect of bollocks and gave her a full blast of patronization saying I was a teacher of future murderers in one of the toughest schools in the country when she was in nappies. I didn't need her to tell me how to deal with this sort of kid. She raised her complaint with the pastoral system. They threatened to take disciplinary action against me. I responded by saying that Steve Sinnott the DGS of the NUT would be my representative and Graham Clayton the senior solicitor, my legal adviser - no of course I hadn't asked them. The threat of disciplinary action soon disappeared. In combat, bluff and even deception are sometimes necessary. As Winston Churchill said, '*In wartime, truth is so precious that she should always be attended by a bodyguard of lies.*' The 'challenging' pupil's behaviour did improve.

Whilst working really hard professionally, I set about working with others to get the workplace better organised and start to change things to secure improvement. For workers, the understanding that they do have real power and strength if they stick together and stand up for themselves, and that they can actually change things, is what it is all about. I was fortunate in having great assistance in this from Lesley Thompson, now Gouldbourne, who also managed to get transferred from Sladebrook to Copland. Davies, realising that my reputation as the Devil incarnate, a trouble maker simply for the sake of making trouble, was nonsense and that I was actually a good teacher and a reasonable bloke - did I say that? - and heeding my statement that Lesley was a good teacher, took her on as well! In retrospect, if he could have foreseen that he was going to rob the school and try to privatise the management of it, this was a serious mistake. However, all that was in the future. Lesley has tremendous organising skills and is a great trade unionist. Davies however did choose to employ another PE teacher in preference to John Willoughby another Sladebrook teacher – great bloke, great teacher and strong union colleague. Davies obviously didn't want to risk a complete rats' nest in his school.

Not long after arriving at Copland, the authority proposed it for closure. Am I paranoid or were they out to get us? The Head and I shared a deep interest in common, not losing our jobs, and became firm allies in the campaign that had to be conducted to defeat the closure proposal. The only way to win in war is, as Mao said, "to unite all who can be united". So we set about a whole school campaign which included a march of teachers, parents and pupils to the Town Hall for a council meeting debating the subject; virtually laying siege to the Town Hall to massive musical accompaniment from the school band. This was led by Liz Sharma, a great music teacher and another Sladebrook refugee, but who was not one of the hardcore union activists.

The government had just introduced Grant Maintained Schools. GMS status took you out of the LEA control. It was a first step on the road to privatisation, to fragment the education service and marginalise or end the LEAs. However, it was an escape route, a lifeline for us. I had no hesitation in saying we should go for it. The national unions' line was to oppose GMS. In general, this was correct. However, when facing the loss of your job and colleagues' jobs, and your school, it is not. In our society there is a class war. It exists whether all understand this or not. This is not to say that every individual in the capitalist class is at war with every individual in the working class or vice versa. It is simply a recognition of the nature and engine of our society. Individuals not fitting into this general categorisation is very well illustrated by Frederick Engels, a capitalist and collaborator and funder of Karl Marx. This leads me to say hi Dermot, one of my very best friends who is a small time[64] capitalist. Human friendship existed before the creation of classes and it will continue to exist after society abolishes them.

Survival is the nature of the game and it is a recognition of the reality that it is most important that those that are the best fighters and the best organisers, survive. In a war, the loss of a battle hardened crack division is felt more than the loss of a newly conscripted one. The general concept of the *égalité*, so stridently and correctly raised in the French Revolution under their slogan Liberty, Equality, Fraternity, should not as I have said, be taken as meaning that all humans are equal. They demonstrably are not. It is not elitism to want to save your best troops. It is the best way to ensure the welfare, even the survival, of the collective, the group, army, school, factory or whatever. We won, beating closure. We continued with our slow but certain building of union membership and seeking to improve conditions.

A major challenge came when we were one of the earliest schools in the country to be selected to be inspected by the newly created Ofsted regime. I advocated that we should boycott it. The Head panicked and launched a 'reds under the bed' or in this case 'red in the school' scare saying following my line would lead to closure of the school etc., etc. We had excellent, heated and massive debates within the staff. At first, we won the vote, but lost a subsequent one. Such is democracy.

I did produce a good document called TOSH (on website) and gave it to the Inspectors before the inspection started saying that they had been

---

[64] I know that calling him 'small time' will wind him up. Being a millionaire makes him a pretty big capitalist in his and I am sure in most people's eyes. But for billionaires, millionaires like the rest of us are not even s..t on their shoes. It is the billionaires that really run and control our society. Read *Pity the Billionaire* by Thomas Frank and *The Trouble with Billionaires. How the Superrich Hijacked the World (and how we can take it back)* by Linda McQuaig and Neil Brooks.

specially sent in to get us and were going to fail us[65]. Paranoid allegations can be very useful. The only way that they can prove that you're wrong, and that you are just a paranoid idiot, is for what you are saying is going to happen, not to happen. This even if they were intending to do it, which they probably were. We passed the Ofsted.

By astute lobbying and a strong collective stance, we managed to ensure first that all staff got an extra recruitment and retention point and later another, making us the only school in the borough to have two Recruitment and Retention points. Other London boroughs did better. Camden, for example, had two R&Rs in all schools. What you get you have to fight for, and if you don't fight, you don't get. This applies to every field. What follows is another example, a tragic example.

Death on the Line

A young boy is running along the train track near Wembley station. His name is Patrick Mullings and he is 15 years old. He is severely autistic and obsessed with trains. He is also prone to run off at any chance he gets to escape from his carers. Moments later he is dead. Hit full pelt by an express train, his death is instantaneous.

What was he doing there? How did he get there? He had been allowed to go on a day school trip to a drama workshop. His school was Hay Lane special school who wanted to do their best and widen the experience of all their special needs pupils. Patrick, if he was allowed off the school premises or even go out with his parents, had to be attached by a strap from his wrist to his carers wrist because of his propensity to run off if the opportunity arose. On this tragic day the opportunity had arisen, and he had taken it.

On any school trip a risk assessment has to be conducted. In a special school this is especially important and with individual children like Patrick who were high risk, even more so. How had it come about that he had been able to run off? And what was it to do with me?

I was the Brent NUT Health and Safety Officer. I was contacted on the day that it happened by Jenny Cooper, the school union rep, to convey not only the horror of what had happened but her concern at how it had happened. Had the risk assessment been adequate? Had the school

---

[65] I had used this tactic when the DfE decided to have a special inspection of Sladebrook.

properly exercised its duty of care? Had any members of staff been negligent? The questions were straightforward but getting to the bottom of the matter and getting answers, and also justice for Patrick's parents were anything but straightforward. I began investigating to find out what had actually happened and who was responsible.

A wall of denial of responsibility and buck passing, descended. The more they manoeuvred the more determined I became to expose the truth. By now, because of my previous experience in investigations and reports concerning asbestos and other matters, I had become virtually an honorary investigative journalist.

What is important in these things is the quality and nature of your key allegation(s). The evidence is of course also crucial, but you have to grab, indeed demand attention with your key headline. I chose *Covering Up?* with a question mark. The straightforward title Covering Up might have been better, but you also have to keep a weather eye out for libel. Something many people don't know is that you can still be guilty of libel even if what you have written is the truth. That is also why I titled it a *First Draft* and asked for any comments. This is to slow them down from bringing libel charges as they have had an opportunity to suggest possible changes to it.

Included in my Report was a quote from the Evening Standard article where Mr Mullings questioned what had happened. "*I want to know why my son was allowed on a school outing without being closely watched … He suffered behavioural problems … Whenever I took him out he was attached to me with a strap so that both our wrists were tied together … If he had been properly supervised, he would still be with us today.*"

In the Report these are some of the statements made by members of staff. '*A supply teacher was asked to go on the trip at a day's notice*'. Only one child had parental consent. '*Despite recommendations, all children listed went on the trip. This was an extremely difficult group … and no staff were present who were experienced with those particular children*'. '*A wrist strap … was used for A* (Patrick) *by the parent and 1:1 assistant.*' '*There was no set school policy for this*'. Once in the building the wrist strap was removed. They assumed the building was secure. It wasn't and they hadn't properly checked. '*A's (new) 1:1 assistant who had been allocated two children to supervise ... took E to the toilet.' 'A ran out of the building and onto the railway lines.'*

There had been no risk assessment of the security of the building where the drama workshop took place. My research showed that there were health and safety guidelines and Health and Safety legislation that had been broken in this area and many other areas regarding this, both in the school and at Local Authority level.

The upshot was the authority still denied any liability. I spoke to Mr Mullings about it. All he wanted was an admission that the school had failed. It was not Patrick's fault or wrongdoing. Because the local authority retains liability for health and safety matters in its schools, if the school had failed to fulfil its duty of care and breached health and safety requirements, they were liable. They were but they denied it. Take them to court I say, they are as guilty as sin. The Mullings didn't have enough money for that. We can't just let them get away with it. I thought - we have the money - so I discussed it with Jean. We decided we'd upfront the money to bring a court case. If we won, we'd get the money back in court costs. And if we lost it would cost around £8000 in the end, not inconsiderable if you consider it was about 16 years ago.

But you can't put a price on justice. It is our duty to fight for it and get it if humanly possible. Thanks Jean as always for agreeing. We won. The Mullings gratitude knew no bounds. Jenny and the staff held a memorial event in the school and a tree was planted in the grounds to his memory – RIP Patrick. For this work and my other H&S work including on asbestos, I won the TUC Health and Safety Rep of the Year in 2003, the first time a teacher had won this award.

Chapter Twelve
TENT CITY OCCUPATION

It was a bitterly cold winter's evening in March 2007. The winds must have been blowing over from Siberia. Jean and I walked onto the site and set up our tent. It was the Wembley Park Sports Ground where the Labour controlled Council was proposing to build an Academy. Lord Levy, Labour fixer and fundraiser and tennis partner of Tony Blair, was on the stump around the country trying to get 'sponsors' for Tony's new Academies, the start of his privatisation of education agenda. It was done under the guise of the programme being to aid the most disadvantaged, deprived and underachieving secondary school children, and under the disguise that the rich or rather super-rich would be helping out by putting in some of their own money. Two million was the minimum requirement. Multi-millionaire Labour and Tory donors came forth. Nothing wrong with backing both 'sides' especially when both sides are on your side, extending the reach of your control over the system. In this case via the education system, and also opening up a new area to the potential for profit making. The situation was captured in one of what I called Scurrill sheets for the obvious reason that we wanted to make the most scurrilous attack on the person(s) involved, but also make sure we couldn't be sued. This was done on the basis that *"they don't like it up 'em"*, and also emulating in a small way the 18th century cartoonists and satirists like Hogarth, Gillray, Cruikshank and Rowlandson.

I must mention here Francis Beckett's ground-breaking book, *The Great City Academy Fraud*, which was seminal. I wrote a review for The Teacher magazine in June 2007 which shows how useful it was for our campaign being published at absolutely the right moment. *'It is impossible to commend this elegantly written book highly enough. It's packed with killer quotes and facts. I have the rather desecrating habit of turning the corners of pages down if they have a particularly important item. Almost every other page is now dog-eared.'*

We appeal to others to join our one tent occupation – one did, then another, and another. It grew and in the end we had a dozen people camping there permanently and many, many others camping overnight, occasionally or on a short term basis. Shane Johnschwager, a drinking buddy from Copland who was also active in the union, was one of them. His tent was decked out like a Bedouin Sheikh's. We had been campaigning hard before the occupation but, as was going to set the path for the future, we weren't getting very far. The lessees of the businesses on the sports ground site - a private nursey, a car wash and a motor cycle driving school - sublet from the main lessees Atul Baktah and Minaxi Dang. Atul Baktah managed the sports ground activities, football matches, and previously quadbike racing before our occupation, and wedding receptions and meetings in the main hall.

The council was endeavouring to compulsorily purchase the site and give it to the 'sponsor' to set up an Academy. The identity of the 'sponsor' was a closely guarded secret. Before the occupation we hold a public meeting on the site - hall provided gratis by Atul - and invite a list of speakers, one of whom is Ann John, Labour Leader of the Council, and who turned up much to our surprise. The hall was full. Perhaps it was because we had leafleted the whole adjacent surrounding area of Barn Hill. The residents were not enamoured of losing the sports ground and having it replaced by a large, new, secondary with the increase in noise and traffic. Never mind our pointing out that this was the start of the privatisation of state education and that anyway the need for more school places was in the south of the borough not the north.

I shouldn't perhaps have been so ungracious to Ann John, as she had agreed to speak, but I had a trap prepared for her. At the meeting I publicly ask her, "*Will you reveal the name of the 'sponsor? Why should it be kept a secret? What did the Council or the 'sponsor' have to hide?"* She is a bit embarrassed or appears to be, but resolutely refuses to reveal their name. "*That's a great pity*" I say, "*because I already know their name, but I think it only right that you, the Council, should reveal it to the local residents and Council tax payers rather than me*". She still keeps mum and declines. Perhaps she thinks I am bluffing. I'm not. "*It's Andrew Rosenfeld*", I announce with some drama. "*Why couldn't you just have told us?*"

I had been secretly informed of this. I have found over the years that many in positions of authority within the system secretly despise it, or aspects of it. If they know from reputation that you will never reveal a source, they are happy to give you information - which I have had on a number of occasions, some on matters of more moment than this.

Our attacks that followed on Rosenfeld personally were merciless. In addition, our dirt digging, dirt dishing Scurrill sheets were sent far and wide including to the media. We tracked down this property magnate's headquarters at 42 Wigmore St, London. We decided we were going to have a demonstration outside and tell the press. We wrote to him saying we wanted to have a meeting to explain why we opposed his proposal. We decided that our line was that it would be a 'white elephant'. Not only would it remove a sports ground facility when there was already a shortage in Brent, but it was not even in an area where a new school was needed. The school proposal was 'a white elephant' we decided.

Could we hire an elephant for the demo? I search and research, but could I find an elephant daily hire firm? You're right, I couldn't. I can't remember how I found out about it but Hamleys, the toy shop in Regents Street had a very large stuffed elephant for sale. There were also proper elephant masks for sale. Talcum powder was used to change our elephant from grey to white. The 'white elephant' demo took place outside Rosenfeld's offices. Just prior to it I got a call. My first from a multi-multi-millionaire. It was Andrew Rosenfeld himself. He would meet me and answer any questions if I would call off the demo. The first question I wanted to ask was "Will you lend me a tenner?" but calling it off was a nonstarter. I said to him *"you call off your proposal and we'll call off our demo"*.

The demo went ahead and was covered by the Press.

We also blew up a massive picture of him, with accompanying derogatory but true text, and had it on huge billboards inside and on the outside perimeter fence at the sports ground. *'They don't like it up 'em'.* On the way back from the Easter teacher conferences on April 11th 2007

we hear Rosenfeld couldn't take the heat and has pulled out. A great victory and one showing **personal targeting works!**

Great. But they do give up and go away. No they're like cockroaches; unless you exterminate the lot another one will be back. Enter ARK, a rats' nest of cockroaches to mix my metaphors. Absolute Return for Kids. Absolute return is a mantra for Hedge funds. Some say it was named ARK after Arkie Busson, the Hedge funder and international playboy who headed ARK at the time. He denied it. But as Christine Keeler said of Profumo's denials at the time, "*He would say that wouldn't he*".

What to do? What's our strategy? Yes, strengthen and extend the occupation. Put your body where your mouth is. Yes, research, dig the dirt, and spread it, wide scale publicity. Yes, try legal challenge, normally unlikely to be successful and costly. Worth a go but not sufficient as a strategy in and of itself. Others? - take direct action if and as possible.

Six months later

I'm clambering through the undergrowth. I'm leading television journalist Riz Lateef to a surprise, well actually her third. We are in an area of woodlands that occupied the north east corner of the sports ground site. "*Here we are, look up*", I say. She slowly elevates her eyes and cranes her head backwards and says, "*????*". Everyone that has seen it has uttered a similar gasp of surprise or oath like "*fuck me!*" The third treehouse is the masterpiece It's over 50ft in the air. Two others have been built but they are both lower. This was Richie's Sistine chapel. Richie Cook. A New Zealander carpenter who was one of the Tent City occupiers.

I had considered how best we could resist and slow them down when they eventually decided to seek to forcibly evict us. We had already delayed them hugely. Part of our game plan was to slow them down so much as to make the whole thing such a pain in the backside, they'd give up and go somewhere easier. Removing people at height is always more difficult than on the ground because of the danger of injury or worse still death. They have to do proper risk assessments and prepare very carefully. Lesson: **organise your protest/occupation at height and as high as possible.** The M3 motorway protestors had taken to the trees and proved a bloody nuisance to remove.

When I had originally broached the idea, Richie had given a totally enthusiastic response. *"Yeah I could do that. I'd love to. I've always wanted to build a treehouse since I stayed in one in Thailand."* He was on. We'd find the money for the materials and he'd build them. Richie was part gibbon and part human. Fearless, an unerring sense of balance, and magnificent. I helped out a little bit but I wasn't even 1% gibbon. Richie's main assistant was one of the two Poles who were part of Tent City. When we first started the occupation the caretaker at the centre was a young Pole named Michel, a plumber by trade. We get friendly and he decided to live with us on the site. He was very helpful. He fixed running water for us, and a shower. But he has no head for heights. His friend (many apologies; I can't remember your name) who by that time was also living on site, was up for the job and became Richie's assistant. The pair of them did some death-defying aerial ballet work in building the treehouses, but at least we persuaded than to use the safety harnesses and ropes that Shane and Dave Kubenk, another teacher from Copland and firm supporter of the occupation, had from their mountain climbing. It was a mighty task to build one, never mind three, but we, or rather they, had the time.

The third tree house under construction.

Boy could Richie work and boy was he a master craftsman. Treehouses are not simple to build; they are not like garden sheds. Every tree is different – obviously - and if they are going to hold the weight of several people they have to be built extremely strongly. Richie explained with glee some of the difficult technical solutions he sorted. Luckily, for a collapsing treehouse and several dead protestors would have given us national publicity, but not the sort we could do with. The treehouses and our protest and cause were on the national news. We only learned later that Richie's assistant had been scared of heights but had faced and overcome them. Not one fucking hero but two!! In the event the Mexican standoff in the trees I was envisaging never occurred. We had a stand off but not in the trees.

After we had agreed to leave the site, when the lease for the businesses was extended for at least another year, Brent tried to get us to pay for the treehouses removal - £5000 and threatened court proceedings. Jean said, "*Take me to court I won't pay. I'm happy to go to jail.*" They dropped it.

Flashcamp

The term flashmob was first coined in 2003 and added to the Oxford English Dictionary in 2004. I'd like to claim credit for the term flashcamp but it's not in the OED - yet.

We had gathered in the darkness of night outside the sports ground centre. No-one apart from Jean knew what the target was, but they all knew it was going to be direct action and they were up for it. My brother Pete had turned up with his lorry that he'd borrowed from work. Rupert his employer didn't know, but he wouldn't have minded anyhow. He, and his partner Tina, had become friends, through playing table football with us in

Camden. He knew about Tent City and supported us. Our press release describes what happened.

'Tent City' protesters camp outside Brent Town Hall.

In a 4:00 am swoop tents, banners, a 20 foot scaffolding tower and even a portaloo were erected in less than an hour to create another 'Tent City'. The protesting teachers and parents are camped opposite the steps of Brent Town Hall and are collecting signatures for their petition, handing out leaflets and explaining their cause via a megaphone atop the scaffolding tower.

Hank Roberts, ATL and NUT executive member said, "The 'Flash Camp' is the latest in our protests. We camped on the proposed academy site for six months. We took to the tree houses when the Council threatened us with eviction and now we've taken our protest to the steps of the Town Hall. Our message is clear – give us a democratic vote on whether the proposed academy should be built on the Wembley Park site leading to the loss of the sports fields or not. If they don't give us this they can expect the campaign of direct action to continue and escalate."

What it doesn't describe is the surrounding 'picket fence'. Friendly lawyers told me that it was harder and a longer process for the police if the area you are occupying or squatting on is enclosed. The other thing we had  decided to act on was that they were very unlikely to organise an eviction on the Saturday and even less so on the Sunday. Our aim originally was to be gone by Sunday evening. In the event we stayed there a couple of days longer. All the councillors heard about it and most will have seen it in its full glory immediately opposite the front of Brent Town Hall. Whatever next! Indeed.

Highlights of our anti-ARK campaign.

At an ARK function in the Brent Town Hall, Jean empties a bin full of rubbish over the display and models featuring the proposed new school shouting *"It's a load of rubbish."* a moment captured on our Tent City DVD or on YouTube. Jason Parkinson, a brilliant independent filmmaker, made two excellent DVDs about Tent City and the events surrounding our campaign.

In July 2008 they again said they'd take over the sports ground and terminate the leases. We reoccupied the site. I defied a court order to vacate the sports ground. This led to a consequent court appearance on15th July 2008. A Mandela-esque 'history will vindicate me' lengthy speech is read out by me. The judge was pretty tolerant but even he got pissed off, asking repeatedly how long it was going to go on for. In the end he agreed I could hand in the rest of my type written speech. A fine of £3,750. As I said to the media afterwards, it's not exactly the cost of a pint of beer.

My defying of this county court injunction to vacate the site was heading for more trouble. The bailiffs repeatedly assured me that it would see me in jail. You don't lightly defy a court injunction. My thinking was yes, I might get a prison sentence. I thought it unlikely that it would be more than nine months and I could wear that. It could have the advantage of giving added publicity to the Tent City anti-ARK Academy fight and to the campaigning against Academies generally. Yes, it was worth the very small risk of a longer sentence. After all it wasn't like I was going to be transported to Australia for years of hard labour like the Tolpuddle martyrs fighting to form a union.

The day comes for my forcible eviction. The police turn up mob handed. National TV are present. A large number are with me on the roof of the sports ground building where I have taken up residence in a pop-up tent, with supplies including D-locks - the ones used to lock bicycles to metal railings or posts - ready to d-lock myself to the flagpole now flying the tent city flag on top of the building. Seeing that TV crew as well as a large group of supporters are present, an obviously high-level decision is taken not to proceed.

Jubilantly we celebrate our victory with speeches and later an impromptu party. They won't give notice of their next move.

Tent City occupation

It is early in the morning of 18th July 2008. As soon as they are spotted, the few present ring round for reinforcements and gather in the car park adjacent to the sports ground building. The police then en masse and with dogs move in; with some shoving and threats of arrest they clear the site - bar one d-locked to the flagpole.

An amusing side story is that when we had first tried out the d-lock to see if it would fit around the flag pole and a neck, I had tested it on Pete. It fitted. A close fit which would make it difficult for them to cut it without risking injuring the person's neck. On the day, I tried to put the lock on. Horror. It didn't fit. Though we hadn't noticed it or thought about it, my neck was a bit thicker than Pete's. Panic. It's going to be a bit easy to get me down if I'm not locked to anything! Fortunately, we have more than one d-lock so the idea quickly emerges. Put one d-lock around the flagpole and link that one to the other d-lock around my neck. It works, thank God. Success.

But the Laurel and Hardy sequence was not over yet. I arrange with Pete that at the last minute on the roof I would d-lock myself up and throw the keys down to him on a side of the building the police couldn't see. I throw the keys to him. ARGHH! Disaster. I misjudge it and the keys land on a ledge probably precisely where they will be coming up to get me. A terrible thought flashes through my mind. They come up, find the keys and the protest, embarrassingly and quickly, is over. I say to Pete, "*Quick, get the ladder*" which we normally use to get on the roof which we'd hidden round the back so as to not make their getting on the roof easy, "*then go along the ledge and get the keys*". At frantic speed Pete manages to get this done without being spotted by the police and bailiffs. A hero Pete.

In the event they turned up with a cherry picker. Up they come with a pair of bolt croppers. The d-lock is too strong. Victory. Round One. They call for the Fire Brigade. A surreal aspect of what was going on was that a camera crew from a Brighton College were on the roof. They wanted to film the action. After a bit of negotiation, the police officer in charge allows them to stay, provided they didn't get in the way. I think he might have had a bit of sympathy with our cause; after all it was a sports ground that local kids used in a Borough that was relatively deprived of these. The police had their own problems with government policies of cutbacks and privatisation of bits of the service.

The Fire Brigade turn up - and go. After a bit of debate, we heard they decided that this was a protest and not an emergency or any of their business so they refused to get involved or to do what they were asked. Solidarity. A private firm is employed and a man turns up with an angle grinder and blue fireproof sheeting. The sheeting is wrapped around exposed parts of my neck and the angle grinder started producing a hail of sparks. The surreal part; not only is this is being filmed[66] but a sound boom mike is thrust near to my face. I am being interviewed whilst this is going on! The sparks look like they might catch alight the furry sock thing that goes over the mike and burn my face or even catch my hair on fire. Fortunately, no such thing happens. There is enough drama for the day. All this time the evicted supporters and others have been chanting and shouting encouragement from behind the fence.

---

[66] We would really love to get the footage of this. If you are or know anyone from the film crew, presumably doing film or media studies from a Brighton College please contact me.

They ask me if I am going to struggle after they have cut me free.
I answer no. What would have been the point? I'd made my point. I am
put into the cherry picker and led out of the premises by the Bailiffs
holding my arms. In truth, I had asked them to do this as it looks better
for the cameras. A great PR stunt. Never underestimate the use of PR in
any struggle. They were happy to do it. Ours wasn't their normal
business, and who knows they may have personally sympathised with
our cause.

I'm at the gates surrounded by police. The officer in charge rings up and
asks, "What shall we do with him?" Answer "Release him". Result! No
being taken to the cells, awaiting trial, in the dock and then prison. Not
even another, but much more massive fine, which they can deduct from
your pay or bank account or force sale of your house to pay for. Jean
and I had also discussed this possibility. No: free to walk.

Actually, after a thank you and a brief 'we will fight them on the beaches'
speech to gathered supporters, it is get into the car, change clothes in
the back seat, and off to the High Court. No, not for defying the ban but
for our legal appeal against the Council's decision to hand the council
land - they owned the sports ground freehold - to ARK. Not surprisingly
we, or rather Leigh Day Solicitors and Matrix Chambers representing us,
lost. Not their fault. They were good. We had had far too good a run for

our money and the establishment wasn't about to take any more. The site was cleared. The court had issued an order that as well as the fine, I was not allowed to go on the site for 2 years. If I returned again it probably would be prison and more than likely for longer, possibly considerably longer than nine months. We're done they think, and we're done you may think. But wait – not so.

ARK paid nothing for this land. We the people had paid for it. Now de facto ARK owns it.

In the run up to our eviction, Jean had been talking to people about who might support us. A name of an activist group of squatters came up. Jean made contact and subsequently we went to meet them and speak to them. We espoused our cause and they agreed it was a good and worthwhile one. Ergo very shortly after we were removed and I and other named occupiers threatened with legal metaphorical hanging, drawing and quartering if we returned, we, or to put it correctly they, were back. The sports ground was occupied again!

We heard from an insider who as usual shall remain nameless that they couldn't believe it. They were utterly exasperated, and the Director of Education said, "*Are there no lengths these people won't go to?*" Answer some - but not many. We said, they're nothing to do with us. They've just decided independently it's a good cause. None of them were previous occupiers.

They didn't have any proof that we did have any connection, but on the other hand how could we prove that we didn't. If there was no connection, and provably so, they would have to go through the eviction process again causing further delay. The building programme was already well delayed. How likely is it that there was a connection? You're right, bloody overwhelmingly. So the judge just granted an immediate eviction order. They leave them for a week and then the police turn up mob handed and in no mood to mess around. They probably knew they were hardened squatters from their surveillance techniques; telephoto lenses, phone tapping, and informants. As we have learnt recently undercover police actually joined such action groups. We were certainly very security conscious regarding minimum contact and no phone contact.

These protestors were the real McCoy. The police were rough with them. We witnessed some of it as did They knew how to link their arms and legs creating the greatest difficulty in being prised apart and to being physically carried out.

A bulldozer had been brought to the site presumably to remove the massive barricade we had constructed. It was made of old tyres mixed with bits of metal girders etc. to make it a problem to move and smeared with honey to make it attractive to wasps and bees -  you're right, nothing if not inventive. Anyhow they managed to let down one of the bulldozer tyres – lucky it was not a tracked one.

ARK invasion

Surely done now? Still not – quite. I come to what was our most inventive and most audacious moment, and I think probably the one that surprised them most. ARK headquarters was at 15 Adam Street off the Strand. We had heard again from an informant whose name will remain secret (unless of course they ever want to divulge it) that the security at ARK HQ was very tight. Not surprising really with the amount of direct action we had taken. The front doors were kept locked. The reception was permanently manned and all visitors had to sign in. The two lifts would only open and operate by the use of a key.

I speculated about the possibility of climbing onto the roof and abseiling down and smashing our way through the windows, but quickly decided against it because the use of force and damaging property would be held against us. Probably it was virtually impossible, short of hiring a helicopter and coming down onto the roof by wire[67], anyhow. I think we

---

[67] You'd have to pretend you're a film company doing a stunt and the licences would have to be obtained and what with precautions against terrorism it would be a very, very long shot.

could probably occupy the lobby by getting one smartly dressed person to get them to open the door to them, and the rest, hiding from view, suddenly charging in. Difficult.

We knew the name of the ARK manager of the office, again courtesy of our informant. The smartly dressed person, or better still in terms of getting them to drop their guard she, could suddenly drop to the floor preventing the door from shutting and we all pile in and push our way through and occupy the lobby. Good, but not really what we want. Other firms shared the building but we want to hit just ARK. How could we do it?

Masterstroke. The day comes. We are a smallish group. Too big would invite suspicion. We are all extremely smartly dressed, except for Pete my brother who is dressed in his normal work gear. Big black boots, shorts and a cap. I don't know who they thought he was, the gardener? Or perhaps they just didn't notice him in the generally smart group. Jason was dressed as he normally was and looked - well - clearly like a cameraman. Apart from Jean and me, the two other brave hearts that were part of this crack team were Lioba Rebstock, an ex-girlfriend with whom I had retained good relations and who had actively supported Tent City, and my current girlfriend Lena who also supported Tent City.

Our bold crew of six sally forth to the ARK HQ. I bought a massive and beautiful bouquet of flowers. The ruse was that it was the manager's birthday and we wanted to wish her a happy birthday - and Jason with his camera was obviously there to film this happy event. The door opens. We're in. Jean, carrying the bouquet, explained why we are here as she has a posh accent. Our story is swallowed hook line and sinker. Only one of us had to sign in. Jean did. Then the security guard says he will take us up. The key is in the lock. The lift opens and we go in. the suspense is palpable but friendly chit chat is exchanged. The security guard comes out with us at the appropriate floor and says pointing to reception and a receptionist *"the lady there will help you"*, and promptly gets back in the lift to go back to the foyer having dutifully delivered his cargo which most certainly is not what it seems.

"Hello" I say, *"we are friends and colleagues of Katie Oliver. Could we speak to her?"* The receptionist answers, *"Have you got an appointment? She's not in"*. A bit of a blow but there's no accounting for happenstance. I quickly recalibrate. *"That's ok. We'll speak to the senior*

ARK person who's here". Again she comes back with, *"Have you got an appointment?"*. *"No, we don't need one"* I say, as a confounded if not dumbfounded look comes over her face.

Suddenly Pete unfolds his protest flag and we reveal our tent city occupation t-shirts while holding up a banner reading *'No academy. Save our Sports Ground'*. It is crystal clear now we are protestors who have tricked our way in. At this point the poor security guard who so helpfully saw us upstairs is called back upstairs. He tells us to leave. I announce we will leave as soon as we have spoken to the senior ARK Representative present about ARK's proposal to have a school built on the Wembley Sports ground site. The security guard then notices that Jason is filming and moves across aiming to take Jason's camera. Jason gives him a, probably well practiced, blurb about the legal definition of assault and damage to one's personal property and that he is a registered member of the NUJ and he would definitely make a complaint to the police. The security guard, realising that the receptionist had by now called the police, and that there was no point in staying at this Mexican standoff, goes back to the lobby to await the police and inform them on their arrival of exactly what the situation was. I reiterate my demand that we want to speak to the senior ARK person present then we will leave. *"No one is going to speak to you. You'll have to make an appointment and we have phoned the police."* As if we haven't heard.

Time passes still no police. She rings again. I continue reiterating my demand. She repeats that you'll have to make an appointment. We wait and we wait and we wait. Me repeating my mantra and her repeating hers. My surprise at not having the sirens and the boys in blue piling in by now - and possibly being arrested for trespass - difficult though as we had been voluntarily let in and would voluntarily leave as soon as they got there - was only exceeded by their own.

Here is the HQ of an outfit run by multi, multi, millionaires with some of the best political connections and the greatest political influence in the land and they can't get the police rushing to their aid with a snap of their fingers. After about literally 25 minutes, innumerable calls to the police and equally innumerable reiterations of me repeating my mantra, lo, but who should appear before us but the Senior ARK Representative present. Finally willing to talk, as it has become self-evidently clear that the boys in blue are in no hurry, to put it bluntly, to be coming cavalry like to the rescue.

We lambast her and ARK. Taking children's playing fields when there aren't enough. Building another school in the North where there's no local demand instead of the South where, the demand is chronic. Taking over land, that belongs to the people having paid for it through our taxes, and having a school costing millions built for them at taxpayers' expense and getting it for free. Her only answer; the council had agreed it - shamefully true - and it was all legal -equally shamefully true.

Suddenly they arrive. No, not the police but 3 community support officers. We said, "*We've said what we wanted to say and as we told them we will go*", and trooped out down through the lifts. Past the poor

embarrassed security guard who'd shown us up to the offices and out into the London sun. We were beyond pleased with ourselves. Not just at having pulled off such a brilliant con against the hated ARK, but by the fact that we had it all on film which we could and would use. And we have got away with it; Scott free.

The amazing thing though, was why hadn't the police come, and come straight away, or if not much sooner? I know we weren't being violent or damaging property. My theory is, you may think it fanciful but I find it hard in the circumstances to think of any other, that when they rang 999 and got connected to the police, the police either knew - our occupation had been on the news - or found out that it was a bunch of teachers protesting about building a school on a sports ground and secretly thought good on them or if not, it was nothing to get excited about. I strongly expect though, that the ARK big wigs will have complained to the powers that be or directly to the police top brass. Somebody will have got at least a wigging.

Reckon they've improved their security? I reckon. Perhaps it should be tested again? It couldn't happen to more deserving people.

Spreading the word

I'm invited by a group of parents and teachers in Lewisham to come down to discuss how they might stop an academy proposal by direct action. They obviously knew about our occupation at Tent City. On the way down to meet them I scouted the premises concerned - Lewisham Bridge Primary School, in Elmira Street.

The meeting was in a house with about seven people. I told them I had scouted the premises and there was quite a large area of flat roof which was easily accessible by putting a ladder on the pavement to the top of the wall. Once up there they could do what we did and set up some pop-up tents and living equipment. They could easily be supplied with food and other necessities by either rope or ladder. There was not united enthusiasm for this. No conclusion was reached, and I set off for home firmly believing this was going nowhere. The phone rings. It's them. I'm astounded. A group of parents are on the roof in occupation. Result. It's on the national news. Some of us from Tent City, including Jean, Shane

and Dave K, go to show our support. We took some supplies, bought some drinks and spent the night on the roof. Two months pass. The roof top had become a proper campsite with running water and kitchen area and was used for meetings and even for a rehearsal space by a local choir, The Strawberry Thieves. Goldsmiths students supported the occupation by assisting with regular shifts and helping to build infrastructure. A garden area behind the occupied buildings was seized, a compost toilet was built, flowers planted, a mural painted, and coffee, tea and cake shared, amongst other activities.

This was too much for the authorities. An eviction order is served with a time and date to be off the premises. Back we go. I'm on the roof with the others – see photo below – when the police arrive mob handed. There's a Mexican standoff with over a hundred supporters on the street as well as those on the roof.

Then, suddenly, the police retreat to our unbridled joy and celebrations. End result: a month later victory is secured. There will be no academy. As I have said earlier, protests at height are the best protests. The dangers and the possibility of protesters or those being evicted means health and safety precautions have to be as stringent as possible. They very often wait some considerable time hoping that the protesters might lose impetus and the protest diminish or even end of its own accord. So, my question is why don't more parents and teachers in schools use the occupation tactic?

The pop-up tent is an ace card - weapon of resistance. Light, transportable and goes up in seconds. Folding it back down is another matter!

We used them as part of the protest campaign against Pimlico school becoming an academy, staging an overnight occupation of the school playground. Bridget Chapman, a teacher at the school, was a key and brave organiser. The Head called the police to evict us. But the police came, weren't interested as long as we weren't causing any damage. We told them we'd be gone from the playground before school started in the morning. They left.

Pop-ups were also used at an ARK academy consultation meeting. It was before Christmas, so we had two people waiting in the wings in Santa outfits – Dave K and Andy Lamb. They duly made their surprise entry, interrupting proceedings with gifts from Santa of technical drawing equipment and suggestions to the ARK consultants that they go back to the drawing board.

L to R: Dave K, Lab: Cllr Powney pro academy, Andy, Shane and Kevin

Then another disruption. Three pink pop-up tents spring to life on the floor of the school hall. 'Say' 'No To' 'Academy' they read. The meeting was made as farcical as the consultation was.

REBEL WITHOUT A PAUSE

Chapter Thirteen
THE BIGGEST ROBBERY AT ANY STATE SCHOOL IN HISTORY

Just when you think it's over, you find that the fat lady hasn't yet sung

It must have been how the Beatles felt at the height of Beatlemania. Kids screaming, cheering and mobbing us. Myself, Shane Johnschwager and Dave Kubenk were striding into school to a rapturous reception from the kids to speak at a packed joint unions meeting in the staffroom.

Having been suspended at Sladebrook school many years previously and now approaching 60, it didn't cross my mind for one second that I would end up suspended again. This time, however, it was with only two other colleagues and not nineteen. Is that progress?

I write this, having hours of free time and plenty of alcohol, during the flights to visit my dear friend Sylvia Hohenthaner in the USA who is seriously ill with a brain tumour. Apart from thinking about her and her family, it is an opportunity to reflect on the past year surrounding the occurrences that led to my whistleblowing on my Headteacher's unlawful bonuses and other payments totalling £1.9 million[68].

Since my arrival at Copland I had got on very well with the Headteacher, Dr Sir Alan S. Davies Kt., Ph.D., M.Ed., J.P. - yes that's eventually what was on the letterheads! But back then just plain old Alan Davies.

Our one big falling out was when I tried to organise a staff boycott of Ofsted which I have already mentioned in Chapter Eleven.

I even managed to organise a staff walkout in 2003 when Blair launched Britain's military intervention into Iraq, without any disciplinary action being taken; it was in effect an unofficial strike. We marched from school to protest outside Brent Town Hall. As far as I'm aware we were the only school staff in the country that did this, though at some schools the pupils - bless them - did. A school in Brent, Preston Manor, being one.

Two million had demonstrated on the streets of London, the biggest demonstration in British history, to oppose Britain participating in an utterly unjustifiable and trumped up war against Iraq. Good, but not good enough. If the whole country had been out, and large strike action taken, we wouldn't have been involved at all.

---

[68] The figure known at the time

Where were the trade unions that had, and still have, the power to stop virtually anything or everything, should they choose to use it? Apart from the heroic Scottish train drivers who refused to drive munition trains.

Some people say 'now the war has started we should support our boys'. If we wanted to 'support our boys' we should be demonstrating to bring them home.

Anyhow, by administering through the union a couple of metaphorical kickings[69] to the Head, plus complimenting and rewarding good actions, we had a behaviour modification plan that worked. I call it the 'slap and stroke' method. Slap them when they behave badly - speaking metaphorically! - and pat them when they behave well. It works just as well for children and for dogs, who have a certain similarity in behaviour patterns - only joking.

The parting of the ways came over the issue of privatisation. One doesn't have to be a genius to work out that I, like every good union member never mind elected representative, am going to be implacably opposed to the privatisation of state education.

It is true that, as I covered earlier, when our school Copland faced closure in the 1990's I, along with virtually all the staff, supported going to Grant Maintained status. Grant Maintained status was rightly opposed nationally by the unions because of this, However, in warfare, and teachers are engaged in class warfare in more than one sense, survival is the number one imperative. It is sine qua non requirement. You must preserve your best troops. A step back, as dear old Lenin said, may be necessary to enable two steps forward at a later date.

In fighting to prevent the ARK Academy on the Wembley Park football ground site, at one time it looked as if a less bad alternative might be Copland, i.e. Davies and I. P. Patel, Chair of Governors and gang setting up a couple of academy schools. These would be run, Davies said at the time, on a cooperative basis. Jointly controlled by the staff and the Governors and the staff having even more representation on the Governing Body, the terms to be negotiated. I. P. Patel thought he might be able to buy sufficient Councillors - probably literally - to get the plan through and derail the ARK proposal.

---

[69] Educational not cranial

I felt personally at the time that anything that might defeat the hated Hedge Fund fat cats that were, and are, ARK was worth considering, and pursuing, if there was no other possible achievable option, as a lesser evil. All our enormous, and quite frankly magnificent efforts were not going to stop the ARK Academy being built. Over five years' delay, however, and seeing off an earlier 'sponsor' Andrew Rosenfeld, is pretty damn good and in a war you do not win every battle. Resistance itself, especially strengthening resistance, is winning. If resistance is continually increased, the tide will eventually turn.

These Hedge Funders had bought serious influence if not control nationally of the Labour Party - Lord Levy, Blair's chief fundraiser and general fixer, had first proposed an academy in Brent and a multimillionaire to sponsor it. The same for the LibDems - Paul Marshall, of Hedge Fund Marshall Wace being the main LibDem donor. And, of course, for good measure the same for the Conservatives - Stanley Fink who helped finance Boris Johnson's campaign for Mayor of London and donated a million to the Conservative party. This basically 'bought' his way into being co-treasurer of the party and he is now Lord Fink, after, surprise, surprise being given a lordship. All three are ARK trustees. ARK and other multimillionaires have consciously organised to ensure that all three mainstream parliamentary political parties support the academies programme, i.e. the privatisation of state education. They want to be there on the ground floor as it unfolds and, of course, ultimately to profit from it.

Not just to be able to make even more of their millions - their main interest - but to take over the relatively democratically controlled, and democratic per se, state education system and replace it with a system more like a bygone era. Where education 'delivery' is again the preserve of religious groups, payment or charity. God's work all. The caveat is that there is precious little genuine charity from the vast majority of today's super-rich 'philanthropists'. An example is the much lauded Bill and Melinda Gates Foundation and I expand on this in Chapter Nineteen.

So Arkie Busson and gang trumped I.P. Patel and gang. Their proposed alternative came to nought. Yet somehow Davies appeared, irrespective, to have convinced himself that I would still support the school becoming a Trust school and acting as sponsor to create a couple of new academies, albeit supposedly much more democratic.

I can still remember Davies's mystified and almost hurt expression when I met him in the school playground and explained that he should not confuse tactics with strategy or general principle(s). I was in principle against the privatisation or part privatisation of state education and would not be supporting the move to turn Copland into a Trust school with no alternative reached to the ARK takeover of the Wembley sports ground and building their school on it.

To say that this presaged a distinct change in our relationship would be an understatement. My removal now became a prerequisite to realise not just their plans to turn the school into a Trust school and to then get built and control two academies, but to their greater personal enrichment out of the process. To stand between a man and his money is almost as dangerous as between a man and his principles.

The Director, John Christie, had meanwhile decided my continued employment and position as senior elected education union rep in Brent was still a threat to the Wembley Park Academy and, indeed, their whole Brent Academies programme. They were supporting another two, John Kelly Boys and Girls to be taken over by Edutrust, another crooked outfit run by Lord Bhatia – subsequently removed for dodgy dealing – and replaced by another reincarnation E-ACT. The 'Director General' - the titles these people give themselves - Sir Bruce Liddington being on a £300,000 a year package[70].

A summit meeting took place. John Christie and the now Sir Alan Davies met. I saw Christie going into his office. I was not invited to the party, but the essence of the understanding reached clearly was as follows -
I'll (Director) complain about his actions bringing his unions and the school into disrepute and you (Head) see if you can take disciplinary action against him and get him the sack. As this might be a bit of a difficult one to pull off - the members at the school might actually want to take strike action and the national unions might back it up - another part of the twin track approach was for me (Director) to say that he (HR) had been misusing his facilities time money in taking actions against the ARK Academy. We (the Council) can cut off his funding and then you (Head) can declare him 'surplus to requirements' and make him redundant. Voilà! Problem solved.

---

[70] For the year 2010-11

In warfare, when the enemy is launching an offensive anything that slows them down is good. Delay is your friend and can enable the balance of forces to change back again in your favour.

The Head's line was that the school could not possibly continue to pay me whilst the Council was withholding the facilities funds from the school and the dispute between the authority and the unions was not resolved. The school's finances were too tight. In retrospect, it might have been true – as he and others were nicking so much of the school's money!

I would have to return to the classroom. In this house of smoking mirrors this did not actually mean what they said. It would rapidly be established that there was in fact no vacancy for me to return to, and therefore I would be declared supernumerary. The school would be overstaffed by one – me! This could be rectified quite simply and legitimately, well legitimate looking, by my redundancy. He (me) was a full-time union man, the authority stopped his funding to the school, school couldn't pay, no available post at the school – end of story. A possible bonus is that maybe national unions can't or won't take action. The advice I was receiving from the NUT at the time was that the best way to safeguard my position was to return to the classroom - and safety! As if they were ever going to allow that to occur.

In life a bad thing can turn into a good thing, or at least bring unexpected benefits. Jean's mother, Audrey, died in 2007, her father Ted some years beforehand, and after the interminable delays that are constructed to enable solicitors to get their hands on as much of the money as possible, Jean finally received the money. Not being one to simply give in to proposals to follow a clearly suicidal course I came up with a ploy only possible because of two things – Jean's mother's death and Jean's loyalty not just to me personally but to the struggle – the fight for a fairer and more equal world.

We told the Head that he need not worry about the school possibly being out of pocket, there was no way this would be allowed to occur, and underwritten by the unions - in the end this didn't occur so we'd fudged it - the potential loss to the school of a year's salary would be paid into the school's bank account to be kept by the school if the authority failed to pay the school the earmarked facilities money for my salary.

What could they do? Their whole argument had been based on **having** to do this because the school couldn't afford to lose the money. Now we, or rather Jean, was offering to put £60,000 (salary of £42,000 with on-costs) into their bank which they would keep if necessary.

I thought it was a masterstroke. Game, set and match?

Not quite. The staff did not want to become a Trust school. We had said so repeatedly by every democratic means. We had conducted our own secret ballot which had the result of 5 For, 99 Against. The hierarchies comment was that the ballot was not conducted properly – Richard Evans said *"no parliamentary ballot would be conducted like that"*. If I haven't represented your comment correctly Richard, do write in and I'll issue a correction. We said we were happy to have one overseen, indeed conducted, by the Electoral Reform Society, and pay for it, and would abide by the outcome. Not surprisingly this handsome offer was declined.

Now surely, that was game, set and match? Still not quite.

All protestations, all demonstrations that this was not the will of the people were ignored. I must say this is a bit of a parable of our times. The Governing Body, now packed with a majority of placemen and women, were going to go down the Trust route come hell or high water. To save my job in this situation was not enough. If the Trust went ahead it would be even more undemocratic, our weakness in being unable to stop it despite our near unanimous opposition could be, and would be, exploited. Getting the sack, not just for me but for the other active union staff, would not be long postponed.

Being an avid reader of military history I have long admired the strategy used by the Russians in the battle of Stalingrad, the major turning point in the Second World War - sorry folks, it wasn't D Day. The Germans were engaged in a massive and unbelievably hard-fought battle with the Russians at Stalingrad but they only looked at the immediate. They concentrated on what they were engaged in, in the here and now. Strategy requires more than this and strategy is the most important.

Whilst Friedrich Von Paulus' troops were fighting the Russians inexorably, step by step, house by house with only two tiny enclaves left on the west bank of the Volga, Stalin, or to be more precise General Georgy Konstantinovich Zhukov, was assembling a massive army, or rather armies, ready to encircle the whole of Stalingrad and trap Von Paulus's 8th Army. This was brilliantly brought to life on a guided tour led by retired Colonel Bob Kershaw where we walked the very streets. It was, perhaps, the best counter-offensive in the history of warfare, but then I'm biased.

We had to counter attack. Do our own mini Stalingrad. Could we attack on another front? Something different? Something unexpected? Something strong?

At this point I need to mention that through all of this period I was represented most ably by Geoff Scargill, no relation to Arthur, a senior official from ATL who fought like a trooper to keep me in the school and to continue to have facility time to carry out my union duties, as well as cope with me as a stroppy bastard in meetings. There were other union people from other unions whom I thank, but I want to publicly thank Geoff for his unswerving support.

To get back to the story. There had, for some time, been rumours in the school that the Head and senior staff, i.e. Deputies, were paying themselves bonuses. 'Paying themselves' somewhat misrepresents the situation because it is the Governing Body within a framework that is set by Parliament that decides pay levels in a school. Teachers' pay and conditions are laid down by a statute in Parliament[71]. However, as we shall see this can be subverted. A Headteacher, especially if in cahoots or worse, collusion, can do a great deal to influence outcomes. And of course, in talking up the value, worth, etc. of their Deputies re the level of their financial remuneration they are talking up their own.

However, we had no evidence. I personally believed it was small beer – in my wildest dreams I could not have conceived of the sums involved. We the staff, received more than most teachers, having organised as I said to get two recruitment and retention points for all staff. Lest anyone thinks this greedy let me tell you that teachers, unless they already own a house, generally cannot afford to buy a house in London.

[71] Excepting now in the increasingly numerous academies and free schools which are exempt from the requirement to stick to the Teachers Pay and Conditions Document

Recruitment and retention points do as it said on the tin – more staff did stay and the pupils received the increased stability needed for their education. I felt, in essence, that if senior management received a little bit extra as a very large and successful comprehensive, so what? Attacking it would probably lead to retaliation and we had bigger and more important battles to fight.

I recognise now that my attitude to this may well have been wrong; well actually it was wrong. Shane had banged on about it for a while. He had suggested trying to get the local papers on to it, particularly Alex Wellman and Lorraine King of the Willesden and Brent Times. I'd ignored it. Well, Shane, you had it right. The problem though anyhow, was that there was no evidence. Nonetheless, when your back's against the wall any crack in it has to be explored.

We decided to dig. In any institution almost everything there is to know about what is going on, nefarious or not, is known by somebody in addition to the perpetrator(s). The only way to keep a secret is to tell no-one, something most human beings generally can't do. Or, if not knowing the details fully, they might have a part of the jigsaw. In schools I've found that caretakers are particularly good with regards inside knowledge. Nowadays, with devolvement of financial spending and control to school level - what a recipe for potential chicanery - a crooks' charter - bursars are also. Ex-bursars with either a conscience, or a grudge, or preferably both, are better still.

Enter Val Goldie. Val is one of those people who are the salt of the earth. She retired recently after spending 30 years at the school. I personally think, sorry if this offends, that those that flit from job to job, especially with the single-minded aim of promotion, are not as worthy as the Val's of this world.

It was The Bear[72], previously called The Post Office, the local pub frequented by the Copland staff, where I entered in a state of high excitement. Val had just presented me with what Shane called the 'Crown Jewels'. The evidence that was going to bust this case wide open and hopefully deal a fatal blow to the Trust proposal, its architects, and those planning a clear out of their perceived rats' nest of union organisation.

---

[72] Now called the Liquor Station

It was photocopies of the pay statements of Davies and the Deputies. It showed that in one year Davies had received a bonus of £60,000 and in another year had received one of £45,000. This might not seem much to some, reading and listening to the media reports of bankers' bonuses. But this is a comparatively well-paid teacher's entire year's salary, paid as a bonus! And what is the bonus for? Improving exam results? Isn't that what Headteachers are supposed to be trying their best to achieve for their normal salary anyway? Improving attendance? Ditto. Improving discipline? Ditto. It should be remembered that as the Head of a large London comprehensive he was already receiving over £100,000 a year.

Where did that put him in the relative pay scales across the country? £100,000 was in the top 2% of all earners in 2008. £160,000 was in the top 1% and £400,000 was in the top 0.2%[73]. Over ten years ago now, in one year Davies earnt £403,000. Compare that with CEO's of academy chains today. Sir Daniel Moynihan, CEO of Harris Academies earns in one year £440,000. Considering inflation, Davies was doing extremely well to put it mildly!

The question then was what to do with this dynamite. We knew from our research that, additionally to the outrageous size of these bonuses in a state and taxpayer-funded school, they were actually unlawful.

I reaped further gold dust from two ex-caretakers, Tullah Persaud, who had also been a Brent Labour Councillor and Peter Camplin known as 'Pops'. What they didn't know about the scams, the fiddles and the downright theft that those in charge had perpetrated wasn't worth knowing. But how to get them to speak? First, I said that anything said to me would be in total confidence. Next, I said that if they were contacted at any time by the police all they would have to do is tell them, again in confidence, the truth of what they knew or what they had heard. They sang like canaries! The Head had made the fatal mistake of crossing both of them.

Some may say if they - the sources - had the knowledge or evidence of wrongdoing why didn't they come forward or say something earlier? I say search your own soul. How many things do you know that are or have been seriously wrong? What have you done about them? Have you come forward? Why bother? Might it only cause you aggravation if

---

[73] Source: Survey of Personal Incomes, HMRC. Since 2008 teachers real pay has gone down but average academy Heads pay has gone up significantly.

not serious trouble? Most people are not heroes or heroines. If they were it would not be anything unusual. But the thing is with a little bit of help and encouragement, with a bit of support, we can all be persuaded to do a little bit more than we might otherwise. Indeed, in some cases a lot more. It also needs someone - why not you - to be prepared to stand up first and blow the whistle or just take a lead. If you won't do anything why should others?

I used what they provided with Val's 'Crown Jewels' and the rest of the documentation we had amassed to compile the 'Dossier' I was to send to the Ministry of Education (DCSF[74]), the Audit Commission, the Education Unions, Brent Council and, ultimately, the Press.

There was no doubt. Where do teachers, and what's going on in education, get the highest profile? Why, the annual jamboree of the teacher union conferences. Each year, either because teachers are too daft or in my view more accurately, the short-sightedness and/or self-interest of some of those at or near the top[75] of the unions, most of the school's Easter holiday is taken up with a succession of the three main teacher union conferences. I was down to speak on a motion on academies at the ATL conference, the first of the three conferences, and it was a good opportunity to publicly let the cat out of the bag. At the time the levels of headteachers' salaries in academies were exempt from the Freedom of Information Act[76] i.e. we couldn't find out what they were, though we believed they were inordinately high and getting higher. Also, the legal limits imposed by the Teacher Pay and Conditions Document passed by Parliament did not apply. We believed that details of Davies's very large bonuses would be most relevant to a motion questioning and attacking academy heads very high salaries and the secrecy surrounding them.

And so it was. I quoted from the dossier that I had just sent to Ed Balls, Education Minister et al[77]. I called a Press Conference timed to occur just after my speech. This was a big story. The media were going to run with it. Then manna from heaven. The media got on to our Chair of Governors, Dr I.P. Patel. In a statement he not only admitted the bonus

---

[74] Currently DfE. There have been many changes to the name

[75] Having written this some time ago and having been on the negotiating body which brought about the NEU, I do have to say from experience, it is sometimes the top and those near it leading rather than slowing down progress.

[76] After huge protests this was eventually changed

[77] Shane went round in a cab dropping copies off to the relevant people.

of £60,000 we had documentary evidence for, but admitted another we didn't have written evidence for, which was even higher. This time for £80,000! Sorry, but nothing can so correctly encapsulate his revelation as 'what an idiot'. We now had evidence for total bonuses for Sir Alan of £185,000 which is starting to rack up and attract, not just a bit of public attention, but serious public opprobrium.

Whistleblower. Suspended again

I've blown the whistle. I've sent a dossier to the Authorities. The Easter break - actually not a break for us as we attend all three teacher union conferences[78] - is coming to an end. How is the Head going to feel when we have the morning briefing at school at the start of term and I'm there, bold as brass, in the meeting? Intolerable?! You're right. On the Friday before term started at the end of the working day I receive a letter delivered by taxi. I open it. I'm suspended. I find it hugely amusing and burst out laughing. An advantage of having, metaphorically, been in the wars is that staring down the barrel of a cannon doesn't faze you quite as much as if you haven't.

I ring Shane, who is the school NASUWT Rep and Brent NASUWT Branch Secretary and find out he's suspended too, and so, for good measure, is Dave Kubenk, the school NUT Rep.

The thing about being suspended is that a) you are suspended on full pay. This meant that instead of the Authority paying me via the school from Facilities money the school had to pay from its own funds. Not a particularly smart move, and b) you don't have to be in lessons teaching. Now, for me being on full time release for trade union duties it made little difference, but for Shane and Dave they were now freed from classroom duties and lesson preparation to concentrate full time – on combating our tormentors.

As a teacher, being suspended from work is a pretty big deal, if you're a normal teacher that is. However, both Shane and Dave, who are normal teachers, or at least fairly normal, took it remarkably well. Shane took it worse at the beginning. In true Aussie style he dealt with it by drinking

---

[78] This was made much harder as the NASUWT changed the timing of their conference to be held at the same time as the NUT. I tried to always spend at least one day at the NASUWT. It was a bit of a logistical nightmare e.g. travelling on Sunday from Harrogate to Cardiff and back, but rarely have I been thwarted in this aim. This is now not a problem as the NEU conference is now not over the Easter weekend.

more than he should. He had recently taken on a big new mortgage and I think he saw the house being repossessed if he got the sack. This was despite me saying I'd sell my house and go back to living in a tent rather than see him, or any comrade in arms, lose his home. Jean might well have had something to say about it[79] but I meant it. Personal possessions, especially having paid off your mortgage, and having money are good but I have to say, and I mean it, they come second to the righteous pursuit of war, in defence and offence, against our, the people's, persecutors.

Anyhow, it didn't come to that and after a couple of tough days Shane was true grit. No, better than that, as John Wayne[80] in my not so humble opinion was both a useless actor and a wanker. Dave was cool as a cucumber except, as can generally occur with a young teacher, he was genuinely and deeply concerned about the pupils missing the lessons he was unable to give them because of his suspension. His moment was to come though.

Fuck me – to digress for a moment, as I pick up writing again I've just been upgraded to first class on an international flight home from Minneapolis. Sylvia, who has brain cancer as I said previously, is in better shape than I feared by the way. Champers all round!

In the airport they called out my name and said my seat had been changed. I was mad because I assumed they'd changed me from an aisle seat to accommodate some family with kids or some such, and stuck me on a window seat. But I should have known. Again, the devil looks after his own! I drank the free champagne for the whole flight home and got absolutely rat arsed.

---

[79] Actually I know she would have supported it.
[80] The original film True Grit was made with John Wayne in the title role.

To continue: during the course of the struggle at school - which involved demonstrations outside the school building of staff and parents, supported by pupils, a lunchtime walkout and joint union meetings being held at lunchtime down the local pub, as well as meetings in school chaired by acting union reps as we obviously weren't allowed on the school premises - one of the reps had been 'turned'. With the age-old combination of threat and a metaphorical bribe i.e. being offered a promotion, the ATL Rep had turned Queen's evidence. She had been threatened with legal action for defamation, a completely hollow threat, and also put on a shortlist for a job carrying extra money. Funnily enough she was, and presumably still is, deeply religious. Is the irony of Judas's action and the similarity to hers, lost on her?

To side with, and be prepared to give 'evidence' to, the Head and his crooked co-conspirators, to get your union colleagues dismissed makes you, in my estimation, low enough to get under a door with a top hat on.

When Dave saw the statement, so-called 'evidence', that Moji Alawiye had provided for the Head his epiphany moment came. He went white and said "*Oh no, Moji's done for us*". Fortunately one turncoat does not make a summer's day, or a case. The *trumped up nonsense* as I described Davies's allegations to the Press, unravelled and collapsed like a house of cards as their wrongdoing started to be seriously investigated.

This is an instructive tale in itself. Having sent in one dossier, for several weeks I heard nothing. No responses or even acknowledgement despite there being very serious allegations, backed by evidence.

I smelt a cover up. Indeed, I expected it. The powers that be would make every effort to try and cover up. It is the normal reaction of those in power when some of their own or those serving them have been caught out. It's only when it can't be covered up that anything is ever done, and then it is the minimum that they can get away with in the court of public opinion - as moderated by the media - and very, very occasionally, the law.

Knowing this I kept back some of the allegations and sent in a second dossier. In it I said, "*I know there is more but I do not expect to have to write a third report on behalf of others whose names and details I am prepared to give.*" Actually I had nothing left and there couldn't have been a third dossier, but fortunately they didn't know that. It was a deception, a tactic mentioned earlier, which I decided was necessary to help force a response and action. They must have thought that this mad bastard must have even more dirt, we'd better do something before we start to look, or end up looking, bad ourselves. Covering backs has a higher priority than any loyalty to those lower down the pecking order.

An important point here is that even if you are not mad, you want them, the opponent(s) to believe you are, i.e. that there are **NO** lengths you wouldn't go to and **NO** punishment you would fear. This makes them more likely to give up or give in or at least settle for a draw.

By all accounts - neither Shane, Dave nor I were present of course - it was a classically memorable day. All staff were summoned to a meeting first thing in the morning in the main hall. They were told that the Head, Sir Alan, the Deputy Head, Dr Richard Evans MBE and the Accountant and Legal Adviser, Columbus Udokoro, had been suspended. Later, Michelle Bishop, the Head's secretary, would also be suspended.

Unlike any of the staff in the hall though, I knew what they were going to be told before they were told it. I had been informed by a Government source that has to remain forever nameless that the Head was going to be suspended. In fact, I was originally informed that it would be the day before it actually happened. It had to be delayed, I was informed, because the parliamentary order that was necessary to be able to legally do this, had been delayed by a day so it would have to wait.

The day before their actual suspensions, we were all meeting, Shane, Dave and myself, round at my house. It was Shane's birthday. I had been sworn to secrecy but it would have been too much of a cruel and unnatural punishment to have withheld from him the news of the fact that we had won, and on his birthday. I said *"I've got something to tell you but I'm telling you that you've got to keep it completely secret. If it gets out I'll be in deep trouble and so will my source. In fact, if you tell anyone I'll have to kill you"* (OK, I like melodrama). I then told them. Davies, Evans, Patel and co were finished. Shane said it was the best birthday present he's ever had.

We then went down to the pub to celebrate his birthday. Shane and Kubenk had a knowing look in their eyes but didn't breathe a word. I trotted out my normal mantra, which, incidentally, I had firmly believed all along. *"Victory is certain. They are finished"*. No one noticed any difference but, of course, this time it was different – I actually knew for certain. It was true!

Just before I conclude this section I have to tell you a very funny story. Over the period of weeks when I was suspended there were various disciplinary meetings with the Head. I was in a 'hearing', or rather kangaroo court, that was - surprise, surprise - going to find me guilty, when we had to have a break.

Lesley Gouldbourne, my Representative of choice, went downstairs to go to the toilet. Suddenly I heard her call out with some urgency *"Mr Roberts, can you come down here"*. I went down the stairs and there was a couple in an alcove busy trying to put their clothes on. It was a 6th Former and someone from outside the school having a fuck. It was my unfortunate duty - actually I did feel sorry for them but in the circumstances Lesley felt, and I agreed, we could hardly ignore it - to have to knock on the door where the disciplinary panel were still gathered and say to Davies et al *"I'm sorry to interrupt but there are a couple of students downstairs engaged in sexual activity and I think you'll have to deal with it"*. I managed to keep a straight face, but I don't know how.

And so to conclude, though this story is not yet over.

Eventually Davies, Michelle Bishop and Columbus Udokoro resigned before their disciplinary hearings. Richard Evans failed to turn up for his and was sacked for gross misconduct. At the time of writing, months later, no prosecutions have been started. You nick, personally (Davies), £600,000 of taxpayers' money from a school and you don't get prosecuted! You nick, collectively, a total of £1.9 million[81] from a school, the biggest 'robbery' from any school in the history of education in the UK[82], and you don't get prosecuted! How low has this country sunk? The ministers responsible for education as a whole, and for schools specifically at the time, Ed Balls and Vernon Coaker respectively, say in an email to me of 3rd December 2009 that not only haven't they seen the Report of Brent Audit and Investigation Department into the matter, nor even a summary of its findings and recommendations, but don't believe that they should!! The biggest and most outrageous 'robbery' at a school in the UK's history and the Education secretary and schools minister don't want to know how it was done, how they've got away with it or what is necessary to stop it being done elsewhere! Welcome to the banana republic - actually Kingdom, of course - of 'Great Britain'.

Mary Bousted, General Secretary of ATL, understood the wider national significance of this corruption earlier and better than the other unions. As she said in writing to me when I first told her about it, '*I agree with you entirely – fraud on this scale must not go unpunished*'.

If the authorities will not prosecute, we will just have to organise our own, and we have told them that we will. This just may prompt them, or is it force them, to bring a prosecution themselves. The potential embarrassment of them declining to bring a prosecution and us doing it successfully would be huge. Hopefully they will do the right and proper thing – but I'm not holding my breath. We should all remember, I reiterate again, there is no justice – just us!

July 2010 – update

As I write this I am waiting, expecting Sylvia's imminent death. We have stopped exchanging phone calls about a month ago as when I last rang, John told me she was bedridden and no longer able to speak.

---

[81] As stated earlier subsequently found to be 2.7 million.

[82] At the time. Subsequently this has been exceeded. As reported in the Daily Mail in 2014 an accountant at a chain of academies championed by Michael Gove was the centre of a fraud investigation after £4million of school funds ended up in his personal accounts. Nigerian-born Samuel Kayode is said to have spent much of the cash on an extravagant lifestyle and buying a string of properties. The 57-year-old part-time pastor was told by the High Court to pay £4.1million back to the Haberdashers' Aske's chain of academies. The High Court case is believed to be Britain's biggest ever education fraud

I expected it to come but it was fast and still a shock. We exchanged emails. Mine included,

I obviously don't know if Sylvia is lucid at all at any time now. But if she is please tell her that she and you all are in my thoughts and give her my love.... Take care and thinking of you

He, ever gallant and caring response included,

Thanks for all the love and support you have given Sylvia over the years. She had a very special place in her heart for you and not only because you were a former Boyfriend. She always said that there were few people one could absolutely rely on in a lifetime and Hank was the one person she could always count on. At the moment Sylvia is in a state mostly reserved for the living dead. She is in a Zombie like state and does not recognize most people, cannot walk without my assistance, cannot bathe herself, is incontinent, and needs to be manually fed. I have no way of predicting her survival rate but at the moment she seems to be fading rather quickly. I will convey your message to her as I do think she still understands....

Climbing Mount Improbable is the title of one of Richard Dawkins excellent books on evolution. I feel that trying to get justice over Davies and Co's robbery of the school is a bit like this or perhaps like climbing the north face of the Eiger with no boots on and upside down. The Fraud Squad act with glacial slowness. On 10/6/10 I write to Commander Allan Gibson, Head of Economic and Specialist Crime Metropolitan Police, copied to Sir Paul Stephenson, Metropolitan Police Commissioner, Keir Starmer QC, Director of Public Prosecutions, Michael Gove, Minister of State for Education, Nick Gibb, Schools Minister, Sarah Teather, MP for Brent Central, and the local and national press.

'It has now been 5 months since Brent Local Authority referred to you the case regarding Copland school and Sir Alan Davies and others receiving unlawful bonuses and other payments taken from the school funds (i.e. from the pupils' education) totalling £1.9 million.

We understand, although we unfortunately have not been informed, that Copland's IEB[83] has decided, … that it will not bring a prosecution aimed at recovering any of the £1.9 million taken. … The time spent by the IEB in deciding to do nothing to seek redress over the biggest financial scandal in a school in the UK's history, was inordinate – nearly a year.

We are also concerned about the possible influence on the new coalition government, which is dominated by the Conservative Party, the party of Dr Richard Evans the school's dismissed Deputy. He is an old Harrovian, twice selected candidate to stand as conservative MP, Conservative canvassee for a Peerage, and also a Freemason[84]. I am fearful that he could seek to use these connections (in concert with Sir Alan who is also a Freemason) to have the case dropped. I do not say that the police and/or the CPS are simply the political tool of the Government. However, I am concerned about any possible political influence.

We are also mindful that your "detectives and analysts have uncovered more than 1.9 million fraud offences suspected of being committed in Britain last year" (as revealed in the Evening Standard 10/5/10) which must put a tremendous burden on the Economic and Specialist Crimes Unit.

… We have previously stated that if justice is not done in this case we will bring a private prosecution but believe that this should not be necessary. At this time of … stringencies and cutbacks regarding public expenditure it cannot be a good example, irrespective of anything else, to allow a state school Head to be paid a total of over £400,000 in a single year and to be complicit in taking £1.9 million in a combination of unlawful and unjustifiable payments from pupils' education and get away with it. … I look forward to a response at your earliest convenience'.

The reply comes on 25/6/10 from Commander Allan Gibson. *'I am now able to advise that this matter has been taken on as an investigation by the Met's Economic and Specialist Crime Command'.* Result or what!

---

[83] Interim Executive Board, the body that was imposed on the school following the concerns of the Secretary of State regarding the financial irregularities exposed by my revelations in the two dossiers sent to the Secretary of State, the Audit Commission, Brent Council etc.

[84] As was later revealed in the High Court so was Columbus Udokoro, IP Patel, Chair of Governors and Martin Day, Vice Chair.

One more brick in the wall. I have no doubt that this is motivated by the threat of taking out a private prosecution and their belief from our past track record we'd do it and, worse still, might succeed. Ditto the IEB. We had been told by a confidential source on the IEB[85] that the IEB was not going to take any legal action because their lawyers had said that it would cost too much compared to the likelihood of any money they might get back. Needless to say the police contacted them about my letter. How could I say such a thing which was wrong complained the Chair of the IEB. It wasn't; it was right but I couldn't reveal how I knew. Qui tacit consentit – those who keep silent consent I said. I wrote to the Chair, Roy Evans, *"Further, we believe that the IEB has now had more than enough time to have sought legal advice regarding your stated aim to take legal action to seek recovery of all or as much as possible of the £1.9 million taken by the former Head and others from the school's budget. We firmly believe that you must have received this legal advice by now. Could you confirm if this is true? If so when did you receive it and why have you not informed staff of its outcome. We presume, because of the delay, that you do not intend to pursue any legal redress."* 27th May 2010

No response. Again. *Qui tacit consentit.* Anyhow it prodded them into action – well, looking at it again anyway.

---

[85] Eva Davidson, MBE had been a long time governor at Copland but was someone who had not 'signed up' to Davies's plans. She was prepared to speak out as the situation unfolded and the facts became known. Good old Eva.

Chapter Fourteen
TAKING ON THE PRESS AND BUILDING UNITY

As I write this, I'm on the Orient Express travelling through the mountains and tunnels of Lichtenstein on our way to Venice. After constantly worrying that the banks would collapse before I got my retirement lump sum, I got it. I decided by way of apology for a lifetime of taking liberties, to take Jean on the trip. It wasn't all the way to Istanbul, but my excuse was we've got to get back to London for the pensions Lobby of Parliament on 26th October 2011. Actually, it cost quite enough to Venice - to be precise over four grand. I am constantly both amazed and grateful for the good fortune of my accident of birth. Not just a free education, when the poor bastards nowadays have to pay £9000 tuition fees, plus everything else a year, but a retirement lump sum (£65,000). Of course, the thieving bastards that have enriched themselves and destroyed the country and are pauperising the commoners, are now removing this retirement lump sum for teachers. I will never tire and never stop saying we owe so much to those that fought and risked and lost their lives in the fight against fascism in the Second World War.

The welfare state that I and so many others have enjoyed and benefited from was built by sacrifice of those who came before. My generation, and even more the following, have so far shamefully been allowing all those gains to be destroyed. Bill[86] to you and your comrades, let me express my heartfelt gratitude and appreciation of your courage and sacrifice and shame at our timorous self-centeredness. I'm alright (just) Jack attitudes.

Hopefully - and I better believe it so - with the half a million TUC demo earlier in the year and the biggest strike action of our lifetimes coming up on the 30th November over the Government attack on our pensions, things are on the change[87].

---

[86] William 'Bill' Ash, MBE, a dear friend and comrade, now sadly deceased, who came from the USA via Canada to volunteer to join the RAF in the fight against Nazi fascism. He, by the way, in doing this was stripped of his US citizenship. He was awarded an MBE for escaping activities. You can read his fascinating story in *Under the Wire* co-authored with Brendan Foley. Subsequently another book has been written *The Cooler King. The True story of William Ash: spitfire pilot, POW and world war II's greatest escapist* by Patrick Bishop.
[87] Unfortunately, it proved to be a false dawn.

I'm really pleased that I was able to second the ATL motion at conference calling for strike action over pensions. The first National strike in ATL's 127-year history. I know that ATL going in with the NUT for the first strike was crucial, not just to making it so successful but in giving a lead to others so that at the TUC in September, every man, woman and their dog was getting up and saying that their union was going to strike too. Paul Kenny, GMB General Secretary getting up and saying he was prepared to go to prison was the icing on the cake. Some joked be careful what you wish for Paul, but quite frankly with Andreas Whittam Smith previous editor of the Independent writing on 19th October 2011 in an article headed '*Western nations are now ripe for revolution*', nothing would surprise me. Well, actually being transported to Australia might.

Teaching the Daily Mail a lesson

We're coming into Venice soon. I've checked my phone for messages but haven't got what I'm looking forward to. It is a response to my solicitor bringing an action for libel against the Daily Mail. Quite rightly they identified me as one of the class enemies that could do with a good old bit of vilification.

The Sunday Telegraph tried it on previously but had the decency to contact me first - simply good journalist practice. They were put off by my saying that it seemed to me clear that this was Evans & Co, because of the inside information the paper had, trying to get me some adverse publicity to help them in any forthcoming court case - or perhaps in revenge - or even both.

I think when a member first joins the union, one of the stated benefits, i.e. an implied contract, is legal advice. Could not a member, if they chose, take legal action against the union for breach of contract? No matter, it seems unjust to me and injustice should be tackled and rectified, if possible, no matter from whence it came. Stand by your union and your union will stand by you. Well, that would be good but in this instance, it wasn't so. This is not an attack on unions. They are an essential part of the working class, and their decline in number and strength in no small part explains the awful position we are presently in.

Nevertheless, when libelled in the Daily Mail in an article saying that I had bullied staff at my school to go on strike over pensions, my union, indeed unions, should have been climbing over themselves to give me legal advice and backing. None more so than ATL for I was, at that time, National Junior Vice President, and as I write this I am now Senior VP[88]. After all, if a national newspaper can get away with libelling a senior union officer it will be open hunting season for all.

I had first sought the union's help in getting a legal opinion as to whether it was libel. I was convinced it was but I needed a qualified lawyer's opinion. First I was told by Andy Brown, then the Immediate Past President, a nice bloke but needless to say not a lawyer, that it wasn't libellous and second that having a go at the Daily Mail would be to invite them to target the Union and basically bringing down the wrath of Khan upon us. And the Union couldn't conceivably think of bringing a libel action because of the cost. What was written about me was completely out of order, but I and the Union should wear it. Needless to say in general principle I do not believe that the best way to respond to an attack is to wear it, and said so.

Subsequently it was proposed that I approach the Defence Committee to ask them to consider the situation and my request. A lifetime of

---

[88] ATL Senior Vice President September 2011 - August 2012

paranoia had served me well. I predicted the outcome of the Defence Committee deliberation with a degree of accuracy akin to quantum theory. Sorry no help. Sorry no reason.

So I asked for Counsel's Opinion. I was told to contact the union's retained lawyers, as the in-house lawyers felt not sufficiently qualified in this area to give an opinion. The retained lawyers, Morrish, said that they didn't have sufficient expertise and said they'd get external counsel. It would cost £3000. I did offer if necessary to pay the costs. However, getting Counsel's Opinion was not agreed. Allowing me to pay for it was not agreed and I was unable to get an opinion on whether it was libellous or not. I proceeded to find a firm of lawyers Collier Bristow and brought the case myself.

The Mail failed on all counts in the article making factual mistakes in almost everything they claimed was a fact, plus a couple of whopping libels to boot; one was that I was responsible along with my two work colleagues and comrades in arms, Shane and Lesley, for falling results at the school. The article said that *in 2007, 140 Copland pupils went on to study at university. In 2010, this figure was just 70'.* In fact in 2007,109 pupils went on to university; in 2010 96 pupils went on to university. My solicitor's letter said, *'These inaccuracies are more than simple errors. They reveal a malevolent state of mind in your treatment of our client. It is to be noted that no attempt was made to contact our client or Mr Johnschwager or Ms Gouldbourne before publication of the articles on 27 June 2011. This is particularly so when your newspaper knows (see Daily Mail 2/3/11) that many of the problems at Copland arise out of the arrest and forthcoming trials of the former Head Teacher, Sir Alan Davies, the former Deputy Head, Dr Richard Evans and the former Bursar, Columbus Udokoro, in connection with the misappropriation of £1.9m public funds, which our client as the whistleblower, as the Daily Mail well knows, was instrumental in exposing.'*

To quote The Mail I had, *'spent the past two weeks urging members to strike on Thursday, to close his school, leading to claims that he is 'bullying' staff'.* The lowering results was a good one especially for poor old Shane and Lesley both of whom, whilst having some facilities time, still teach and are both by common consent and results, good teachers. For me, and the bullying one as extra, as my solicitor's letter stated, *'Our client did not bully anyone and there is no allegation that he did.*

Our client did not attend the Union meeting held at the school during this period and he did not canvass or speak to any member urging them to support the strike… In this article you falsely charge our client as responsible for a decline of standards at Copland and aggressively abusing his position as a trade union officer by bullying Copland members to join the strike and thus close the school. This is grossly defamatory of our client.'

As to the Daily Mail response, I'm going to try and resolve it by getting them to let me have an article in their paper putting the case for the maintenance of teachers' pensions and why in the circumstances it is right to be taking action. This would be much better than any amount of money in damages. I used this tactic once before with the Times. In an article they called me an *'avowed Maoist'*. They didn't contact me before to check this. I'd never said anywhere ever before that I was a 'Maoist' and, as it wasn't true, I failed to understand how I could be. I managed to get a two-page spread by way of recompense all about professional unity – and the libel was so obvious and self-evident I didn't even need solicitors.

The Mail wormed and squirmed. The answer came back that I wasn't high-profile enough - even though I had been high-profile enough for them to attack me in their paper. Okay, I responded through my solicitor, was the ATL General Secretary high-profile enough? Further, they obviously could run their own story side-by-side refuting it and putting their side of the argument. Response to this handsome offer came there none.

After a threat to immediately move to trial, came an offer to settle out of court. Pay all legal expenses - £3000 and damages, very reasonably put by myself at £1500 - it's the principle not the money. And an apology on page 2 of the Daily Mail *'In an article on 27th June 2011 we said that ATL union officer*

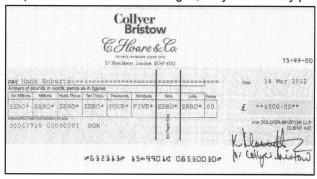

Hank Roberts had bullied staff at Copland College in North London into going on strike. We accept that Mr Roberts did not bully anyone and are happy to set the record straight'.

A victory to savour! A photocopy of the cheque and apology adorn my wall at home. Well, how could you not[89].

When I come across things that are wrong, no matter from whence they come, I try, if not too overwhelmed with other fights, to right the wrong without fear or favour.

It was fortunate in that having received of my lump sum and not yet having had time to piss it all up against the wall, I had the money upfront, and the brass neck, to sue the Daily Mail for libel. Suing for libel as everyone knows can be ridiculously expensive which is why it's known as rich man's justice. The law so obviously needs reform.

My second libel action was against The Sunday Times. They had run an article on the 29th April 2012 headlined *Teachers' leader in row over job 'deal'* which had alleged that, '*One of the country's most prominent teachers' leaders has denied claims that he persuaded a school to give a pay rise to a union representative - and helped it get rid of two teachers in return'....*

'*Roberts and Brent council, the local authority, dismissed them as a "total fabrication by aggrieved people". Roberts added that when he advised a departing teacher against pursuing grievance procedures this was "straightforward union advice", as the chances of winning were slim.*'

As this was concerning my actions and role as an NUT representative Officer, I asked if they would give me legal aid. They agreed. Naturally with libel, a difficult, tricky area, I wanted to have Counsels' opinion. They agreed to this as well and I got it.

It said, '*In summary, my advice is that although the Article is defamatory of Mr Roberts there is a good chance that Times Newspapers Ltd*

---

[89] I intended to do this but failed. Occasional bouts of ineptness unfortunately are inevitable.

("TNL") will have a defence of Reynolds privilege[90] in respect of it. TNL has already written letters indicating that they would defend the Article on this basis (see e.g. 5 September 2013; 21 December 2013)'.

I thought bollocks. The Sunday Times are in the wrong. What they wrote was untrue and actually I believed it was a conspiracy to defame me. If it got to court, and I believed we would get them to give up beforehand, we would win. This was because of the weakness of their witnesses. One, Alan King, previously Headteacher at Furness Primary in Brent, being proved to be a blatant liar and the other main two, a temporary Deputy Head and the previous Chair of Governors Russell Smith had no first-hand knowledge of events. Alan King and the Chair of Governors had been sacked, as had the whole Governing Body, in response to an investigation the local authority had conducted over financial and other irregularities. This had followed a complaint I had made on behalf of the members at the school. Counsels' opinion, not that I had then received it in full, indicated no likely prospect of success so therefore the NUT - and I don't blame Bob Stapley, Regional Secretary for London for this - had to say no to support for legal action. Bob is a long-term mate and I know this hurt him as he realised I had been maliciously maligned.

In short, I again contacted Rhory Robertson of Collier Bristow and his equally able sidekick Alex Cochrane and brought a case. I had to upfront the money and again it is outrageous that only those with money generally can defend their integrity against newspapers libels.

To cut a long story short – success. The Sunday Times agree to pay all our legal costs and make a retraction. The 'apology' was somewhat mealy mouthed, but I got back the money that I had upfronted for the case. I deliberately in both cases have not asked for much. I'm not interested in the money. I'm interested in you telling the truth, you bastards.

I take Rhory and Alex a magnum of champagne and a large bunch of flowers for their secretary. Job well done. They were brilliant.

This account is a really useful way to illustrate what victory is in warfare, class or otherwise. Victory is when you win more than you lose, or even

---

[90] Though this may leave you none the wiser it is qualified privilege. This protects the maker of an otherwise defamatory statement so long as he had a legal duty to communicate the information to someone who had a material interest in receiving it.

expected to lose. Forcing them to a settlement out of court on the terms I got was a victory. If they were strong - as they would have liked to have been - they would have taken it to a court hearing. Money is no object to them. They wouldn't give diddly squat. It's not the amount of money that they have to pay that hurts. As I said money is no object. It's having to pay me at all or to apologise or retract anything.

Professional Unity 2000 and Beyond!

ATL has transformed since I first joined in 1996. I know I have played a part in that transformation. But credit where credit is due. When I stood for ATL General Secretary I did not consider for one second that my opponent might do as good a job as I could, never mind better. But Mary Bousted's been doing a quite magnificent job recently. She has some serious abilities. I know the partner does not make the person, but they have an influence. I think Martin Johnson and Mary becoming an item has been a positive. Especially so, I hope not just in the general fight against the forces of darkness, but in taking forward professional unity. Martin has been a long-time supporter of professional unity and is an Honorary Vice President of UNIFY. I remember his presidential speech 'Buccaneers of Capitalism' as President of NASUWT in 2000 when he condemned the *"expensive, unnecessary, and damaging movement towards privatisation of our education services, which transforms public money into private profit"*. He also spoke as Past NASUWT President at our Professional Unity 2000 fringe alongside Tony Brockman, NUT President and Eddie Ferguson, ATL President at the NASUWT Jersey Conference 2001. With all three speaking in favour it was quite an event.

As I entered the Conference Hall in Jersey, the then Deputy General Secretary Eamonn O'Kane spotted me and walked over to me in full view of all the delegates. Many were deeply hostile to professional unity and to me personally. He shook my hand and warmly greeted me. This was indicative of his bravery and principles. Frances Rafferty wrote a good biography of Eamonn, *Eamonn O'Kane: Teacher and Teachers' Leader*. In it she quotes him saying, *"My big ambition is very controversial. I do believe we should discuss the possibility of forming one single teachers' union". This was Eamonn's declaration of intent, on becoming general secretary, during an interview with Brian Walker for the Belfast Telegraph in August 2002'.*

At the NASUWT annual conference in Scarborough in 2002, as General Secretary-Designate Eamonn produced a way ahead for professional unity in a paper entitled, *The Future Direction of the NASUWT*. The delegates rejected any discussions on merger talks by 89,273 to 65,295 in a card vote. *'Bolstered by the TES's own poll which found that 70 per cent of teachers wanted a merger, he* [Eamonn] *said, "I am clearly bound by the decision of conference but I am also responsible to the membership. It is important at some stage that the wider membership of the union has the opportunity to register its views".*

Unfortunately, professional unity, which then seemed so near, was not to be. Tragically Eamonn died in 2004 without realising his dream. As Rafferty reports Eamonn and Steve Sinnott, then NUT General Secretary got on. *'After Eamonn's death Steve made an extraordinarily generous gesture. When asked in 2008 by the TES which historical/fictional character he most identified with, he said, "Eamonn O'Kane, the former General Secretary of the NASUWT ... His death was a great loss to education and trade unionism. He was a teacher trade unionist, radical in his thinking, committed to professional unity and not afraid to put forward controversial ideas and argue for them. I hope to have some of his characteristics".* She ends this section with, *'If both men had lived and had had more time to work together the history of teacher trade unionism could have been very different'.*

Hopefully the changed situation, where professional unity is again back on the agenda - if trade unions don't see the need for unity in this situation they never will - will lead to progress that does not fall again at the last hurdle.

Though sworn to secrecy, I knew that those at the top of ATL and NUT are on for it. But I pointed out this was the problem last time with both the ATL and NASUWT; the top were on for it, but you have to win it with the whole Executive, secretaries and Conference. A huge amount of work has to be done but I have a feeling the time has eventually come. How daft is it to have three main teacher unions. Perhaps even the secondary headteachers union ASCL might be weaned away from this Government's adoption of the fuehrer princip[91]! 'Leaders' indeed. There is natural leadership. That freely conferred by others out of recognition of their ability. There is elective leadership, necessary on a larger scale where people do not know personally those seeking leadership roles.

---

[91] Basically whatever the leader says is law and must be followed

Not perfect but the best in the circumstances. As Churchill said of democracy *"Democracy is the worst form of government, except for all the others."*

Then there's the Army type leadership by appointment but necessarily so. 'Followers' have to obey instruction. The whole system rests on unquestioning obedience. A model for schools? I think not, though this Government and some in and seeking headteacher positions do. As for the future leaders; no doubt that's what they said to the Hitler youth[92]. Get real. You're all gonna get stuffed by the new breed of Executive Heads and so called 'Superheads', but they will also be stuffed by the system. Burnt out and discarded. Led by Damascene or gradual conversion into realising a life of subservience, saluting the flag and those above you while shitting on those below, is no life at all.

At this point I should explain a bit more background regarding professional unity. It has been my main passion and driving force of my union work for many years.

I had been attending NUT conferences for some years and regularly uniting the unions would be discussed. For many years previously, the Union had this goal as a policy, but nothing ever happened that moved it forward in any way. Professional unity was in words only.

I had an idea. Surely what we needed was a cross union body? All that supported unity across the teacher unions could come together in one pressure group and work jointly to make it happen. Easy. I'd set one up.

One evening in 1996 I invited a small number of key Brent union people from the NUT, NASUWT, and ATL to meet in my classroom to discuss what we could do to take unity forward. My memory of what was to be an historic event is not perfect. It was over 20 years ago but I know as well as me there was Malcolm Horne, Ray Thyer, Phil Allman, Lesley Gouldbourne (at the time Thompson) Dai Badham and David Gilman. I apologise if I have missed anyone.

---

[92] In fact that is precisely what they did and special schools/training centres were set up for the indoctrination and training for future leadership positions of young Nazi 'prospects'. The ultimate purpose of education was to fashion citizens conscious of the glory of country and filled with fanatical devotion to the national cause.

We discussed what to do and agreed to set up a formal organisation. What to call it? We decided that setting a time in terms of achieving our goal was a good idea. It seemed that by the end of the millennium, the year 2000, it should be easily achievable. After all it was so self-evidently such a logical and obvious move. A trade union basic is that unity is strength. So we decided to call ourselves Professional Unity 2000. I'd like to say that the name was my idea but in truth I can't remember but I'm more than satisfied with the fact that the idea to meet and form an organisation was mine.

As history shows we had seriously underestimated how easy it would be, and the time it would take, to make progress towards our goal, never mind the complete achievement of it. Hundreds of meetings, travelling many thousands of miles, hundreds of publications, articles, leaflets, newspaper reports, attendance at dozens of union conferences and repeated motions put to them. We also asked to meet other education unions.

Professional Unity 2000 Officers met with colleagues in NATFHE and AUT – two higher and further education unions – and encouraged them to look at amalgamation. They went ahead with this idea and became the University of College Union (UCU) well before we did - well done comrades. Especially so Sally Hunt and Paul Mackney, the respective General Secretaries of AUT and NATFHE. Leading strategic and organisational roles were also taken on by Alan Carr, AUT and Jacqui Johnson, NATFHE who are both Honorary Presidents of UNIFY.

During our long march, the year 2000 came and went and we changed our name to UNIFY. Apart from it becoming rather a joke, particularly with those who were anti-unity, the key point in the name change was also the recognition of the role of support staff and the need to create an education union covering all sectors involved in education. We have at last made a giant step on the way. The ATL and the NUT have united into the National Education Union, NEU. This is precisely what we intend to do with the other education unions and in less time than the 20 years it took for the first part. As I said in my September Presidential speech, the journalist Richard Garner with *'his steadfastly principled journalism'*, did great service to the cause of professional unity by his many articles in support of this.

Chapter Fifteen
COPLAND UPDATE

I'm on a plane again. It seems to be the only time I've got lots of hours with nothing pressing to do, and free alcohol helps. Earlier I was looking at Nelson Mandela's cell on Robben Island and being guided round by an ex prisoner. Surreal. I tried ringing my mate Byron in England to talk to him because I was round his house when Nelson Mandela was released in 1990 as we watched this happen on T.V. Mandela spent 18 years of his 27 years of incarceration here. Most people think he spent his whole time in prison here. Most people also think Robben Island is, or was, one big prison like Alcatraz. It isn't.

The coach guide, before you get the ex-prisoner guide, was spectacularly informative, entertaining and alternatively deeply moving. I was particularly interested in his description of another prisoner Robert Sobukwe who not just had his own cell in a special isolation block for the political prisoners regarded as leaders as Mandela did, but his own personal prison 'block' on the Island. House arrest meant he was not allowed to speak to anyone else. Even his guards were forbidden from speaking to him; he was regarded as that dangerous. Our guide likened him to Malcolm X and compared Mandela to being more like Martin Luther King. His story is told by Benjamin Pogrund and it is entitled 'How Can Man Die Better'.

How dangerous the Apartheid regime regarded him is evinced from this section in the book. There was 'a decision not to use existing powers to banish or ban Sobukwe but to act an entirely new method of political emasculation: to keep him in jail after his sentence had ended. This was done by providing that anyone convicted under security laws could be imprisoned after his sentence had ended if the Minister of Justice considered he was likely, if released, to further the achievement of any of the objectives of communism (as defined by the Government). The law was initially for a year but could be extended without limitation. The law was called the Sobukwe Clause and he was the only person against who it was used.

As the London magazine The Spectator reported, 'It is difficult to imagine a more refined form of torture than to wait until a man is within days of completing a long prison sentence and then announce he will be kept in in fact indefinitely'.

201

This violated a fundamental principle of justice - nulla poena sine crimine (no punishment without crime).

As the protests and public opposition grew to his treatment the account continues, '... *to try to blunt criticism and to acknowledge Subukwe's unique status, he was not to be kept in a cell but in quarters which had been used by coloured warder trainees.* "He will have complete freedom of movement [!] in a large prescribed area", said Vorster [President of South Africa]. "Newspapers can be supplied to him, and he will be able to receive visitors weekly. He will by no means be treated as a prisoner but receive special treatments in respect of food, movement, using leisure hours, hours of rising and retiring, clothing etc". Interesting – how worried were they. As the situation developed who was holding whom captive? A similar position unfolded with Nelson Mandela's extended imprisonment.

Again, I will never tire of saying that the debt people owe to those who went before them and sacrificed hugely is basically everything.

Remembering who went before you is important in a more general sense too. An example in science is well put by Gareth Williams in *Unravelling the Double Helix* where he talks about the scientists whose work had paved the way for the elucidation of the double helix, who he knew nothing about. '*What had happened to them? Some were airbrushed out of the historical record because ... everything that happened before 1900 was irrelevant. Others were plunged into darkness when the spotlight swung on to Watson, Crick, Wilkins and Franklin ... Newton acknowledged that he had seen further only by standing on the shoulders of giants, but few modern researchers are gracious enough to pay their respects to those who have gone before'*.

We, Jean and I, were on our way back from St Helena, a venue Jean had chosen because it can only be reached by sea - it has no airport[93] - is one of the most isolated inhabited islands on earth and it takes five days by sea to get there, and five days back. This was good because

---

[93] One has now been built but they can't open it because of the dangerous cross winds. You'd think they might have figured it out before they spent millions building it. One solution suggested is to blow the top of the mountain off. Since writing this footnote the issues have been resolved and the airport is now open.

I had to prepare a speech as incoming ATL president in September (2012). A fantastic place, known for Napoleon being exiled there and dying there and by some for him being exhumed and his body, apparently in an excellent state of preservation, being repatriated to France to be re-interred at Les Invalides in Paris.

On the Island Jean and I climbed Jacob's ladder, a 799 step climb, from the capital Jamestown which nestles below, straight up the cliff to the fort above. It nearly killed us, well me anyway. I didn't know whether to start with me nearly dying - and this part unfortunately having to be ghost written, like people finishing Dickens unfinished last book, *The Mystery of Edwin Drood*. But I make light of a serious subject.

Near Death Experience

It's Wednesday 6th June 2012. I wake up. There's a growing feeling as if my skin is on fire. It's getting worse. My face is tingling like an electric current is going through it. My lips are swelling. I'm finding it hard to breathe. I try to get up off the settee but I'm so weak I fall to the floor. With huge difficulty I try and pull myself up off the floor onto the sofa and grab for the door handle. What the fuck is going on I'm thinking. I'm confused but I know that it is definitely not good. I manage to twist the door handle hanging onto it and open the door but am too weak to stay standing. I crash to the hallway floor, banging my head on the bannister hard on the way down. I'm on the floor, fortunately still conscious, but too weak to move and my breathing is getting harder and harder.

Norman, my step-father, wakes up; fortunately he's there as Jean was going down to Portsmouth so I took the opportunity to invite him up to London to take him out. I've been sleeping in the front room and he's been sleeping in our bedroom. In addition to him very luckily being there, also very luckily he has heard me fall. Without those two bits of luck I'd be dead. He comes out of his room. Poor man I can hardly imagine his state of shock and concern. I can hardly speak. I mouth *amb-amb-u-lance*. He races into the front room, grabs the telephone which has a long extension line and comes back cradles my head and tries to reassure me whilst at the same time dialling 999.

By this time, I think it must be a heart attack and it is clear to me that I am dying. I can remember thinking how ironic. I finally get elected to be ATL President and I won't see my Presidency. I wasn't worried about dying at all. I can remember being annoyed/angry at the ambulance line operator on the end of the line who kept asking Norman questions, some of which he couldn't answer and was trying to get answers out of me. To say with not much luck somewhat understates it. I thought how fucking stupid asking all these questions, I'll be dead before the ambulance arrives!

I realised later that of course its normal procedure to keep the caller on the line and they knew exactly where a landline call is coming from and have already dispatched the ambulance. The ambulance gets there with amazing rapidity. I was still conscious - just. I couldn't move. They gave me a shot of adrenaline and hauled me onto a stretcher and down the stairs into the ambulance. I don't remember much after apart from my breathing getting better.

Turns out I am allergic to nonsteroidal anti-inflammatory drugs (NSAID's) like Diclofenac. I had been prescribed this after having my knee 'cleaned out' due to damage from arthritis. Now I have to remember to take my epi-pen with me when I go on holiday just in case I go into anaphylactic shock.

Back to the Copland Saga

I digress. My task is to pick up the trail. Talk about fat lady singing, it's been like a Hallelujah chorus. Singing the practice scales have started. Davies has been charged. Escape is seemingly ever less likely. However, the system has become completely bent. From my point of view, the politicians and state apparatus has been corrupted and bought comprehensively by the likes of Evans and his public schools chums running the country. Or, if not, telling those that do, what to do. So we still can't know for sure what is going to happen.

Knock me down with a feather. I couldn't have dreamt it in my wildest dreams that not only would Davies and Co. be facing a total of £2.7 million wrongfully pocketed, but also be charged with money laundering! You could say this is small beer, and it is in the cosmic scheme of things.

In the book *Treasure Islands: Tax Havens and The Men Who Stole The World*, by Nicholas Shaxson[94], he gives the following figure for criminal money and tax evasion and avoidance purposes that is put into the offshore system each year. *'In 2005, the Tax Justice Network estimated wealthy individuals hold perhaps $11.5 trillion worth of wealth offshore'*. He also points out, *'When billionaire Warren Buffet surveyed his office he found he was paying the lowest tax rate among his office staff including his receptionist. Overall, taxes have not generally declined. What has happened instead is that the rich have been paying less, and everyone else has had to take up the slack'*. Buffet, the fourth richest man in the world in 2016, also famously said, *"There's class warfare alright but its my class, the rich class, that's making more, and we're winning."*

However, for a school, £2.7million is pretty substantial and if you are laundering it as charged, I guess you kind of know you haven't taken it legally. A question remains, how is it that if in a 'riot' you take a bottle of water you can end up in court quicker than you can say fried bread, but if you rob blind school kids, it takes over three years? There is no justice - just us and what we do about it. Needless to say over this extended period
I have stirred the pot at every conceivable stage with both the police and the crown prosecution service. Well you'd have to be an idiot not to. If you sit on your backside and wait for justice, you'll have a very, very long wait and a very sore backside.

The powers that be got annoyed and sent round a police inspector, an Inspector Jarvis to try and lean on me into stopping writing to the police. To stop questioning how long this was going on, the accounts I'd heard of not enough evidence to prosecute, and accusing them basically, and the crown prosecution service of intending, because of pressure from high up, to let them off. Listen mate, or rather Inspector, if I could be leant on in any way I wouldn't have done what I did, or quite frankly be

---

[94] Shaxson's new book *The Finance Curse. How Global Finance is Making Us All Poor* in another excellent book and a notable call to arms.

who I am. It would have confirmed my youthful predilection to think that all coppers are bastards. But enter DC Carl Hughes, a thoroughly decent bloke and doing his best in a fraud squad, massively underfunded. Carl said it could take another year before it gets to court.

The fraud squad is now quaintly, or perhaps not so quaintly, renamed and known as the Specialist, Organised and Economic Crime Command. In our society today, the misuse or reconfiguring of words has become an epidemic of not calling a spade a spade, for purposes of deceiving, manipulation and downright lying.

Fat Lady goes for world record in holding breath.

Fear of asphyxia! How long does it take to get some common thieves in jail? A bloody long time, or even not at all if they are well off or well connected. I heard via two separate sources, Kumud Deshmuk and Denise McKenna, both witnesses involved in the Sir Alan etc. case that the policemen that interviewed them said that Sir Alan and gang were not going to be done because there was not enough evidence. What a load of baloney. We always knew that their friends in high places would do everything they could to let them off. After all, they only robbed the taxpayer and children of the poor and relatively poor who can't have a private education. I am going to have to write to the Director of Public Prosecution at the Crown Prosecution Service and accuse them of intending to let them off i.e. it's a fit up, thus making it harder for them to do so because it only makes my conspiracy theory look right.

I finally got around to writing in September 2013. Here is what I said.

Dear Keir Starmer,
Re: Misappropriation of public funds at Copland Community School in Brent

I write to you to convey my serious concern that I have had reported to me via two different sources; that, in conversation with investigating officers, witnesses were told that there was a lack of evidence that means there might not be a prosecution brought against Sir Alan Davies, Dr Richard Evans and others formally of Copland school in Brent. I was also informed by journalists that when things are put back i.e. from appearing in court in October 2011 to March 2012, that this is often done when cases are subsequently dropped.

We have made the point previously that obtaining a conviction for fraud is more difficult than say misconduct in public office. We do not think it ought to be necessary but staff, parents and ex pupils will bring a private prosecution to respond to this outrageous injustice if there is not a public prosecution. Staff are angry that not one penny of the money wrongfully taken has been paid back to the school. We are also aware that a very large sum of taxpayers money has been spent on this lengthy investigation; now approaching three years.

To bring no charges in this situation (a total of £1.9 million being taken. This included Sir Alan being paid £403,000 in one year) would send out a completely wrong message. After Sir Alan Davies and Co. were suspended, with all the publicity, especially in Brent, surrounding the case, Brent put in place more stringent financial oversight and auditing procedures. Despite this another Brent headteacher (Furness Primary) has recently been sacked for, amongst other things, financial impropriety with public funds. This can only mean that there is already a more widespread problem of misappropriation of public funds in education. We believe that the move to Academies and free schools will only make the possibility and the actuality of fraud/misappropriation of public funds and misconduct in public office worse, unless serious action is taken'.

I reiterate, there is no justice - just us - and how hard we fight to stop the bastards getting away with it. Accusing them publicly of doing something you know they are intending to do is one of the best ways of putting pressure on them not to do it. As is the threat, which in this case they know you will carry out, viz bring a private prosecution.

REBEL WITHOUT A PAUSE

Chapter Sixteen
WARFARE IS A SCIENCE. WE LEARN BY PRACTICE AND STUDY

The Coalition Government has massively quickened the pace and the pressure to increase the gap between rich and poor. To make the working class poorer and to make the seriously rich even richer. Blair and New Labour started it and would have continued if they had been re-elected. The super-rich, our rulers, have worked assiduously in making sure that whichever party may get elected to power their position at the top, and their control, will not be threatened. No obstacle to them making ever-greater sums will be placed in their way. Read *The Vote. How it Was Won and How It Was Undermined* by the late Paul Foot, as mentioned earlier.

Their plan was and is to do this by means of extracting more surplus value from UK workers. This is primarily done by lowering their real pay and making them work longer. Preferably if possible until they drop. This deals with their perceived 'problem' of old people - apart from themselves - not working i.e. continuing to provide them with more profits but getting money through state pensions.

Basically they believe, and the capitalist system works in this way even if they didn't believe it, that they should get everything. Workers aren't even entitled to sufficient to live. Marx identified in *Das Capital* that the intrinsic tendency of capital is to exploit to death. He gave the example of early capitalist style development in Roman Times, where workers in gold mines were quite simply worked to death. The early industrial revolution gave innumerable later illustrations. Examples are *The Conditions of the Working Class* in 1844 by Frederick Engels, published in 1845. It is only the collective organisation of workers to resist and societal social pressure that stops this. The nature of the beast is well explained in *The Corporation: The Pathological Pursuit of Profit and Power* by Joel Balkan. This means that no area should be excluded from them and from them being able to make money out of it[95]. To quote from his introduction, *'The Corporation's legally defined mandate is to pursue relentlessly and without exception its own self-interest, regardless of the often harmful consequences it might cause to others. As a result, I argue, the Corporation is a pathological institution, a dangerous possessor of the great power it wields over people and societies'*. Later in the book, he asks Dr Robert Hare an internationally

---

[95] Notably prisons are now to be wholesale included in this.

renowned expert on psychopathy, for his views on the Corporation. *'Unlike the human beings that inhabit it the Corporation is singularly self-interested and is unable to feel genuine concern for any others in any context. Not surprisingly, when we asked Dr Hare to apply his diagnostic check list of psychopathic traits to the Corporation's institutional character, there was a close match.'*

The working class - by which I mean all those who have to sell their labour power, in short have to have a job to live - not unnaturally object to their families' standard of living decreasing and tend to oppose any attempt to enforce this. Thus we have the origin of the class struggle. Marx wrote about there being an intrinsic aspect of capitalism causing this and not just a fight over the share of what is produced. It was the tendency for the rate of profit to fall. This is illustrated and explained in a number of books but well done recently in Fawzi Ibrahim's book, *Capitalism Versus Planet Earth: An irreconcilable conflict*. See particularly the Appendix. The Critical Zone, Capitalism at the edge of a vortex.

Yes, it is a war. They know it even if some of us don't. That is why we have to learn the best tactics and strategies to carry out the war and this is best done by studying warfare.This would constitute a book in itself. However, some of the tactics and strategies are mentioned in my book. Much more can be learnt from reading and study of the classics of warfare. Examples are *Art of War* by Sun Tsu, *On War* by Carl von Clausewitz, *On Protracted War* by Mao Tse-Tung, Ho Chi Minh's essay, *Guerrilla Tactics*, and *Marshal of Victory: The Autobiography of General Georgy Zhukov.*

As Mao said, political power still, unfortunately, *'grows out of the barrel of a gun'*. Mind you we went to Las Vegas with Kathy and family for her 40th birthday. One of the things that I really wanted to do was to fire a machine gun. Yes, I know I need help. I blame the military school upbringing. There was an age limit to this. You couldn't do it under eight years old. With kids this young the only thing that grows out of their gun barrels is a massively high accidental gun death rate in early youth and a high level of deliberate deaths in later years.

Chapter Seventeen
MR PRESIDENT

I'm on a flight heading for North Korea. It's August 2013. In a roller coaster life, this has been my biggest roller coaster year.

It started inauspiciously when the evening before my inaugural speech as ATL National President I met up with long term mate Dermot, and Laura his work secretary. The demon drink; when we meet we're like naughty schoolboys and encourage each other's misbehaviour. I am utterly pissed. Dermot also completely pissed manages to hail down a black cab. He opens the door or was it me - a monumental irrelevancy. I stumble forward like a felled tree and manage both to hit my ribs on the bottom edge of the open door and my face on the floor of the cab. Despite this the cab takes me and, somehow, I get home. I think it had something to do with Dermot giving a considerable sum up front to the cabbie to ensure I got home.

Thank god in these situations money talks and Dermot had it.

I had cut my face, and, I discovered the next day, I'd cracked my ribs. Jean was horrified at my state and just before such a big and important occasion; she rang Dermot and roundly abused him. The actual words used are, even for me, unrepeatable in print. As if it was his fault. In truth it was no one's but my own. Next day makeup covered my cuts, painkillers dulled the pain of my cracked ribs, but nothing could cover up that I delivered my speech less well than I could or should have. Moral of the story; don't get pissed out of your head the night before you have something very important to do. I was pleased, though, with the wording[96]. I had worked on it for months including on the boat trip to and from St Helena as previously mentioned. Nonetheless the delivery was distinctly not up to scratch. I was, however, very pleased that the General Secretary of the TUC, Brendan Barber, and the new upcoming General Secretary Frances O'Grady turned up. I was mightily pissed off however that the NASUWT because of a childish - in my view - sectarian spat declined to send anyone to go officially to represent NASUWT as was normal protocol. This may be smacking of conspiracy theory. Maybe it was they just did not have anyone available at the time. However, I had good reason for suspecting conspiracy.

---

[96] The speech is on my website

A rule had been introduced into NASUWT rules in 2006 when I was secretary of Brent ATL, NUT and NASUWT. It meant I could not stand for any officer position if I was an officer in another union. As I had become an Executive member for NUT and ATL, they were worried I would get elected onto the NASUWT Executive as well. According to insider information it was known as the 'Get Hank Rule'. I decided to take them to court using the firm of Leigh Day, costing thousands, but the rule change was upheld. Unfortunately, but not surprisingly, not one of the insiders was prepared to be a witness that the rule change was known as the 'Get Hank Rule' as they would have been 'got' too.

So full marks to my mate Shane, Brent NASUWT Secretary and Rex Phillips the NASUWT senior official in Wales, who turned up anyhow, and my NASUWT Cardiff colleagues Brian Williams, Jane Setchfield and John Talbot who chose, very comradely of them, to travel all the way up from Cardiff to London to be there.

During the course of the year I finally hear that Maria Callas has been booked – a plea had been put in – incredibly not guilty! Can you believe that? A date for the trial of Sir Alan and Co fixed. It's taken – over 4 years. What a disgrace. Justice delayed is justice denied. Will they worm their way off the hook? I'm betting no. I really want to win that 50p bet with Graham Clayton[97]. Jean just interrupts my writing to tell me that she has just seen a news flash on the aircraft TV console that she was watching that North and South Korea are likely to improve relations. I say *"that's because I'm going there"*; that's a joke by the way.

I was determined during my year as President to tell it like it is. As ATL President you get to write a column for each issue of the house magazine Report. I told it like it was, as I did at the many branch meetings I was invited to around the country. Interestingly enough the things I said at branch meetings never got me in trouble. ATL and teachers generally are developing a better and clearer understanding of what's going on. It's still just that they lack the confidence to believe that it's within their grasp to halt the ongoing decline. However, my forthright and pretty militant tone in Report ruffled feathers and led to an attack, but certainly not from a quarter that I expected. The Vice President, Alison Sherratt. Now, within a union everyone is entitled to speak out - within the rules - and everybody should. But I had helped Alison in her election campaign by giving her, I believe, some helpful advice

---

[97] Graham has paid up

regarding her election manifesto. Nonetheless she led the charge by attacking the manner in which I attacked Michael Gove in my column in the magazine.

I found myself on the back foot with the Officers[98]. I was determined not to be cowed into writing platitudes. I stood my ground but was more careful about how I said it and for a couple of issues of Report asked Mary and Martin to look at my column, making it clear that there would be no censorship, but that I would welcome their views. They were extremely helpful. The storm clouds passed eventually helped by the fact that if you're in a fight, if one person, or side, is prepared to fight to the finish, the other side has to be prepared to as well otherwise they will not win.

Alison and I became good friends again. She was a strong supporter of professional unity. Sadly she died of cancer in June 2016. Fortunately she was able to complete her presidential year and played a very important role in the discussions leading to the amalgamation of the ATL and NUT.

I didn't think that my combatants at that time would have either the balls or the ability to remove me as President even if that was their thought-out intention - in fact I don't think it was. But what the heck anyhow. I'd sooner have stood by my principles and have been chucked out as President than played the yes man. At conference the same choice faced me. Play it hard line in my Presidential speech and risk alienating the delegates and possibly the membership at large, or to tone it down and go for a safe, or at least safer, option.

I was bet by John Richardson that my speech would not be as radical as a colleague, Malcolm St John Smith, who chaired the Independent Schools Sectorial Committee. John had helped with his speech. Malcolm's speech was indeed radical, but I won the bet. I had concerns my speech might bomb, but I thought I've got to take that risk. I couldn't live with myself if I didn't take the opportunity to tell the unadulterated truth which many, indeed most people, very often don't want to hear. I was relieved when it received a standing ovation. Not by all, but overwhelmingly. Again if interested, read it or hear it on my website. I always welcome comments. Yes, I know it was too long.

---

[98] This spat blew over as contradictions amongst the people normally do. As Mao wrote contradictions amongst the people and contradictions with the enemy are distinctly different.

Retribution

Retribution was inevitable. We had not just exposed grossly negligent Government control and oversight of the 'expenditure' of taxpayers' money in state funded schools but hit a Tory party high flyer, Evans. He was being canvassed on a Tory party website for a Lordship. After getting it he would no doubt have been a runner for Secretary of State for Education. But further we had been causing a lot of trouble both as a school group and at national level for Gove and the Government's academy privatisation scheme. They decide to go for another academy. Where? Guess. You've got it. To turn my school, our school, Copland into another ARK academy – followed no doubt by my and the other 'troublemakers' removal post haste.

A time comes when they set out to crush the resistance. Our time had come. Turn the school into an academy. Remove staff that might oppose it. In fact, preferably remove all staff to eliminate any possible resistance virus remaining, and potentially spreading. The vehicle for the government's academies programme, after bribery and blackmail fail, is force, and the vehicle for the exercise of this force i.e. forcing schools to become academies, is the use of Ofsted.

When I heard that Ofsted eventually was coming, I drafted a letter. I showed it to Shane. He thought it was OTT, too aggressive. Not by half I thought. Anyhow, joint union work means – correctly – you can't always do exactly as you want. I toned it down.

And so it came to pass. I met the Ofsted Inspectors and reiterated my concerns and noted the unusual composition of the team i.e. the presence, number and seniority of HMI's on the team.

There was a possible theoretical escape. A follow-up inspection would occur by a lone inspector who might decide that sufficient improvement had occurred and therefore you would not get the blackspot or rather, perhaps the blackspot would be taken back. However, it was as I predicted. Special measures. Forced academisation. The governors and head objected. The governors' letter of objection was powerful. But needless to say, to no avail.

An Interim Executive Board (IEB) was imposed. Grahame Price appointed as its chair and Richard Marshall, the interim head. The governing body dismissed (again) and the head Grahame Plunkett, leant on to go. Interestingly his post was advertised and someone contacted the school enquiring about it before he was even told anything! The process of destroying the school, of attacking the unions, of attacking and removing staff started.

I asked at the first briefing at which Marshall the appointed interim head appeared and addressed staff, would there be a staff meeting to explain to staff what was going on and what would be happening. "Yes", was the unequivocal reply. The rest of the term, staff meetings came there none and no explanation was given, no opportunity to question. Top-down briefings, yes. Ordinary staff involvement and participation, you're having a giraffe. Staff were given enhanced voluntary redundancy packages like there was no tomorrow. The bullying and intimidation led to grievance procedures being launched. The answer was offer them enhanced redundancy as a payoff for dropping the grievance.

Now the point is, this is public money. Public money should only be paid out if there was genuine need for a redundancy to take place, but a huge proportion of staff were being given it despite the fact that they justifiably could not, or rather should not, have been allowed to go if the curriculum was still to be covered. Of course, not all of the posts were or could be redundant. Replacements would have to be found even if there was some reduction. What about any sense of continuity?! Were we all useless? Surplus to requirement? In fact, any of us? No capability procedures had been brought – yet – against any of them even under the new regime – which has started a decimatory witch-hunt, writing to heads of the faculty asking them to name their two weakest teachers – to be targeted in a future culling procedures. Now the lack of scientific rationale in this is patently exposed by the fact that the best faculty in any school in the country, if it has three or more members of staff, will always have 'two weakest members of staff'.

Apart from the outrageous and utterly profligate expenditure of public funds from any educational point of view, this policy will lead to an increase in indiscipline as a very large proportion of new staff are appointed. That is, if all vacancies are filled and probably with some of less than good ability in view of the huge pressures to fill the many vacancies. The many new staff will not know the pupils, will not know the complicated layout of the school, will not know the school rules, regulations, policies etc. etc.

This can only be designed for the school to descend into chaos and be closed to be handed over, thereafter to new privatised management, or to get the school filled with the new young subservient flunkies who when told to jump some meaningless or worse anti-educational hurdle, will simply ask – how high?

COPLAND
The Education Sell-off
The inside investigative story of how academy
chains like ARK are taking over state education

All this of course is for the same end. An academy. The paranoid theory of history is correct. They are always conspiring to get you.

Find this DVD on YouTube – it's another great film by Jason Parkinson.

On complaining to Mo Butt and the new Labour Lead member for Education Michael Pavey and presenting the evidence to them, they had to admit that it was disturbing. Their initial stance was that procedures and due process should be followed. We should lodge a grievance. This was reminiscent of the advice I was given and had no option but to ignore, regarding Davies et al siphoning off the funds. It was complain to the governors i.e. lodge a grievance. It is no good lodging a grievance to a body that is not even just complicit in the wrong doing taking place but are the authors of it!?! It would be as absurd as the Jews of Germany in occupied Europe addressing a complaint to Herr Hitler.

Before the trial

It's Tuesday morning 1st March 2011.
It is approaching 2 years since I sent in the first dossier of Davies and Co's misdemeanours on the 5th April 2009. The phone rings. It is the answerphone saying we have a message. A female voice says, "*Davies and Evans have been arrested.*" Result. I subsequently realised it was

Lorraine King, of the Willesden and Brent Times. The fat lady has sung, well at least is warming her voice up one might say.

I received innumerable text messages congratulating us and some of them being very rude messages about Alan Davies and gang. I believe they're finished - bar the shouting - and there is no coming back from this one. I wish Sylvia had been alive to know the result. Three were arrested I was told. At first, I thought it was Michelle Bishop but the police statement about the arrests said two people had been arrested at one address and the woman was aged 50. This ruled out Michelle Bishop, Davies's girlfriend having possibly moved in with him, if his wife had chucked him out. It must have been, I worked out, Evans' wife. As the Evening Standard article later that day said, "*Police swooped on the homes of Sir Alan Davies, former head of Copland Community School in Wembley, and his deputy Richard Evans after claims they took home hundreds of thousands of pounds in unlawful bonuses. Mr Evans's wife Lesley, 50, was also arrested today at the couple's Barnet home on suspicion of theft and conspiracy to defraud. The arrests follow a fraud squad investigation into alleged "serious financial irregularities" at the north London school, where one pupil said: "We are all ecstatic and joyful."*"

The theft charge I believe must relate to an alleged theft of the paintings of Mary Fedden. She is a renowned artist who has said that she gave the paintings to the school on condition that they were displayed in the school. They subsequently turned up in Sotheby's auctions for sale by Evans with Mary Fedden demanding to know why. In the event, this charge was never pursued, and the facts are unresolved.

Alex Wellman, a key local journalist in covering the scam alongside Lorraine King, rang me. I missed his call as my phone was hot with journalists, friends and well-wishers ringing. Later I returned Alex's call and after genuine mutual backslapping, Alex said he believed that might be two further arrests. Let's hope so. But this would still leave one out. The three co-conspirators not yet arrested were Columbus Udokoro, Michelle Bishop and the Chair of Governors, laughing boy or is that laughable boy, Dr I P Patel. He, in my view, was also probably a key spider at the centre of this particular web. Let's hope he's not the one that got away.

Further news. Alex was right. More arrests. Now it appears that the whole coven/cabal/other name as you think appropriate has been cracked. All have been arrested – Davies, Evans, Evans wife, Columbus, Michelle Bishop, IP Patel and one I didn't expect, Martin Day the then Vice chair of governors – The Un-magnificent 7.

It is the Friday before the bank holiday Royal wedding. Jack Grimston, the Deputy Editor of the Sunday Times rings me up and says they're thinking of running a story about Davies possibly losing his knighthood. It is apparently a very rare thing. In the event the story doesn't run but I tell him I've heard from a colleague Jenny Williams, Head of Art at Copland, who's being questioned again for the third time by the police, that there was more still to come out on Davies and Co. I tell him I'll meet my colleagues to confirm. Jenny tells me there are more paintings that they have acquired and disposed of. My, my, talk about opening Pandora's Box. My question remains though, how long will it be before justice is finally done? It just seems increasingly incredible to me that an investigation can take this long. I feel pretty certain they will be sent down - as they should be - and Davies will lose his knighthood.

Ironically, in 2002 on my election to the NUT Executive, I received a card. It said, '*You fully deserve the honour. Congratulations on all you have achieved,*' and signed *Sir Alan and Governors*. Perhaps they could give his knighthood to me; Sir Hank of Harlesden, whoops I'm mixing my metaphors or rather honours – this is a joke; I am not fishing.

I was told in confidence that they also intend to go after the bonuses that the deputies were given. In the event they didn't. Sorry but I agree. They were only given 'crumbs from the table' to help facilitate their royal banquet. Concentrate on the main culprits and authors. It would only cloud their central culpability and be used to attempt to lessen their clear responsibility and guilt. Minimising the number of your enemies is also sound strategic sense.

Chapter Eighteen
THE BIG D AND THE BIG C

I am in Tahiti[99] sitting out on the veranda having an early morning coffee. Large birds are circling and swooping nearby. They look a bit like frigate birds but after discussing it we come to the conclusion they are not. The sea is gently lapping the shore some 30 metres away. An island looms dark on the horizon, partially obscured by the numerous tall coconut palms clustered along the beautifully manicured strip of lawn between us and the sea. I think anyone would love it but growing up as a child in Bermuda instilled a special nostalgia and love in me for the sea and islands.

I reflect on the events of the last year and a bit regarding my illness – surgery, chemo and radiotherapy. That my throat feels like someone has a hand round it and is trying to strangle me or has got me in a permanent headlock. I cannot twist my neck fully from side to side and doing so causes pain. My mouth and throat are permanently dry, and I am starting to move like an old man. Perhaps that's because I am. Though being so old seems like a miracle to me. Jean reminds me, I've had a charmed life. I know of course she's right and it's the proper way to think; to think otherwise would be self-indulgent, self-pitying even.

We are off tonight to board the ship that will take us, among other places, to Pitcairn. I am really looking forward to it. I have always loved the story of the mutiny on the Bounty and its almost mythical status in British seafaring and naval history. As if the mutiny itself were not enough, there is the 4000 mile voyage that Bligh and the other crewmen cast adrift endured before they finally reached safety and kicked off the process of the hunt for the mutineers.

Just over a year ago around July 2013 I was propelled onto a giant rollercoaster that was to top a lifetime of rollercoasters. I look back to what I wrote at the time.

The Big D - Davies Trial

I've just had my throat cut virtually from ear to ear. The scars are nowhere near healed. The stitches are still in and there are numerous strips of surgical tape helping to ensure the wounds don't open. Jean is

---

[99] I was subsequently to return to the self-same island and hotel (and view) on our return trip to Pitcairn.

deeply concerned about me leaving hospital before she thinks I should, but I'm not missing this. This is like having a ticket to watch Maria Callas perform at La Scala opera house. Davies and gang are finally in court and I'm going to be there come hell or high water. The hospital said that I shouldn't travel on the tube because of the danger of infection. I should stay in bed and rest and recuperate. Bollocks. I'm going to the show. I get Jean to look up the nearest hotel to the courtroom. Drive there and book a room I say. Jean accepts the inevitable.

I'm there as is Jean and Dave Donaldson, bless him, has turned up too. God it looks as if after all this literally years of investigative work by both Brent's Audit and Investigation team and the fraud squad, they are going to get away with it. The Crown Prosecution Service are pathetic, utterly inept. They have failed to comply with the discovery requirements as requested by the defence and ordered by the judge. The defence moves for the case to be dismissed. Judge Deborah Taylor is clearly annoyed that the prosecution had not complied but allows more time nonetheless for the Crown Prosecution Service (CPS) to get their act together.

The case/hearing reconvenes. Jesus, how useless are these people, or is it a conspiracy to let them off. Once again, they still haven't got their documentation ducks in a row as ordered by the judge. It looks like it must be curtains for the case and they'll get off. But no – the judge bends over backwards and gives them yet more time and does not accept another move by the defence barristers - I count a total of 14 in the court with ten for them and two for our side! - to strike out the case. We begin to have the first inkling that she wants to hear the case.

We return. They've finally got the documents ready to the judge's satisfaction and it looks as if we are ready to rock and roll. This should be really interesting. Then a bolt from the blue. The defence indicates that Sir Alan is prepared to change his plea to guilty. Guilty to the six charges of false accounting if the charges of money laundering and conspiracy to defraud are dropped. The defence indicate that the prosecution has said they are prepared to do a deal. I was informed that no less than Keir Starmer, Head of the CPS at the time, was involved in this deal which had the much desired side-effect of ensuring that none of them spend any time in prison – something they so richly deserved in the eyes of the overwhelming majority of staff, pupils and parents at the school.

Because the charge against Davies of conspiracy to defraud was dropped, the CPS couldn't go ahead against the others. They were not, as they claimed, proven innocent; it was just there was no trial as charges were dropped as a result of the 'plea bargain' where Davies took the rap or rather a rap. A particularly outrageous aspect of the brokered deal was that it was accepted by the CPS that the bonuses were lawful, WHICH THEY WERE NOT. This was established by Tim Ross, then a reporter on the Evening Standard, who had emailed the DfE and got confirmation that bonuses were **illegal**. An error of judgement? Form your own opinion. I think you know what mine is. The Fraud squad were deeply unhappy as well they might be after all the time and effort and indeed expense. Especially as so few of their cases are actually investigated at all, never mind reaching trial, and even fewer resulting in conviction.

Did they get off? To an extent yes. The establishment undoubtedly acted to protect their own. However, and it's a very big however Davies, a JP, ended up with a criminal conviction, a prison sentence of twelve months albeit suspended for two years. It was a disgrace and utter humiliation, but Davies tried to downgrade and minimise it in his statement outside court which was given to me by a friendly journalist. "*In some instances I have felt that we were being tried by the media and there were a lot of misrepresentations made in the press, many of which were wholly unfounded. I do, however, have to accept that I did not have all the necessary paperwork in place and I made a profound error of judgment by backdating eight documents.*"

However, Judge Deborah Taylor, said: "*You were in a position of trust at that school. Your dishonest behaviour represents a fall from grace. You have failed in your duty as head of the school – in failing to ensure proper, transparent management and, more importantly, you lied about it and resorted to dishonest fabrication. What sort of message did that send to the children?*"

It was the worst thing that has ever happened to him. However, worse is to come. I write to the Queen[100] regarding our demand that he had been stripped of his knighthood. After a lengthy delay I find out its happened.

---

[100] I believed I had written to the Queen but I have since recently found out that that was what I was going to do until Jean found out that it should be addressed to the Prime Minister, David Cameron.

He's stripped of his knighthood[101]. Champers all round. Sir Alan, or just plain Alan now, do you remember when you told me during my trumped up disciplinary hearing that I was *"in serious trouble"*? And do you remember when I replied, wagging my finger and pointing at you, *"No, you are the one that's in serious trouble?"*

I thank the heroes and heroines that helped bring some justice; namely Shane Johnschwager, Dave Kubenk, Val Goldie, Pop Camplin, Tullah Persaud, Eva Davidson, Lesley Gouldbourne, and other Copland staff and union colleagues who gave their unstinting support.

The Big C - The start of my treatment

As I write this I'm lying in a hospital bed listening to the endlessly repeating cranking buzz of the machine that is pumping Cisplatin into my vein – potential side effects include loss of appetite, nausea and vomiting, kidney damage, low blood count, peripheral neuropathy, numbness or tingling in hands and feet, taste changes probably temporary, changes in hearing i.e. deafness, and hair loss – whoopee! It's important in this to remember that serious side effects are not the norm and not taking medication has worse side effects, i.e. death.

There are quite a lot of people in the two adjoining treatment areas. I'm the only one with a bed. I don't know if this is good news or bad. I suspected bad, but the bed is so comfortable I decide it must be good. I have two massive scars across my neck that makes me look like Frankenstein or Herman Munster. I've got no feeling in my left shoulder, part of my left ear, the left side of my neck and part of the left hand side of my face. I've got a feeding tube inserted into my stomach through a

---

[101] Those who have lost their knighthoods. As said earlier it is very rare.

1916: Roger Casement, following his conviction for treason and was subsequently hanged; also stripped of his CMG.

1918: Joseph Jonas, after being convicted of a misdemeanour as a result of the anti-German sentiments in Britain at the time because of the First World War. (His crime had been discussions with a potential German customer in 1913, a year before the war.) In addition, his British citizenship was revoked but he was not deported.

1980: Joseph Kagan, Baron Kagan, following his conviction for theft.

1991: Jack Lyons (appointed 1967) following his conviction for fraud; also stripped of his CBE.

1993: Terry Lewis, after being convicted of 16 counts of perjury, corruption, and forgery. Also stripped of his George Medal, Churchill Fellowship, Queen's Police Medal, Australian National Medal and OBE.

2012: Fred Goodwin, after widespread criticism of his conduct as Chief Executive of the Royal Bank of Scotland Group.

2013: James Crosby, after widespread criticism of his conduct as Chief Executive of Halifax Bank

2014: Alan Seymour Davies, following his conviction for false accounting

very painful procedure. I don't think it's so painful normally, but there were real problems inserting it. It's a Tuesday. To cap it all on Saturday I had split up with Lena, my long standing girlfriend, after I had been particularly out of order, and on Monday I heard that my job is to end in April[102]. As they say up north, mustn't grumble. I could have had my house repossessed and all my family killed in a freak tragic accident.

It's all about money, unless it's political and about class. No amount of money is too high if it can inflict a defeat on workers. Viz Thatcher's response to the miners' strike. We now import millions of tonnes of coal when we live on an island made of coal and we have spent billions on the social devastation of unemployment and the annihilation of the mining communities. Irrespective of the wisdom of continuing the strike for so long, would Thatcher have settled earlier under any terms other than total and abject surrender? Arthur Scargill was right – their aim was to destroy the British coal mining industry and more importantly still, the NUM as the most organised and class cohesive detachment of the then 13 million strong trade union movement. The logic of no coal industry, no NUM, was clear.

This is not an argument against the long term need to replace the use of fossil fuels as our main sources of energy. The defeat[103] of the miners' strike cost billions. In common with many others we had a miner living with us for months. A thoroughly decent bloke. Who could blame Jean, least of all me, for having an affair with him, especially as I was out so much with various girlfriends.

How did I end up here? No, not on that subject but in hospital. The big C. As my father had died of it at 30 I should not be surprised. I count myself very lucky to have lived to over twice his age. And the way I got it as you will learn I thoroughly deserved. A lump appeared on my neck.

---

[102] At that time ARK did not pay into the facility pot which paid schools to release union officers. My release from school to be able to continue union work would have ended in April as that is the last payment Brent would have made. Subsequently this changed and ARK agreed to pay into the facilities pot. Primarily I believe (I would wouldn't I) because this would have helped me with the victimisation on grounds of trade union activity case I was preparing to bring and the far more serious one of conspiracy.

[103] The use of the word defeat does not properly assess the strike which radicalised thousands if not millions, showed the power of the collective, the dangers of weakness engendered by division e.g. the miners that continued to work and joined the misnamed Union of Democratic Miners and who ultimately lost their livelihood in addition to helping to secure the loss of livelihood for others.

I thought I had a swollen gland, which I had had before, and it would go down. It didn't. After about a month I went and mentioned it to the doctor. She decided it should be tested 'just in case'.

Jean had insisted in coming along to my appointments (bless her) even though I had tried to persuade her not to as it wasn't necessary. After various tests on the biopsy it was time to meet the main man Mr Farrell, the consultant at Northwick Park Hospital. I start to tell him my view that the lump on my neck may be caused by a deterioration in my teeth connected to the metal plate put in my jaw after it was broken in three places. Jean suggests I let the doctor speak - why? I am clearly the expert. Confirmation – it was throat cancer and metastatic i.e. had spread to the lymph nodes in my neck. It was caused they confirmed later by HPV (Human Papilloma Virus) caused by too much pussy licking. Ah well. It was fun at the time.

Further tests and scans were done. Further appointments with Mr Farrell, where he looks with his fibre optic tube inserted down my nose, normally with some considerable discomfort even after the nasal passage is mildly anaesthetized with a spray. This time he sets out a timetable for an operation, spelled out the fairly serious consequences but with the consolation he said that my natural good looks wouldn't change – oh joy – and that radiotherapy would follow.

I explained that I had a holiday booked to North Korea and no way was I going to miss that. If I died so be it. I had had a wonderful life. In fact the life of Reilly, so I couldn't and wouldn't complain. He made it plain, in fact crystal clear, that he thought I was a fucking idiot - not quite in those words, he was more polite - just. He said this was a life threatening situation and that by postponing treatment there was every likelihood of it being a death sentence.

I was a bit taken aback – well, perhaps a bit stunned. However, my mind was made up. I thought, well I might die anyhow and would I like to see North Korea before I did – you bet I would. Was I likely to get another chance to go there? No. And anyhow we had already paid!!!

As I walked from Northwick Park Hospital to the tube I rang Jean. That was the only one of the appointments she couldn't make with me. She was in France on holiday with both Kathy and Brendan and their kids. It had been Brendan's birthday the day before. I gave her a lecture about not being worried and her needing to be strong for the kids, but I shed a tear at her reaction. Not for me but for her and for the fact that the kids, Brendan and Kathy, would obviously be upset. She was devastated by the news and particularly how I was proposing to deal with it. Furthermore, less than a day after she got back from France I was leaving for my holiday with Lena.

Next comes the bit that convinces most people that I am bonkers. I explain to Jean that I want to commit suicide rather than simply die from the cancer and that I would use this as a protest to highlight what the privatisation of education was doing to education, and the need for increased opposition to it. And that this would have to happen before the end of my ATL presidency which ended on 31st August and no-one was to know. Jean was distraught as this would have meant only a few days after our return from North Korea. She pointed out that September 1st was Lucy's birthday and that I couldn't do this to her, let alone everyone else in the family. It would destroy them that they hadn't been able to say goodbye.

I realised that I needed to write to the children in case I didn't make it back from the holiday.

Luckily things did not take this turn and those final goodbye cards, handed to Kathy and Brendan by Jean, were given back unopened[104].

This is the statement I was intending to read out if I had gone ahead and committed suicide.
"Yet once again hundreds of thousands of pounds of tax payers' money have been wrongfully and unlawfully expended at Copland school and union staff and representatives victimised, treated partially and disgracefully and careers blighted.

In protest at this and to draw attention to it I have chosen to end my life. I do so in sound mind, indeed with crystal clarity. The enormity of what has gone on and is going on. The wanton attack on state education, on

---

[104] Being Jean she didn't believe it could be that imminently serious and had immediately started phoning the consultant etc. on the day I left to find out the real situation. Meanwhile she had the task of telling the children that I had cancer and may even die on my trip, and they may never see me again. The call from the Macmillan nurse came in the middle of this revelation, before they opened the cards. He made it clear that it was not the immediate death sentence I thought the consultant had led me to believe. The surgeon had laid it on thick to try and persuade me or frighten me into doing the sensible thing and have the surgery as soon as possible.

my trade union friends and colleagues, on democracy and the attack on my school in the aim, and at the direction of Gove's forced academy programme. The privatisation of state education to be run for profit. To ensure that this comes to light, is properly investigated, culprits identified and brought to justice requires an enormous response. I am sure my friends, colleagues and champions of justice everywhere will be up to it. This is my contribution.

Life is precious. It is given but once and we should live it to the full. I have done so. I apologise to those I have hurt along the way, but gradually I hope I have learned to be a less selfish person.

I have shed some tears for my family and friends who I know will shed tears for me. But there comes a time when we need to say enough is enough. We the people of our country must not standby as this barbarity is rained down upon us. Everyone can do their bit and if they do we will assuredly get back on the path of progress, of our children and grandchildren having a better, not worse, life than we did."

There was one bit of information I thought it diplomatic to hide from the surgeon Mr Farrell; that was that before I went to North Korea with Jean, I was going for three weeks to Thailand with my girlfriend Lena. Aside from this I hadn't told Lena I had cancer, and I had already paid my share. Lena is kind hearted and generous. If I told her, she would definitely refuse to go and say that I must have my treatment even if it meant losing the money. Even if I insisted we still go on holiday, it would hardly be a happy one knowing that the person she was with was going to die soon, and possibly even, I thought at the time, during the holiday.

In my Spockian and semi autistic logic – which I of course believe is entirely rational because it ignores human feelings – I knew I would have to tell her, but I'd do so near the end of the holiday so that we would enjoy most of it, or if I was finding it impossible to swallow. Already I had started having some pain on swallowing.

Nigel, Lena's best male friend and a good friend of mine came round to pick me up first, before picking up Lena and taking us to Heathrow airport to catch the plane to Thailand. I live quite near where Lena lives. She jokes that for any affair to succeed the participants have to live within 3 miles of each other. Poor Nigel. In the space of a few minutes he went from knowing nothing apart from we were going on holiday and he was taking us to the airport, to be being told - as I truly believed at the time - that I was going to die in short order, possible on holiday. As Lena's best friend he might have to be strong and support and comfort her. My relationship with Lena has been my longest and happiest of all my girlfriends by far.

He was devastated. I told him he had to be strong and give the acting performance of his life so that Lena wouldn't notice anything was wrong. You did it good mate. A hero. I have seen many, many plays and some outstanding actors. Never have I seen a better performance especially under such difficult circumstances. However, though I didn't witness it, I know that Jean's performance on holiday in France in concealing everything from the kids and trying to carry on as normal after she had heard the news of my impending death sentence and the manner I proposed to deal with it, must have been an even greater act.

I have always been utterly dependent on Jean, but I didn't have her down as my top cancer consultant. They are going to operate to remove my left neck lymph glands. Jean had previously questioned a small lump on my right neck but had been told it was nothing. Nothing daunted, on the day of my op with Mr Farrell she strongly states, one could say with more than a hint of challenge, that she thinks the right lump might be cancerous. A consultant feels it – no that's just muscle he pronounces. Not satisfied, Jean raises it again with Marie Claire, the junior consultant who has been closely involved with the scans etc. She feels it and thinks she should consult the PET scan. But the PET scan is not in my folder. It is missing! Eventually they track it down. Sure enough it reveals a small cancer spot on the right!

What can I say of my stay in hospital? Northwick Park is as big as Westfields Shopping Centre or appears to be. I know these massive hospitals are good when it comes to big specialist units for the higher level surgery and treatments. But for lower level surgery and A&E, smaller local hospitals, and a quicker journey to hospital is best and can save lives. It is not best practice to remove them wholesale including now closing some of the bigger ones. Clinical treatment at the top end, for example as with my cancer, is still amazing and science continues to make huge advances in spite of the research cutbacks in so many areas. For example, proton beam treatment.

If its life or death, it's still very good but the cutbacks are having a devastating effect in other areas. The breaking of it up into separate trusts has also created a bureaucratic nightmare. The front line is and will be increasingly affected. Many books and authors have shatteringly clearly exposed the awful reality of what is going on. One of the best was written in 2005 by Allyson Pollock and it has only got worse since. She is Professor of Health Policy and Health Services Research at University College London. Her book is entitled *NHS PLC: The Privatisation of our Heath Service*. Quotes from the preface are worth noting. '*Making health care once again a commodity to be bought, rather than a right, has become the standard prescription of the World Bank, the International Monetary Fund, the World Trade Organisation and even the World Health Organisation – and, increasingly, the European Commission*'.

The book shows, '*the commercial forces as work in the accelerating privatisation process …real costs of privatisation … both the dramatically increased financial costs of using private enterprise, which in reality is so much less efficient in providing health care … costs in terms of lost services, lost universality and lost equality*'. '*Meanwhile the health service is being broken up into hundreds of competing trading organisations.* In her conclusion she states, '*This book is an attempt to show that the NHS has not failed and need not fail. What is required now is not reform but revolution – a quiet, collective and reflective revolution of the sort that brought the NHS into being in the first place*'.

It's Saturday and they are talking about releasing me soon. I had hoped not to be released until Monday. Then tonight I could have tried to sneak out and find a party as I did once before from Hammersmith Hospital when I was in for anaphylactic shock. Hopefully a Halloween party. It would fit in with my slashed throat with the mass of blood still behind the transparent sticky dressing that has been put over the staples. The neck is still swollen but gone down from a few days ago. I still look like Boris Karloff as Frankenstein only missing the bolts. I think the costume couldn't get more authentic.

Back to the treatment

As I continue writing the next day to the buzzing and clanking of the cancer treatment machines, I realise the bed was just a first day 'sweetener'. I'm stuck in a chair with the hoi polloi. Straight after my initial disappointment I convince myself it's a good thing. Cancer no worse than the norm. The normal brain's wiring to be more optimistic or positive about the realities of the difficulties of a situation or ones performance, abilities etc. is well documented. Ian Leslie, mentioned earlier, in his book *Born Liars* says, '*We routinely over-estimate ourselves and – because other people are the only standard which we have to go by – underestimate others.*' He quotes from a published research paper written by Shelley Taylor and Jonathan Brown; '*The normal human mind works with a pronounced positive filter on reality. At every turn [the mind] construes events in a manner that promotes benign fictions about the self, the world and the future*'. This is obviously an evolved survival trait. If you are in a desperate situation and you think you have a reasonable chance of survival this is much better than thinking what the reality might be, that you have very little. Equally if you think you are good looking rather than the reality which is that you are not, this is likely to be of some assistance in seeking and getting a partner. The interesting thing is that even when people know about this research they still regularly overestimate themselves – present company excepted of course. But seriously, alongside recognising that I have some good, even a few great, abilities I recognise that I am a deeply flawed person.

On a more positive note for me at least, I am back with Lena. Jean the treasure rightly predicted the split wouldn't last long. She drove me round to Lena's after a long day of chemo and radiotherapy well late. Lena then drove me back. As she did, she quipped *"how many men get their wives to drive them to their girlfriends and then their girlfriends drive them back to their wives?"* She went on, *"You must have some charisma – not that I've seen much of it recently."* Her quick-witted sense of humour is a notable quality.

Jean's tolerance, thankfully, knows almost no bounds. But there are some, and I have a habit of testing them to the limit and beyond,

The six weeks of chemo and radiotherapy start in the middle of December 2013. Somehow, I get through Christmas and New Year with treatment every day except on Christmas Day itself. We even manage to drive to Portsmouth for a family Christmas day driving back that night. I also spend some time in hospital over the holiday period as I develop pneumonia. Despite this I sneak out to watch a play *Wind in the Willows* at the Duchess Theatre. Only after finally giving in to my constant cajoling, Lena had reluctantly agreed. She drove me through central London traffic in the pouring rain and thunderstorm to the theatre, whilst I repeatedly coughed up phlegm from my pneumonia filled lungs. My absence from hospital was discovered. They phone Jean who gives them the number of the theatre and an announcement is made over the tannoy during the break. I have to leave the performance to return early. The doctors find it amusing but the staff nurses are furious. I suppose they are the ones who carry the can for my going AWOL. While all this is going on the treatment continues relentlessly. As they say it is brutal treatment for a brutal disease.

I'm in the toilet in Charing Cross hospital. The radiotherapy department. I'm about to see the consultant. I've got 3 more radiotherapy sessions to go. Then finito. Liberation. I'm told, however, that things get even worse for a short period after your last radiotherapy session. But then onto the road to recovery. Back to life. I look in the mirror. I see a tiny black mark on my face. It could be a bit of dirt or a black biro mark. I rub it. I wet my finger. It isn't either of those. The consultant confirms my self-diagnosis. 'It could be cancer'. I find it hard to credit but quickly adjust. What's the chance of that? Three days left to the end of treatment for the big C and a second C erupts. What can you do but 'stay calm and carry on'. A biopsy later confirmed that it was not malignant and it was removed. I also tell him I've not been hearing very well. He informs me that this is likely to be permanent. A side effect of the Cisplatin – could be worse – total deafness. But he does tell me my voice which is down to a rasping whisper will return - result. It's like winning the lottery. My voice was the only thing I really cared about. A requirement I consider to be able to continue to fight the good fight. We shall see what happens.

Chapter Nineteen
END GAME

I've just swum in the Nile – whoopee! Hopefully bilharzia free[105]. All the info advised against it but fuck it when you get to my age, you're going to die reasonably soon of something. I'm just grateful it wasn't at 30 like my father.

I'm in Luxor. It would have been safer in Aswan, but I didn't get round to it, and nobody told me there wouldn't be another opportunity. I slipped away whilst everyone was drinking and got a towel, spare pants, shirt, and socks and went out of the ship along the quayside to get in front of three large ships. An earlier reconnaissance had established this was the only place where I could enter the water, and, more importantly, the only place I could get out i.e. I couldn't enter, swim with the current and exit further downstream.

Quick change artist and into the water.

Fine - everything is going swimmingly - pardon the pun. I swim a relatively short way out to the edge of the three ships moored next to each other parallel to the bank. I turn to swim back, confident. I'm a strong swimmer. Fuck - the current is much stronger than I noticed or expected. I'm being carried in the strong current to a narrow channel between two of the ships. I suddenly get alarmed. This current is getting stronger. In fact, much stronger. The advice, well more than that, I have been given by Lena not to do this and how on earth could she face Jean and our kids if I drowned whilst on the holiday with her, flashed through my mind. I struck back for the landing steps with a power surge that can only be bought on by a full on adrenaline blast.

I remember the advice I had given earlier in the trip to another cruise member who had discussed the possibility of swimming there in a built-up area in a big river with a strong current. It's like London, I said. Most people who drown in the Thames, do so not because they can't swim or even because they are not strong swimmers. It is because they can't

---

[105] Checking the internet beforehand it warned that it is not recommended to swim in the Nile or its canals because of the risk of exposure to bacterial and other infections. However, if you must swim in the Nile, ask the captain of your ship where you can swim. He will know the best and safest places. **Do not swim from the riverbank.** And another: Swimming in the Nile is not a good idea. You'll almost certainly get diarrhoea and run a high risk of something more serious (filariasis, schistosomiasis and paragonimiasis). It is a stupid idea.

find a place to get out of the river. Good advice. Why don't I listen to my own advice?

In my bravado and not wanting my girlfriend to come with me and suffer the massive anxiety of having to accompany a nutter on a potential suicide trip, I had slipped away without informing her. Was anyone watching? I didn't know, but certainly not her. Would anyone raise the alarm if I was swept downstream by the surprisingly fast moving current? Would there be anywhere to get out? As I said earlier in my reconnaissance I had only found one entry/exit point. If I made it near to the shore would there be anything to hang onto? What would Jean and the kids think? Fucking idiot. How perceptive!

My body and mind went into overdrive. I appeared to be making little progress. Very gradually I started to get nearer. And I started to get more tired. And I started to get nearer, and I started to get even more tired. As I neared the built-up bank and the stairs into the river where I entered, the current eventually slackens. My progress increases. Eventually, at last, I make it. I am utterly, utterly exhausted. Thank fuck for that. My lifetime of periodic idiocy had not ended yet.

I have to relate another incident. As part of a guided tour we visited someone's house who kept crocodiles in a pool. You were allowed to hold one - its jaws were taped up - so I paid for a photo holding this 2-3-foot croc. The fucking thing pissed on me! Who would have thought a crocodile would have the intelligence to take the piss out of me? Is it that bleeding obvious that I deserve it?

Later that evening when penning this I had time for reflection. Irrespective of the particular outcome and other near misses, my life is approaching what they call in chess, the endgame. But more on facing the grim reaper later.

Having mentioned chess, I have beaten a Grandmaster at chess. Like many statements that are true, the qualification tells a somewhat different story from the bald statement. From developing a keen interest at my military boarding school which I have never lost, through my teaching of others, and putting motions to union conferences on the importance of teaching chess in schools, I have got involved with the Chess in Schools charity run by Malcolm Pein and others. At their annual gala dinner held yearly at Simpsons in the Strand, Grandmasters who have been involved in the London Chess Classic, a world-class tournament, play collectively and simultaneously against guests at the dinner tables. Lena enjoys going to this formal event as she enjoys a good game of chess. They play a quick move and then move on to the next table. The speed of their decisions is greatly aided by the fact that at their level, play is primarily based on pattern recognition. When I say I won, it should have been we won – twice on two separate occasions. With grandmasters sitting at my table, I should also say my role in my team's collective deliberations was – nil!

Will ARK take over the school in September? Almost inevitably. Will I be offered a deal that no one in their right mind, even me, would say no to? Who knows? I don't and that's part of the excitement and interest of life. It's what Stephen Jay Gould in his book *Wonderful Life: The Burgess Shale and the Nature of History*, called contingency. If you played life's tape again, he was writing about evolution, you would not get the same outcome. He said it would be an almost completely different outcome every time. Jonathon Losos, also now at Harvard, in his book *Improbably Destinies: How Predicable is Evolution?* said that on the basis of more recent rigorous analysis and evidence that there would be a great deal more similarity than Gould predicated. But our individual life's outcomes are not so heavily constrained or predictable.

My journey to North Korea

I write this on the way back from Beijing after having been to North Korea. Wow. Another blast. Not what I expected nor any of the group of ordinary tourists we were with expected either. A highpoint: the Arirang Festival was a mass gymnastics and artistic festival held in the Rungrado May Day Stadium in Pyongyang. Just amazing watching up to 100,000 people moving in choreographed displays, some creating pictures and some with lots of different activities going on at the same time. You just didn't know where to look.

Interesting? Hugely. Bizarre? Certainly in aspects, but not quite as bizarre if set in context and thought about. For example, the worship of their leaders in particular Kim Il-Sung is a form of ancestor worship having a common cultural theme across the far east. For example, Japan's ruler was in living memory regarded as a god. In Thailand to insult the Royal Family is an imprisonable offence.

There is a large degree of equality in North Korea except for those at the very top. It is run like a family firm ergo the dynastic sequence. However, what they have in spades is the idea of self-reliance wherever and whenever possible. We were surprised that they admitted in the past experiencing a famine - in which they did accept foreign aid - and explained how they had since changed their methods of agriculture. No unemployment, or exploitation of others by private firms. It's like a sort of state monopoly capitalism. Payments/perks for those at the top. Inherit private property? Yes, but not houses or businesses. Everybody must work except those who cannot. They nearly all have mobile phones, but the network is exclusively for use in North Korea. Education at all levels is free including university and college. Their education system produces, as we witnessed in part by the various performances they put on, some remarkable outcomes. But it is clearly a highly selective system. If you show early potential in any field, you are hot housed rigorously to ensure that you best serve the system. I read in a New Scientist article once about a delegation of western volcanologists going to study volcanic activity in North Korea and them saying that they were very impressed by the high level of knowledge and understanding of the North Korean scientific hosts.

Michael Palin said of his filming experience when he was making his documentary 'Michael Palin in North Korea', "*What I'd expected was conditioned by the general idea that this was a dark place, a grim place, repression, lack of freedom. I felt that it was going to be an interesting but threatening experience and that just didn't happen*" … "*We were not going to be able to discuss politics, we were not going to be able to discuss weapons. For me, when you are filming a country it's not really the big statements or the big policies that you are hearing about that make the difference, it's the way people move, people talk, people eat. There was no way that our minders could control everything that we saw, nor did they really try to.*" In short it was better than he expected as it was with our group of tourists.

Part of understanding North Korea's attitude was brought home when we visited their prized possession, USS Pueblo, which had been captured as a spy ship in their territorial waters and the crew detained. The US denied it was a spy ship but after much bluster and threats, they finally had to admit it was when the documentation and photographs proving it were released across the world. The North Koreans demanded a written apology from the US before they would release the crew. That written apology takes pride of place in the exhibition. It is the only country that the US has ever apologised to.

I could write a lot more about the country, but I simply recommend a visit. The North Koreans remind me of a Staffordshire bull terrier – well capable of being destroyed but completely convinced of its own indomitability.

I now turn to what some might think is a morbid matter, but which I don't think is, of death.

My thoughts on the Grim Reaper

On death. I am pleased. I have faced death, looked it square in the eyes and not blinked. I prepared for death. I did so with equanimity. Life is a lottery. There is no point in not accepting the hand we are dealt. I told Pete and he had a similar view, which is not to say he wasn't sorry to hear it. Jean took it much harder than I'd imagined. I know that sometimes my mild autism makes it hard for me to understand some human reactions. To me it was obvious, logical. If you're going to die go out with a bang so to speak. Do it to some purpose. Interestingly, and perhaps surprisingly to me was my friend Dermot's reaction. I had always had Dermot as somewhat lacking in the human empathy department. I said to him once, "*Dermot you do know you are a sociopath, not a psychopath*". "*A sociopath; what's the difference?*" he enquired. I explained, "*A psychopath doesn't know the difference between right and wrong. The sociopath knows the difference but is not that bothered*".

I should have known from the grief he suffered from his beloved dog Tara's death. I put it down at the time to her non-judgemental affection, always a must/hit for those with emotional difficulties or problems. But joking aside, I think it was the experience of going through his father's death and him being at his bedside when he died that brought it home to him. He tried to convey to me the pain that somebody feels on the death of their father, or mother or loved one. I knew it from childhood before I had developed reason or logic, and I somehow just assumed most adults viewed it differently – with more detachment as I now did. I think his talk with me, made me reconsider. I had rung him to tell him after my initial virtual death sentence, what the deal was and my views. He suggested meeting at a trendy hotel in Shoreditch.

'Think of others not yourself' was the short of it; fair point. I hadn't been thinking of others, especially my family, enough. However, I would not want to live without my voice. I do not want to live till I'm old. A bit too late to say that at 63, nearly 64, many would say. Too late in the words of The Who lyrics of *'My Generation', 'Hope I die before I get old'*. Only the old, or seriously ill, can have any idea why anyone not seriously depressed would think like this.

For most in old age, you become a shadow of your former self. Your circle and number of friends and acquaintances diminishes until at extreme old age, apart from spouses (possibly) and relatives (hopefully), it tends to end up with just you. The aches, pains, the steady accumulation of medical problems, the deafness, the disintegrating health, the memory going, balance going, strength going.

What's it like to be going from Mr Macho man, the dog's bollocks to pre-senescent decrepitude. Is there nothing to look forward to? Yes. The personal highs of your loved ones. The marvellous increase in scientific knowledge and its application. The unfolding of history, especially when tyrants, the corrupt, and tyrannical and corrupt regimes, or indeed capitalism itself receives a blow as in the 2007/08 meltdown. Otherwise, I alongside everyone else of my age and older would have committed suicide.

But they get fewer. As so many have rightly observed, the youth are our future. Which only makes the crimes of our rulers even greater in seeking to enforce on them, and so far getting away with it, a worse life than my generation experienced. Wake-up. Start to do something about it, or if you are, try a bit harder!

Following Sylvia's death there are two other people that I was very close to whose deaths I want to recount, not just because of how they affected me but because of wider social implications.

Lynsey

I'm in the playground. I'm rung up by Lynsey's mum. *"She's only gone and done it"* she says. *"She's gone and killed herself."* I am utterly stunned. I can't grasp it, comprehend it. I'm in a daze.

Lynsey was an ex-girlfriend. She had, as I said in my speech at her funeral, *"A smile which like Helen of Troy could have launched a thousand ships. A laugh that was utterly infections and lit up the world."* I had stopped seeing her quite some time prior to this tragedy. Our relationship had been tempestuous. I know I had not given her what she wanted and needed. Not just love but permanence and stability which I could not offer. As I also said in my speech, *"We should all remember that Lynsey was ill. She suffered from an illness called depression and it periodically made her suffer greatly"*.

I have no doubt that the medication Seroxat, that she was taking for her depression was at least part of the cause of her suicide. A class action had been launched against GlaxoSmithKline over this[106]. I tried to get Lynsey's Mum to join this, but the hurdles were difficult. I nonetheless believe that this was yet again an example of corporate greed, putting money to be made above health and indeed life. Her suicide note was tragic as is the story of a wasted precious young life.

To quote again from my speech, *"The present world was not designed for Lynsey. She wanted and needed 100% as she told her Dad. She was a 24/7 her Mum said"*. And finally, *"Lynsey I want to thank you, from*

---

[106] The United States Department of Justice fined GlaxoSmithKline $3 billion in 2012, for withholding data, unlawfully promoting use in those under 18, and preparing an article that misleadingly reported the effects of paroxetine – marketed as Seroxat - in adolescent with depression following its clinical trial study.

all of us, for the sunshine and light you brought to our lives. Though it was not enough it is my fervent hope we brought some to yours". I then read my adaptation of one verse from *For the Fallen* by Laurence Binyon.

'*She shall not grow old, as we that are left grow old*
Age shall not weary her, nor the years condemn
At the going down of the sun and in the morning
We will remember her.'

Dave

David, better known as Dave, Leavers, who I mention visiting in prison earlier in the book, died at the age of 62 of pancreatic cancer. There are many mad accounts I could give of the times we got pissed out of our heads in Camden and elsewhere and caused mayhem. I met him in the Hawley Arms – where else. At one time he was a bouncer at Dingwalls, another great Camden club. I saw Bo Didley there and Wilco Johnson amongst many others. Dave used to let me in free. At one stage he got me barred from almost every pub in Camden from Haverstock Hill down to Camden tube - including the Hawley. Even he, however, couldn't manage to get us barred from The Marathon, which says a lot about The Marathon.

Befittingly we distributed his ashes in – yes, you've guessed it – the Hawley Arms and also around Camden. Then our merry band – Dermot, John Bougher, Murray Sharp, Shane, Johnny Beatlejuice, Pete Foot, Dave S, Patsy, Poneytail, Declan and Rob among others – wended our way to the Elephants Head. Some who couldn't make it were Eoin, Mick McGee, Ian the Mechanic, Scottish Jim and Dimitri who turned up late and they wouldn't let him in. All of them brilliant friends and most as mad as hatters.

When I visited Dave in hospital for the last time he was clearly dying and in extreme pain. He briefly came out of his drug induced torpor when the nurse asked him, "*You've got a visitor here. Do you recognise him?*" He barely audibly croaked "*Hank Roberts.*" It was excruciating to witness. After spending more than an hour talking to him without any further response, the medic said that he was stable and that nothing would change any time soon so I left. However, he died later that night. As he had no known living relatives and was living in sheltered accommodation, Chelmsford Council paid for his funeral as councils do for those who are destitute. The Bereavement services did him proud – it took six men to carry his coffin as he was broad shouldered and 6ft 4in.

A vicar had been organised to do the reading. In preparation I had sent a draft script and a play list as he had requested. We waited and waited for him to turn up but no show. So I volunteered to be the vicar instead! I read out the speech I had sent him. Luckily I had brought a copy. Extracts will help give a picture of the man.

'*Dave was a binge alcoholic and had problems with drink throughout his adult life but especially in the latter part. When sober he was intelligent, witty, and charming. When drunk he was initially hilarious but eventually as a binge progressed, more and more obnoxious. Few could handle it, especially over the long haul.*'

I then relate one very funny episode which sums up Dave. '*Having photography as a hobby and loving it Dave became a photographer on a big cruise line and stayed for many years, eventually becoming Chief Photographer with a team under him. This ended one New Year's Eve, the most important day in a cruise ship photographer's year. Dave, as it was New Year's Eve and everyone is celebrating, decides not to go to work and joins in*'.

'*Eventually officers were called and ordered him back to work. He refused. At sea this was technically mutiny. Eventually he was manhandled into the brig. No easy task, and he assaulted one of the officers in the process. When the ship returned to port he was handcuffed, taken to the airport and immediately deported back to*

England'… 'Dave became a millionaire twice in his life, both times eventually losing all. When he had money, he was extremely generous'.

Having covered a variety of other 'adventures' in the reading, at the end of the service the mourners are assailed by the lyrics of *Highway to Hell*. Perhaps this is why the vicar hadn't turned up. Not only was the reading a bit close to the bone but the lyrics weren't exactly appropriate for a vicar's service!

In later life he had brief periods of mental illness, as do many, and was hospitalised. He also spent some time living rough on the streets and during this time he attempted suicide. In an earlier form of human society that of small groups of hunter gatherers he might have had more support. Additionally, I tried to help him to get social sheltered accommodation rather than his tiny individual flat, to no avail.

Some philosophical points on death

As Mao Tse Tung said. *'The death of some people weighs greater than Mount Tai and of others it is lighter than a feather'.* I spoke these words at the funeral of our close friend James Howes. He was a great thinker. James had an outstanding mind and gave many erudite comments on all sorts of important, and obscure, areas of knowledge. His death was definitely a weight greater than Mount Tai.

As to others being lighter than a feather, when Margaret Thatcher died, I unashamedly broke open a bottle of champagne and went down to Brixton with Jean and many others and partied. Why? Because I really didn't like her. If I had I'd have joined those that mourned, but not the hypocrites like Hesletine, Howe – and all the other senior Tories at the time who stabbed her in the back and got rid of her – whilst 30 years later, weeping crocodile tears and saying she was the best prime minister ever.

Carol Thatcher correctly identified me in her book, *Diary Of An Election*, in the photo captioned as *'Thatcher out badges being sold by one of Mum's less supportive constituents'*. I came face-to-face with Thatcher when I had been selling Thatcher Out badges in her Finchley constituency during election time.

I worked my way into the media scrum and said to her face on, "*You said Labour wasn't working with one million unemployed. Now there are three million with you.*" She replied, "*There's*

Above left: The Opposition in Bristol

Above: 'Thatcher Out' badges being sold by one of Mum's less supportive constituents in Finchley

sixteen million unemployed in the European Union". I replied "*Well, that makes it okay then*". I was on the TV news. I was rather pleased with my response.

Death is inevitable the saying goes, as are taxes. Taxes aren't. I've just been to North Korea and they don't have taxes. Death is inevitable to humans presently, but it is not a necessity decreed by the laws of science and the universe. Never mind the multi-verse or the many worlds theory if either prove true.

In his book *The Beginning of Infinity – Explanations that Inform the World*, David Deutch explains about the severe, life-threatening fundamentals. To quote, '*If something is permitted by the laws of physics then the only thing that can prevent it from being technologically possible is not knowing how.*' He continues, '*A sick person is a physical object, and the task of transforming this object into the same person in good health is one that no laws of physics rules out.*' And even on death he says, '*The problem of ageing is of the same general type as that of disease. Although it is a complex problem by present-day standards, the complexity is finite and confined to a relatively narrow arena whose basic principles are already fairly well understood. Meanwhile, knowledge in the relevant fields is increasing exponentially.*' I agree with him – we will ultimately find a scientific way to conquer death. Probably not as fully biological being and ultimately probably not as a biological being at all. As Deutch says if it is not prevented by a law of science it can happen. It is only a question of complexity and difficulty.

I will miss in both senses of the word, this and the extension of human life or what passes for it in the far distant future, but in the realities of the here and now I do not. I wish to die believing I have fought the bastards, fought for the people, my friends, my children and family, my class, as best I could. I wish I had had more ability and talent, but we are dealt a hand. We can and should seek to improve upon it. But as Marx said we make our own history but within parameters: *"Men make their own history, but they do not make it as they please; they do not make it under self-selected circumstances, but under circumstances existing already, given and transmitted from the past".*

The 'Big Man' and Philanthropy

As I face death, perhaps sooner rather than later, I will die happy. Except for one thing, and it is a really major one. How is it that the biggest issue that confronts our species, is that a relative handful of billionaires and multi billionaires can still so dominate the world? An Oxfam Report published in January 2019 concluded that the number of billionaires owning as much wealth as half the world's population fell from 43 in 2017 to 26 in 2018. In 2016 the number was 61. Is it by dint of any human attribute or talent?

Is anyone 1 million times stronger, cleverer or more talented in any way than an average human could be, with due effort? And if not, why should they receive, or potentially receive, 1 million times more food, shelter, sex or any other fundamental requirement or even deserve it more than you or I or any other normal hard-working human being. And if all their needs are met, why should they have so much more to spend on non-necessities when others, including children who are and must be blameless, do not have the basic necessities of life.

Some people will say that climate change must come first. I say that unless we can challenge and limit the power of the multi billionaires that run the world who first have been primary causes of the problem and second will act to stop or slow down all logical and scientific steps necessary to halt climate change we will be stuffed.

Bill Gates, a man who has more personal wealth than the GDP of most nations, is normally regarded by most as the poster boy of philanthropy. Justification for why he deserves his billions are look at how much his inventions have improved millions upon millions of lives and look how his medical philanthropy has similarly saved countless lives.

The reality of this regarding him and other multi billionaires from Rockefeller and Carnegie to Buffett and Soros, is hardly rose-tinted. In her book *No Such Thing as a Free Gift: The Gates Foundation and the Price of Philanthropy*, Linsey McGoey does a very thorough exposé of the difference between the myth and the reality.

These are just a few of the highly pertinent questions she asks and points she makes. She highlights the book *Philanthrocapitalism: How the Rich Can Save the World* by Matthew Bishop and Michael Green. She says, *'The book has become… A bible for a new breed of philanthropist… reshaping the world by running philanthropic foundations more like for-profit businesses.'* What is the aim of a for-profit business you ask? Obviously to make a profit. This clearly signposts the direction and intent. She writes, *'Critics of philanthrocapitalism raised three main concerns…'* 1) the lack of *'accountability and transparency'*. *'The Gates Foundation is accountable to no-one other than its three trustees: Bill, Melinda and Berkshire Hathaway CEO Warren Buffet.'* 2) *'… philanthropy, by channelling private funds towards public services, erodes support for governmental spending on health and education'*.

She gives this instructive example, *'The tension between private philanthropy and public spending has become clear in recent battles over public education in the United States. Often working in collaboration, three powerful 'mega foundations' – the Gates Foundation, the Walton family and the Broad Foundation – are helping to build one of the fastest growing industries in the United States: secondary and primary schools run on a for-profit basis.'*

3) *'The great industrialists of the late 19th and early 20th century were dubbed robber barons due to the widespread condemnation of their predatory business tactics. Today some of the world's most celebrated philanthropists, from Gates to George Soros earned billions through business tactics that have compounded financial instability, eroded*

labour protections and entrenched global inequalities.' I.e. they were accumulated in some measure by ill-gotten means.

Astonishingly proponents of philanthrocapitalism also claim that capitalism itself can be philanthropic benefiting people through new products, higher quality and lower price!

Two fundamental questions arise;
1) Is this 'philanthropy' reducing economic inequality? Her answer is that the opposite appears to be the case.
2) Does philanthropy make the rich richer and the poor poorer? The answer from her well researched book, is yes. These modern-day charitable giants aim at preserving wealth rather than redistributing it. Also political interventions such as the aforementioned political intervention to support the neoliberal takeover i.e. privatisation of state education, do the same.

The cat was let out of the bag in an article entitled *The Competitive Advantage of Corporate Philanthropy* by Kramer and Porter 2002. They urged that philanthropic strategies should be pursued that helped corporate donors to get greater profits for their business!

Another book that calls for reform rather than the ending of the philanthropy, *Just Giving. Why Philanthropy is Failing Democracy and How it Can Do Better* by Rob Reich has these words on its fly sheet of the front cover.

'Is philanthropy, by its very nature, a threat to today's democracy? Though we may laud wealthy individuals who give away their money for societies benefit, Just Giving shows how such generosity not only isn't the unassailable good we think it to be but might also undermine democratic values and set back aspirations of justice. Big philanthropy is often an exercise of power, the conversion of private assets into public influence. **And it is a form of power that is largely unaccountable, often perpetual, and lavishly tax advantaged** (my emphasis). *The affluent – and their foundations – reap vast benefits even as they influence policy without accountability. And small philanthropy, or ordinary charitable giving, can be problematic as well. Charity it turns out, does surprisingly little to provide for those in need and sometimes worsens inequality.'*

Even a plea for reform, which the book is, puts a stake through its heart.

A final source knocks on the head what is known as the 'Big Man' theory. It's almost invariably a man. In finance they are called, or were before the crash of 2007/8, Lords of the universe, supermen all. Outstanding achievements overwhelmingly involve large elements of luck, often large elements of dishonesty or dubious behaviour, often are collective achievements with the names and assistance of other partners written out.

My last quote on this subject is from *The Trouble With Billionaires – How the Super-Rich Hijacked the World (and How We Can Take it Back)* by Linda McQuaig and Neil Brooks. *'So, if we were to present the story of the development of the personal computer as a stage play, it would be a rich and complex drama with a long list of characters. From early scenes featuring Joseph Marie Jaccard and his punch card technology, the play would go on to include starring roles for Charles Babbage, Herman Hollerith, Thomas John Watson, J Presper Eckert, John Mauchly, Douglas Engelbart and Bill English, with a host of other largely unidentified characters playing crucial supporting roles on stage and off. Toward the end of this rather long drama, there'd be an intriguing subplot about how technological innovator Gary Kildall thought he had a deal with IBM, only to discover his friend Bill Gates had sold IBM an adaption of Kildall's own operating system for the first mass-market personal computer. It would only be at this point late in the final act that we'd get our first sight of Gates, and he wouldn't come across as a particularly heroic character. Indeed, as the curtain came down at the end of the production it would be hard to imagine Gates getting a curtain call or receiving the lion's share of the applause, let alone walking away with the entire box office take.'*

Billionaires will not save the world. Their psychopathic pursuit of self-aggrandisement and ideological support for naked neoliberalism is destroying it.

Our real enemy is not the top 10% nor even the top 1%. Nor even the top 0.1% or even 0.01%: it is more like the top 0.001% i.e. the top 1 millionth of our population. Of course, we have to deal with and confront the more numerous implementors and aiders and abettors of their looting and pillaging of our means of existence and heritage, but strategically it is important to specify and identify our main enemy. They are indeed few. We are indeed, and overwhelmingly, the many.

Finally let me refer to famous literary talents on the subject of philanthropy. First is that stellar literary talent, playwright and satirist Oscar Wilde. Many recognise and know of his unjust and brutal treatment as a homosexual, well portrayed in recent films, but few of his socialism. In his essay *The Soul of Man under Socialism* he said, '*The best among the poor are never grateful. They are ungrateful, discontented, disobedient and rebellious. They are quite right to be so… Why should they be grateful for the crumbs that fall from the rich man's table? They should be seated at the board and are beginning to know it.*'

The other is the author of the *Ragged Trousered Philanthropist*, first published in 1914. A book more famous than some of the Shakespeare plays or some of Dickens novels. It has never been out of print. Over 1 million copies have been sold in over thirty languages

As McGoey says the book '*extended the label of philanthropists*' to a group of house painters who, as Tressell saw it, acceded meekly to the demands of their bosses. With sly wit Tressell suggested that their willingness to surrender their labour cheaply was the ultimate philanthropic act. The story of the *Ragged Trousered Philanthropist* is both tragic and instructive. Not many people know that Robert Tressell was not the real name of the author; it was a pen name. He used a pen name because he was worried he might be blacklisted for his socialist sympathies.

His real name she explains was Robert Noonan. He died in 1911 of tuberculosis-related illnesses at the age of 40 and was buried in a pauper's grave in Liverpool. '*The book was never published in his lifetime. He never lived to see it become a bestseller, credited with helping to bring about Labour's shock victory in the British election of 1945. He never lived to see his story rouse the anger of future generations of workers, labourers determined not to act with good will, determined not to feign gratitude. As Wilde said why should they.*' The main lesson from this for you dear reader is write your book and seek to get it published. Imagine how pissed off you would be if this happened to you. Actually you wouldn't be of course, because you'd be dead. Don't do a Tressell, oops sorry Noonan. Get on with it. Now!

It is time to stop the rot. It is well within our capabilities. The united workforce of this country, the united workforce of this world, can achieve over time, anything it chooses that is not outside the laws of nature. We have but to try.

Journey to the North Pole

It only seems like a blink of an eye when I read back on my previously written account of my earlier life events. Time is relative as you get older. It marches faster. I am on a special charter flight that has just left Helsinki for Murmansk – the most northerly port in Russia – famous for being the destination of the Arctic convoys in the Second World War. I'm on my way to a destination which, if asked as a kid, I would have said was the second last place in the world I could have expected to get to. The South Pole being the last. Yes, the destination is the North Pole. Maybe more people have been to the South Pole than the North as the South Pole has a 200 strong community of scientists which change on a regular basis. Few people have been to either. I put this as, in a way, an apogee, of what the development of British society achieved by the hard work and struggle of the post war generation. A standard of living that a fairly ordinary member of the working class, a teacher, can achieve. The next generation? Getting poorer by the day. It looks unlikely that ordinary workers of the next generation would be able to afford such a thing, unless we have a radical change.

We're getting there on board the world's most powerful and biggest icebreaker, the nuclear powered *50 Years of Victory* (*50 Let Pobedy* in Russian). Named in celebration of the 50th anniversary of the victory of the Soviet Union against fascism in the Second World War.

Before you complain about the carbon footprint, let me remind you it is nuclear powered and therefore there isn't one. And for the anti-nuclear power lobby let me say nuclear is and will be an important source of energy for the foreseeable future. Nuclear fission does produce radioactive waste which is obviously a disposal problem, but it is still the safest method of energy production in terms of deaths per megawatt produced. Fusion, where the atoms are forced to merge instead of split, when mastered will be a much cleaner source of energy as will the use of thorium in reactors instead of uranium or plutonium.

Also without it for example we could not have received the information sent back from the Voyager missions or from the recent New Horizons spacecraft flypast of Pluto which thanks to its nuclear power source sent us the spectacular photos and information about Pluto and will continue to send back signals on its journey to the Kuiper Belt Object (KBO) which it will fly past on January 1st 2019. New Horizons is a NASA spacecraft that was the first to visit dwarf planet Pluto in July 2015. Its pictures of the dwarf planet's icy surface, as well as observations of Pluto's moon Charon, are revolutionizing our understanding of solar system objects far from the sun.

Nuclear weapons are another thing altogether. Of course, they should all be dismantled. Even their first use, on Hiroshima followed by Nagasaki their second - and hopefully the last use - was unjustified; the Japanese were already defeated. The Americans were worried that the Japanese would surrender to the Russians. In *Why America Dropped the Atomic Bomb* by Ronald Takaki, he says, '*Although General Douglas MacArthur was the supreme commander of Allied forces in the Pacific, he was not consulted about whether to use the atomic bomb on Hiroshima. In fact, he was informed of the decision only forty-eight hours before the fateful flight of the Enola Gay (on 8th August 1945). MacArthur considered the bomb "completely unnecessary" from the military point of view: he believed that the Japanese were practically defeated. In July when the general learned that Japan had asked Russia to negotiate a surrender with the United States, he told his staff: this is it. The war is over'. A member of his staff recalled, "We expected acceptance of the Japanese surrender daily". "After the bomb was dropped on Hiroshima", he added, "Gen MacArthur was livid".*

'*Chairman of the joint chiefs of staff Admiral William D. Leahy .... believed that the atomic bomb was not at all necessary. "It is my opinion" he wrote in his memoirs "that the use of this barbarous weapon at Hiroshima and Nagasaki was of no material assistance in our war against Japan. The Japanese were already defeated and ready to surrender because of the effective sea blockade and the successful bombing with conventional weapons".*

Takaki continues, 'Manhattan Project Director General Groves described the atomic bombs larger purpose more directly: *"There was never, from about two weeks before the time I took charge of this Project, any illusion on my part but that Russia was our enemy, and the Project was conducted on that basis."* In Gar Alperovitz's book *Atomic Diplomacy: Hiroshima and Potsdam* he proves the same points. Another book written by Peter Watson entitled *Fallout: Conspiracy, Cover-up and the Deceitful Case for the Atom Bomb* is an excellent account and brings the evidence bang up to date.

Enough is enough, teacher, return to the ship. What a ship it is. The ship has superior characteristics for an icebreaker, such as exceptional manoeuvrability and a top speed of 21.4 knots (24.6 mph). The icebreaker is designed to break through ice up to 16 ft thick. The spoon shaped bow increases the efficiency of the ship's efforts in breaking the ice. She has two OK-900A nuclear reactors (2 × 171 MW) and two steam turbo-generators (2 × 27.6 MW). Each system is duplicated – if you only had one you'd be in serious trouble if it broke down.

For a few trips during the summer the officers' cabins are used by 100 tourists at a time, paying a suitably fat fee to help pay towards research on global warming in the North pole area. That means the officers have to share with ordinary crew, but it seemed to work well.

As I write this I've just returned from a swim – at the actual North Pole. Bloody freezing. The crew have created an ice free, or relatively ice free, pool of sea water at the stern of the icebreaker, the perimeter of which is roped off. The temperature is below freezing – the high salt content of the water means that it freezes below zero degrees centigrade, actually at -2.6. The shock of the cold can cause a heart attack. By the side of the ice pool is a defibrillator. I dive in. I've done it before, so I take my chances. I go hell for leather for the perimeter. We all have ropes round our waists in case of emergency. I touch the perimeter rope and turn to swim back.

Oh f… Potential disaster. On turning and making for home my legs have got caught up in the rope attached to my waist. I can't continue with the

crawl. I quickly change to breaststroke using just my arms. It is slower. As I'm approaching the exit ladder I am slowing down and starting to really feel the effects of the freezing temperature.

I grab the ladder but can't manage to get my legs to climb the steps. I'm helped up. A slightly ignoble end but luckily most people watching didn't realise and I get a resounding round of applause.

Jean also made a heroic effort and swam unlike a number of the faint-hearted brave hearts, who jumped in only to get straight out again. A later picnic/barbeque on the ice gave it a surreal atmosphere – as did one of the captain or crew's sons who cycled on his bright red bike around the North Pole sign stuck into the ice - full marks for originality. We formed a big circle, had one minute's silence and the Captain made a speech wishing for world peace. If only, but the right sentiment. A Qatari prince who was on the trip had got out his flag, as had someone else, but were told by the translator to put it away as this was an international event.

Helicopter ride of a lifetime

The ship has a helicopter on board. The weather has been quite bad, foggy for a lot of the journey. The passengers have only had one flight – basically a ten-minute circumnavigation of the ship. We hear an announcement. The helicopter can be privately chartered. An insane idea comes into my mind. I wonder to myself how much that would cost. I suggest to Jean that she goes to the bridge to find out. She remonstrates quite reasonably and insists I come also. We ask. The minimum time is half an hour and it costs $7000. It's a five-seater helicopter. If we could find others it could potentially halve or more the cost.

We can't. Fuck it I think, we'll go anyhow. Jean goes along with what appears a ridiculous extravagance. We discuss if there is anyone else we can take. A Chinese man from Australia whom we have got friendly with and had shared his very expensive wine he had brought with him, was the number one. In conversation he says that he would have liked to have gone on a charter flight, but his friend thought that it wouldn't be worth it and you wouldn't see much more than you did on the ten-minute flight. I ask him, *"Did you really want to go?"* He replies, *"Yes"*. I said *"Well you can as we're going. You can come with us"*. He offers to pay. I say, *"No. We've booked it. We're going anyhow. There's a spare space. You can have it"*. He was overwhelmed and tried to insist again on paying his share. But we refuse.

I had already asked whether we can we land on top of one of the mesa like plateaus that Franz Josef Land archipelago abound in. The answer is no. For safety reasons – if anything goes wrong with the helicopter on or after landing we wouldn't be able to get down. As we found out later polar bears frequent these islands also and, as I'm sure you know, are very dangerous. But he says you can land on that one over there because there's a way down. Deal done. They have two of the staff crew come along for the ride. One, the official photographer Lauren and the other, Alex the safety person but Jean and I agree we think they're there just for the ride – who wouldn't be?

What a ride it is. Jean describes it. *"After days of fog today is brilliant sun. It shines on the snow and ice creating swathes of silver and areas sparkling like diamonds. The views are spectacular as the helicopter flies over the ice shelves and up fjords. Reflections in the water are of absolute clarity. The pilot skims over the surface as he climbs and descends the slopes, making tight turns. We see the perfectly rounded boulders of Champ Island – the only other place they exist is in New Zealand we are told by a New Zealander later".*

We're heading back to the boat. The pilot has forgotten he was supposed to have made a landing. Jean tells Alex, who realises at about the same time, and he climbs over from the back and touches the pilot on the shoulder. He indicates by pointing that he is supposed to land. He couldn't tell him because everyone had head phones on as the aging Russian helicopter was so noisy. We land and get out. We look around in awe. It's a fantastic view.

I say to Jean, *"Do you know why I got you here? I Patrick Henry Roberts take you to be my lawfully wedded wife. I promise to love you and cherish you in sickness and in health and I've certainly had sickness. Till death do us part".* Then I said, *"Jean I got you here to renew our marriage vows".* She was totally amazed and responded back with an equally unique version of the normal vows, saying she loved me and always would. There were tears from both of us. Yes, I can hear you say ahh. How many points do I get for that?

On Champ Island, part of the Franz Joseph Archipelago, after exchanging our vows

Chapter Twenty
MUTINEERS, DRAGONS, HOBBITS AND MY GREATEST DAY

Return to Pitcairn

On a plane again. To Auckland via Los Angeles then on to Tahiti; staying again at the Intercontinental in Papeete then onto Mangareva and picking up the cargo ship Claymore II to take us to Pitcairn. After the 10 minutes of feeling gutted that we had not been able to land on Pitcairn last time I had resolved to come back, by hook or by crook whatever it took, to get ashore at Pitcairn. The ever intrepid Jean had taken me at my word and, less than 18 months later here we are on our way back. She had secretly organised a return trip, this time booking the final journey of the trip on the cargo freighter that supplies the island. We will get ashore because the cargo has to get ashore or the islanders would be in trouble. If we have to wait till the weather and seas calm down, we wait. This way also we get to stay on the island for 4 days rather than just a flying visit. Jean: every house should have one. She gave me the ticket when we were at No Man's Fort in the Solent with our kids to celebrate Jean's 65th birthday. I couldn't have been more surprised if I'd won the lottery without entering.

On the plane something occurs to remind me of my old self. I get up to go to the toilet. It's occupied so I wait. A big, heavily built, young guy comes up to the toilet and stands in front of the door. What the fuck does he think he's doing? Pushing in. I don't think so! I move right up next to him as close as I can get without touching him. If he thinks he can intimidate me into allowing him to jump the queue, he's got to be joking. I mentally prepare for combat. He is bigger than me and almost certainly stronger. I'm no spring chicken and the cancer operation and treatment have slowed me down, but I'm fucked if I'll let anyone jump the queue in front of me whatever the consequence. I reflect this potentially will be the first time I've had a fight on a plane but in the situation it would be unavoidable despite the possible consequences. Courts don't take kindly to this sort of thing. A stewardess comes along and asks us both to get out of the way as we are obstructing the gangway. We move and he gets behind me. Crisis over. The adrenaline starts to subside. I hadn't momentarily lost my temper; I was just utterly determined not to let him get away with it without a fight if necessary. It reminded me of what I used to be like; you can teach a dog a new trick, but you can't make a dog a cat.

The journey to Pitcairn is interminable. Heathrow to Los Angeles, straight on to Aukland, New Zealand, a long airport wait and on to Tahiti - 30 hours travelling. Exhausted. But at least we had time to catch up on the book – me writing and Jean correcting. No waiting taxi as promised from airport to hotel. But eventually, two nights at the incomparable Papeete Intercontinental. Then on to Mangareva and on to the small cargo boat Claymore II. Another 48 hours best likened to being in a spin dryer. It had been a better crossing from Cape Horn to Antarctica via the Drake's Passage. The waves were bigger - but so was the boat. Sorry Ship. Well, actually it felt like a boat.

But the best bit was to come last. We have to transfer from the ship to the Pitcairn longboat. The swell meant the longboat alongside our ship is being lifted up and down around 10ft. We are meant to step from the ship onto the boat in the brief atto second they are aligned. Admittedly, there are deckhands helping you and shouting at you "GO", but they are not safely strapped to anything. They are experienced sailors, but even they admit *"yes it's dangerous in high seas"*. But we all make it – just. Then into Bounty Bay. The boat trip is downright hairy. It's like being on a roller-coaster but with added sideways sway. We are completely drenched and have to hold onto the gunwales for dear life. We're ashore. Welcome to Pitcairn the sign says and the emissaries of the tiny population greet us. We made it. No wonder not that many visit.

The history of the Mutiny on the Bounty, Pitcairn and Captain Bligh's four thousand-mile journey after Fletcher Christian and the mutineers ordered him and the remaining crew into the longboat, is legendary. Actually many of them did not have to be ordered, as they fancied their chances of survival in the longboat more than the option of staying with the Mutineers. If they stayed on board, they knew the Royal Navy would hunt them down and a noose would be the outcome. I am an avowed Bounty nerd, as I have said before, and have been from my youth onwards. Read many books, seen the films and the plays. I recommend a visit. If beyond your means or abilities there is a surfeit of books to chose from.

On the subject of Captain Bligh and who was the cause of the mutiny. Was it that he was a dictatorial, bullying, verbally abusive bastard? Or was it the mutinous lowlife whose rebellion was fuelled by the desires stoked by the furnace of available and 'promiscuous' by British standards, Tahitian females? By a desire to keep hold of an unprecedented sex life? And the mutiny given an unwarranted gloss of respectability by it being led by an upper-class Christian?

I mention here the fabled 'free love' sexual mores and appetites made famous from the Bounty crew's stay on Tahiti whilst collecting the breadfruit. A matter of high interest now and then was the sex lives of the Polynesian women. The sexual mores of the Polynesians were more distant than the miles they had sailed from their homes. In the Georgian period, the time of the mutiny, the morals were laxer than say compared to the Victorians. Like the Victorians though, the prudity that existed was covered in a mountain of hypocrisy.

In *Sex at Dawn:* by Christopher Ryan and Cacilda Jethá mentioned earlier, the authors have a crack at explaining the sexual liberality of the Polynesians by quoting Desmond Morris. He *'recalls an afternoon he spent with a female truck driver in Polynesia. She told him that she had nine children, but had given two of them to an infertile friend. When Morris asked how the kids felt about that, she said they didn't mind at all as "all of us love all of the children." Morris recalls, "This last point is underlined by the fact that, when we reach the village ... she passes the time by wandering over to a group of toddlers, lying down in the grass with them playing with them exactly as if they were her own. They accept her instantly, without any questioning, and a passer-by would never have guessed that they were anything other than a natural family playing together.'*

'A natural family'. Perhaps this easy acceptance between adult and unrelated children, the diffuse nurturing found in societies where children referred to all men as father and all woman as mother, societies small and isolated enough to safely assume the kindness of strangers, where overlapping sexual relationships leave genetic paternity unknowable and of little consequence ... perhaps this is the 'natural' family structure of our species.'

The relative standing of Bligh and Christian and the mutineers has varied over the ages – the over 200 years since its occurrence in 1789. Firstly, this has been in part connected to the social and economic climate in the country. Secondly, the more conservative, support Bligh. The more liberal and radical, support Christian and the other mutineers. Thirdly, the differing class backgrounds of the authors. In my view a

Ph.D. in this for someone. I considered it but never had the time. Also, the relative strength of the two lobbies – one supporting Bligh, the other Christian and the fact that Christian had a higher social class background.

Regarding Bligh it is clear that he was a master mariner and navigator. And so he should be. He honed his craft working under Captain Cook on his third voyage on the Resolution where Bligh was appointed as sailing master. Bligh assisted extremely ably with the navigation and the mapping of the new territories discovered.

Was he the main contributing cause of the mutiny? From my reading one would have to say yes. It must be remembered that Bligh was the object of not one mutiny but three, including when he was a Governor in Australia. And one near mutiny. He had a very dubious record when handling his men or subordinates. However, as Richard Woodman says in *A Brief History of Mutiny*, the Bligh mutiny *'is a cub among mutinies and had neither the furious, savage and bloody vigour of that of the crew of the frigate Hermione against the sadistic Captain Hugh Pigot in 1797 nor the justifiable anger of the rebellion of the crew of HMS Culloden against the hot-headed Captain Thomas Troubridge in December 1794. Though very different in their causes, these were red-blooded mutinies in the full sense of the word.'*

Nevertheless the mutiny on the Bounty was a mutiny. In the book *Captain Bligh and Mr Christian: The Men and the Mutiny* by Richard Hough, he writes in the foreword of the 1979 revised edition, *'As one exalted Admiral of the Fleet once remarked and, as another Admiral of the Fleet agreed, "surely he was his own worst enemy".* It is most likely that Nelson is the exalted Admiral referred to though he does not name him.

Our four days on Pitcairn were some of the best experiences of our lives. The inhabitants could not have been more welcoming. Jay and Carol were excellent hosts. They took us to explore some of the furthest points on the island on their quad bikes, entertained us at large family meals and at a communal meal in the town square. Carol is a 6th generation descendant of Fletcher Christian.

We also did a lot of extremely strenuous walking, up and down the steep landscape, covering practically the whole 1.9 square mile island. They had no teacher at the time, only primary aged children staying on the island, and they offered Jean the job. Thankfully for me she declined.

Hank, thrilled at having just swum in Bounty Bay, enjoying the view after climbing the Hill of Difficulty as the Islanders call it.

On the voyage back to Mangareva luckily the sea is beautifully calm. Some Pitcairn inhabitants, on their way to Tahiti for various medical reasons, keep us entertained with talks and slides about Pitcairn and the other three islands that make up the Pitcairn islands. Ducie and Oeno are small low atolls, while Henderson is a much larger raised coral island. All are uninhabited but support remarkably pristine, but fragile ecosystems, which the Pitcairn islanders try to protect. The earliest known settlers of the Pitcairn Islands were Polynesians who lived on Pitcairn and Henderson, which is now uninhabited.

Indonesia

It's now summer. I am on my way again to Bangkok, Thailand and then onto Indonesia; Komodo Dragons, Hobbit man museum in Flores, and to summit an active volcano to look into the caldera. What could possibly go wrong? Don't answer that. Some time again on a long haul flight to review events, what a year it's been and especially the cracking pace and extraordinary nature of recent events.

I'm in Borneo with my girlfriend Lena. It's the second day of a river expedition to see the orangutans in their natural habitat. We've the world's largest arboreal ape in front of us; the orangutan. Yes, gorillas are bigger but they spend most of their time on the ground. Orangutans spend 90% of their waking hours in the trees.

I'm sitting down on a bench behind a sizeable crowd of tourists, who are right up against the 'fence', two parallel ropes ten metres away from the platform where bananas are left for the orangutans that have recently been released into the wild. These bananas are supplementing the food they get from the wild to keep them going until they are fully able to feed themselves. Suddenly an orangutan heads straight for the 'fence' and crowd, giving all appearances of an attack. Now everyone knows that two puny ropes are not going to contain a rampaging orangutan. The petrified crowd parts like the Red Sea, only a good deal more rapidly, and with stark fear and horror on their faces. The orangutan goes straight through this gap, stops and calmly waits at the base of a tree. One of the Orangutan National Park field staff runs across to join her. She then leisurely climbs a tree. I, at the back of the crowd, never in the firing line, find the trick played wildly amusing. Not so most of the crowd, who have been scared witless. Especially those parents with small children!

Indonesia and Health and Safety? Go there. Seeing is believing or rather disbelieving. This was confirmed by a second incident, definitely not planned and not a joke by anyone's judgement. I hear an alarming commotion, shouting and screaming. A woman is being chased by an orangutan who, we were later informed, was trying to take her bag. Rescued by a park ranger, responsible for the errant orangutan, rushing to intervene and assist. He too was clearly panicked and it most certainly wasn't staged. I fear a tragic accident looms if health and safety is not tightened.

We are walking back to our boat along the very long jetty like walkway - 8 foot above the ground to enable access when the area is flooded during the rainy season. A full-grown male Orangutan is suddenly spotted on the walkway ahead. It is making its way towards us. No park staff member is with us. We freeze. I think the situation is dodgy - putting it mildly. Lena and others are scared rigid. It advances. There is hardly enough width on the walkway for it to pass even with us standing sideways. Lena in fear stares out into the jungle. I watch it advance hoping heroically if pathetically to stop any attack. It passes less than a foot away. The drama has passed. Borneo 10, Health and Safety 0.

We're being driven on a massive all day leg in Sulewasi to the home of the Taraga people in the Taraga Region. Suddenly we find that the road is blocked. There are huge banners. It is school children of secondary age all in their uniforms[107]. Some of the children were directing their own 'traffic light' system causing traffic hold ups but not blocking the road completely. An inconvenience, but not a serious bloody nuisance. They were receiving strong support from the Indonesian motorists as they tooted their horns driving past the assembled throng. I asked the driver what was going on and he said they were protesting about education cuts. Ingenious. Why don't our kids copy this?

I'm eye to eye with a Komodo dragon. Well I wasn't at first. It looked as if it was asleep but then it opened its eye. I'm in the Komodo National Park seeing a creature I have long wanted to see. The world's biggest lizard. Record length from nose to tip of tail 10.3 feet.

I don't like lizards or snakes. I think this is because when I was growing up in Bermuda all of us kids believed that one of the endemic lizards – a big multi-coloured one – was poisonous. I can remember when young climbing a tree and coming face to face with one! I propelled myself out of the tree and away from the branch having no fear whatsoever of the dangerous inevitable downward trajectory which was as naught compared to my fear of the 'poisonous' lizard. Luckily no injury ensued.

The Komodo walks slowly forward. The slow pace is no reassurance to me. Komodo's attack method is a sudden burst of speed. But the ranger with a forked stout stick provides some reassurance. Komodo attacks on humans are rare but they do happen. My guide informs us that Park Rangers have been bitten. People who are bitten can die from the bacteria in their teeth causing slow but fatal infection. This is the way that they catch their prey, following them until they collapse. Nine Komodos later and an overpriced wooden carving and a fridge magnet to join a legion of other nick knacks and we're off.

As I stare into a mouth of a huge cave. I can't believe it. I'm here.

---

[107] Uniforms are complimentary for all Indonesian school children - they start at the age of 7 - and are free provided by the state our guide told me.

I made it. It's the 'Hobbit' cave. Home of the sensational discovery of Homo Floresiensis in a massive limestone cave named Liang Bua (meaning cold cave) in the north of Flores Island, part of the Archipelago of 5000 islands that constitute Indonesia. They were short hence the nickname Hobbits. This is the highlight of my trip. I can't believe it when I get there. There is absolutely no security. You can walk straight into the cave where the digs have taken place, and more are planned for the future. I could have come in with my shovel and started digging,

I remember being astounded when first hearing of the discovery of a new hominem; not just one which was another branch of our family tree that went extinct a million years ago – such as Homo erectus - though they may have only gone extinct as recently as 60,000 years ago in the Far East - Australopithecus, Homo habilis etc. Homo floresiensis only went extinct 50,000 years ago i.e. they survived almost into modern times.

Most of my life I'd been brought up believing that only one in any way near homo species had lasted into the homo sapiens time frame. That made a young me, and presumably many others, think about what if they hadn't gone extinct? Or what was it like when our ancestors met homo Neanderthals? A brilliant example of the ability of science to make things known that we thought we would and could never know, we now know. Some humans had sex with Neanderthals or if you like some Neanderthals had sex with humans[108]. Yes, scientists have discovered through DNA analysis that some humans are part Neanderthal. Yes, Pete, we have found the missing link. It's you. I've always suspected it. It's your forehead that gave it away.

Unfortunately, in 2018, Pete developed a very rare and unusual illness known as Good Pastures disease – a one in a million chance of getting this. This has led to the loss of function in both kidneys so he is permanently on dialysis unless and until he can get a kidney transplant. First, they have to get rid of the disease before he can even go on the transplant list. Naturally I will be first in the queue to offer one of my kidneys.

---

[108] Subsequent to this I found out that this also occurred with Denisovans, another recently discovered species of homo that went extinct and also another group termed ghost only known through their genetic fingerprint left in human DNA. More to come? I hope so. The marvel of science.

The special conference: A huge step towards unity

It's the morning after. The morning after the greatest day of my life[109]. I give my account of what happened.

My plan is sorted. Of the innumerable JOG (Joint Organising Group meetings), executive meetings, secretaries' conferences and conference motions – not to mention 20 years campaigning – the day has arrived. November 5th 2016. My problem is that the two special conferences are being held at the same time! These conferences will decide if the two unions, ATL and NUT, will amalgamate. Crucial conferences. They say quantum mechanics theory allows for a particle to be in two places at once but does not apply to large macroscopic objects like humans. Actually, this is a common misconception. The particle could be in effect in either of two places, or more. You don't know until you look. Irrespective I am not a particle and I certainly couldn't be in two places at once.

Luckily the two conferences are both in London. The NUT's is in Central Hall Westminster and the ATL's at Etc Venues Conference complex adjacent to Liverpool Street train station. The answer is clear – I will go to both! To the NUT's in the morning and the ATL's in the afternoon. Fortunately, Westminster tube station and Liverpool Street tube are both on the Circle line.

I get to Westminster early to get my card in but not as early as I used to. The previous NUT system for many, many years was that you formed a queue outside the conference venue so you could put your card on a motion in first and you would be called to speak first on that motion. I liked this system because all you had to do was get there early enough to be first in the queue. I was determined and was invariably the first in the queue at some ridiculously early hours in the morning or rather night. I can remember only once getting there, horror of horrors, with someone in front of me! This led me to revising my timetable and getting there a couple of hours earlier still. Success. But the system had been changed. Speakers cards are now randomised and genderised so that speakers are taken in a random order, female first followed by male etc. For obvious reasons I personally preferred the old system.

---

[109] Excepting my wedding day and the birth of my kids.

Randomisation throws up surprises of calls both negative and positive. At a recent NUT conference operating under this system on a crucial professional unity vote, Jean was called first to speak and I was second. What were the chances of that! I opened by saying *"How can I follow that?* Someone shouted out *"Well, sit down then"*. How cruel. Needless to say, I didn't sit down.

Back to the conference. Will I be one of the speakers today because of the new randomised selection? Probably not. Would it be a blow not to be able to speak? Massive – but c'est la vie. To maximise my chances of getting to speak I put in five cards and await the outcome. Bingo. As Fred Jarvis said in the title of his autobiography, *You Never Know Your Luck*. I am called to speak as the first speaker against the first amendment, accurately termed a wrecking amendment. It says in essence delete all – the proposed new constitution, articles and instruments of governance, proposed new rules etc – and replace it with a statement saying that the NUT was, is, and forever will be wonderful. Well, not quite, but if would have kicked the amalgamation into the long grass.

I haven't got a written speech which I normally have for conference. But if I can't speak on this subject without a written speech what subject could I do it on? Now if ever is the time to peak. As I have previously said mock modesty is not my forte. My speech is probably the best I've ever done. The amendment is totally, overwhelmingly defeated.

Kevin Courtney brilliantly outlines the case and the history of what had happened. He emphasises he is giving his opinion, but it was up to the delegates to decide. The Immediate Past President Philippa Harvey also gives an outstanding speech as does Gawain Little, Chair of the Professional Unity committee. I once said to Gawain who is notoriously hard to contact and, through overextending himself, missing deadlines *"you are the only person I know who is both better than me and more f…..g useless"*. Gawain, you could become a future General Secretary but first you'll have to get better organised[110].

An announcement is made at the conference. Because of the Million Mask March - which was being held in various cities around the world against capitalism - a police cordon has been put around the building and no one is being let in or out. The bastards; that's to stop me getting

---

[110] I am pleased to say he is now getting better organised.

to the ATL conference, I joke. Lunchtime comes. More debate is to be had in the afternoon, but I know it is all over. The NUT conference will vote for unity. I had indeed predicted it in a UNIFY press release the day before when I wrote, *'Prediction is fraught with dangers but may I be so bold as to predict that both unions will have an overwhelming majority for going forward to a ballot of their respective memberships'*.

It is off for me and Greg Foster, another NUT and ATL branch secretary, to see if we could talk our way through the police cordon. As it happens there is no cordon – the police have obviously moved on. We arrive at the ATL conference. Speeches had resumed after lunch. One excellent speech after another. Jean tells me when I find her in the conference that the morning has been brilliant. Robin Bevan's speech had been masterful and really consolidated support.

I join the queue of speakers and am called to speak. It isn't my best and certainly nowhere near as good as at the NUT, but it doesn't matter. The job is done. One funny moment is when I asked the delegates if there is anyone who thinks that disunity gives strength and one young delegate raises his hand then takes it down again to much laughter. He had misheard and thought I said who here thinks that unity gives strength.

The vote is taken. Only eight hands go up against, a 97% vote in favour. It is an historic day and a crushing endorsement of trade unionism's cardinal principle; unity gives strength. In my speech I had made reference to another point I had made in the UNIFY press statement. *"My challenge to Chris Keates[111], NASUWT General Secretary is; you say the majority of your NASUWT members don't believe in and don't want a single united education union. In that case prove it. Commission an independent opinion poll of your members"*.

From this great step forward, we must not lose impetus. We need to plan to unite the rest. One union for all education workers. Over 1 million strong it will be a force to be reckoned with. It will not be a magic solution to all our problems, but it will help immensely.

In the evening we have a celebratory gathering at BMA house. A posh gaff. Chosen not just because it's a beautiful building and venue but to

---

[111] Chris Keates has recently announced her retirement. She has been strongly against professional unity. A general secretary does not decide policy, but they have an influence. Her departure hopefully will open new opportunities.

portray our organisation UNIFY as one of solidity and weight and hopefully some prestige. My attempts to do this are always somewhat called into question by my insistence on having Metalworks provide the entertainment at any do I organise. When I warned the event organiser at the BMA, Hannah, that the band we propose to have was a rock band - actually heavy metal - and was there any potential problem with noise? She said no as there was a built-in noise limiter.

At the do we present medals to those who have made a serious contribution to the battle for unity. The roll call of honour – you know who you are. They are presented with their medals in an ante room with a glass of champagne. Some received theirs later. such as Professor Peter Mortimore who could not attend on the night. He is a Patron of UNIFY.

But the highlight is the presentation of six special awards, four of them posthumous. The posthumous awards are for Eamonn O'Kane, past General Secretary of the NASUWT, Steve Sinnott, past General Secretary of the NUT, Malcolm Horne, past National President of the NUT and Alison Sherratt, past National President of the ATL.

The other two were presented to Fred Jarvis previous General Secretary of the NUT and Brian Williams, honorary president of UNIFY who had done so much in the NASUWT. Speeches are made about those who had died. Fred and Brian give stirring speeches.

The limit of two minutes is well broken by both Fred and Brian, but it is Fred who finally has to be told to stop, after 15 minutes, so there is time for the band to play! No wonder both of them are so outstanding. Ignore the 'rules' and don't let anyone stop you saying all that you want to.

Steff and Metalworks[112] open up with a pretty deafening, if not ear-splitting, number. Well, if there was a noise limiter, it isn't working. At least they don't have to bypass it as they did at the Tent City gig in Wembley.

Ralph Surman, previous long serving national secretary of ATL, very happy with his medal.

This had the same effect as it had when I insisted as President of ATL in having them play at our conference dinner. A good number leave or at least move some distance away and a hard-core love it and go mental – or should that be metal. Steff outdid himself in learning and getting the band to play a brilliant heavy metal rendering of *You can't get me, I'm part of the union … till the day I die* – to great acclaim. Nice one Steff.

---

[112] Search for their Facebook page and YouTube videos of their performances.

REBEL WITHOUT A PAUSE

Chapter Twenty-one
EXIT STAGE LEFT?

I'm in Cape Town again. Why? My mate Shane offered to give Ash, his wife, a two week break from looking after their baby, Petra, not yet two, and fancied going to South Africa. Being a man, he naturally needed help with the baby care - heroic, but not an idiot - so he contacted grandma, his Mum Julie, in Australia. She was delighted to join him.

Reinforcement for the childcare, and female company for Julie, he invites Jean. He also thought he needed a boozing partner. Who else?

On the day before we set off, we have a meeting with the legal team, Hefin Rees, QC senior barrister and Jennifer Thelen, junior barrister and Arnold Meagher, solicitor for Brent Council in the role of Head of Litigation and Dispute Resolution. Brent has decided after a lot of pushing to take Davies et al through the civil court route to get the millions stolen back.

I have had a meeting with Hefin and Arnold before, but it is Shane's first time. From our first conversation, I like Hefin. He's smart, very smart with a good sense of humour. He's on top of his brief. He confesses that when he's feeling a bit down he reads bits of the case in particular Evans's statement and he finds it hilarious. It makes him laugh and cheers him up. He runs through the case with us and shares the key aspects of it. The bad news is they need us to do supplementary statements to answer the bile in some of the statements from the ex-Sir Alan, Evans, Day, Patel, Udokoro and McKenzie (nee Bishop). So at least some of it is a working holiday. He wants it, he says, if possible by Wednesday! We only arrived on Sunday.

We study the voluminous statements and manage to get it done by Wednesday with Jean's help and Julie, Shane's mum doing the bulk of child care duties. It hasn't interfered too much with seeing the attractions. The cable car up Table Mountain 65 person carriages. Jesus! Those cables are strong and the floor rotates as you go up to widen the vistas. How cool.

High tea at the Nelson Hotel, named after the Admiral, not Mandela. Enough food for a day and delicious.

To come: watching the feeding of great whites from a shark cage[113], visiting Robben Island for a second time. You can't have too much of The Mandela Story with its just and heroic ending. And the blue train. I love trains. Then all too soon it will be back to the trial, and the grindstone.

The grindstone is yet another attack on the staff of my old school, Copland, now ARK Elvin[114]. To update you, with ARK coming to take over Copland, I felt it beyond likely that as I had led the opposition both to Copland being taken over by ARK and the occupation of Wembley Sport's ground to oppose the building of ARK Wembley School, that their victimisation and planned removal of me would not be long coming.

To take a step back. It is Sunday, 31 August. As I write this, I still do not know whether I will have reached a settlement before school starts or will have to return to the belly of the beast, the tarted up ex Copland, now ARK Elvin, school. This is what for me makes life worth living. The suspense of not knowing what might happen. At this moment in time there are two clear possibilities, either of which could have unknowable but clearly serious and life affecting consequences.

I get an email. It's a borough solicitor. He can't meet me Sunday - and didn't contact me Saturday - and certainly can't meet tomorrow which is the first day of term. We set a time to meet later in the week. I decide, though his email says it's not necessary, to go into school. I want to hear what preaching and bullshit the frontline of the superrich capitalists' club that is ARK, have to say. And whoa! It's highly informative as an exemplar. What I pity I wasn't wearing a hidden camera. During the summer a journalist named Ben Ferguson from Vice News contacted me and said that they were considering a programme on ARK and what the pupils went through - and a staff member - making use of a hidden camera. I was up for it. To my disappointment they decided not to go ahead with the programme. My career hopes as an undercover agent were dashed.

---

[113] Much to Shane's Mum, Julie and Jean's amusement Shane and I spent an expensive day getting sunburnt, seeing no sharks and not even going down in the cage. Shane and my story was that the great whites were too frightened of us.

[114] On 1st September 2014 Copland became an ARK academy. ARK Elvin – you don't know who Elvin was? Then look it up like everyone else had to.

I have prepared and planned meticulously for the worst – paranoid. Of course, they are always out to get you if you have caused them, those in authority, our rulers, any problems.

I had constantly been accusing them, and making sure it was in writing, of victimising me and intending to sack me. The usual thing – accuse them of it first, and if they do it, it makes your allegations correct all along. Asking the LA as my employer to get an assurance from ARK that, on their takeover of Copland, they would not victimise me on the grounds of trade union activity. Assurances on non-victimisation came there none, so I lodged my grievance.

I've written this letter to Mo Butt[115] - personally I get on well with him. I explained to him before I launched the grievance against him, that it was nothing personal. I would accept a pay off, but it wouldn't be cheap. Alternatively, I'd fight what was going to be the inevitable attempt to get rid of me by any and every means possible, including as per last time, taking it to the High Court.

Included in my grievance was the lack of care the LA had shown after I had blown the whistle on Sir Alan. '*This led to a malicious attack on myself culminating in my wrongful suspension. A disciplinary hearing was started against me where it was made plain that I could expect dismissal. After Sir Alan was suspended and ultimately resigned to avoid a dismissal hearing himself, attacks continued against me with libellous statements appearing in the press, including one by someone impersonating a member of staff. I also received death threats which I reported to the police and had to live with police surveillance cameras at my home for some months in a very stressful situation.*'

And further, '*That you/the LA have not exercised your duty of care in not providing or seeking to obtain an assurance that on transferring to ARK employment they will not subsequently try to victimise me and seek to end my employment and or ability to undertake union activities.*'

The initial answer came. To summarise, a legal "fuck off." Dingdong round one. Round two my next letter - oh I omitted to mention I've been asked by Peter Pendle ATL DGS what my bottom line was. £90,000 I said. Peter said he felt to put it mildly I was unlikely to get that amount. That was before I sent my second letter. '*I reiterate, after a long*

---

[115] Muhammed Butt, Labour Leader of Brent Council

sequence of events caused by the Council and its negligence (or alternatively deliberate actions), I now end up facing a very serious and real threat to my future employment. The Authority has not only not got a written assurance from ARK that they will not seek to victimise me by seeking to end my employment and/or ability to continue to represent Brent members as at present, but it would seem not even prepared to ask them for this whilst still prepared to deal with them (the precise contents of which are secret) to buy up land and to lease it to ARK at a peppercorn rent.'

I did get an initial offer of £27,000. My reply was, yes you will have guessed it. In similar vein to theirs. A clear-cut victory in a victimisation case in a court loomed.

Result – an out of court settlement – a sum very considerably higher. I am not allowed to reveal the amount under the terms of my Settlement Agreement. That set me up for a bit more 'trouble making' - rectifying injustices - and seeing the world. The lesson is, if you think you are going to be victimised put it in writing straightaway, and meticulously build all the evidence before it happens. Preparation in advance is all. A key to strategy and warfare – class or otherwise.

Do I have any qualms about seeking a payoff? No. Have I taken the King's shilling? No. Have I, will I, change sides? Never.

I know that ARK will be coming for the remaining reps, particularly the NASUWT rep who is also branch secretary of Brent NASUWT, Shyam Gorsia. Shyam is outspoken, even mouthy, and also follows a bit too much of the NASUWT line of instructing the members what to do irrespective of circumstances in the school.

It's not as simple as that. It depends if members are up for it, think they can get away with it, see others prepared to do it. Also, the easiest and most certain way of making change is *one step at a time* – not a whole long list of instructions of what members should do. It is very different if only one person in the school - you for example - are refusing to do something compared to everybody being prepared to do so or even just the majority. Isolation exposes you to being targeted. Unity as always gives strength.

I tell him to write me a letter, or send an email, and one to the NASUWT regional secretary, Stuart Darke, saying that he believes he will be the next Rep to be lined up to be victimised for his trade union position and actions and picked for redundancy. He leaves it too late and his redundancy letter arrives in the post beforehand.

The first attack was a staff reorganisation undertaken at the behest and direction of ARK to get rid of selected staff in advance of ARK taking over. Repeated strike action against both the academy takeover and their proposed redundancies, for ten separate days, at least prevented any compulsory redundancies. It did not stop the ARK takeover of the school. Even if we had, as in the film *If*, mounted machine guns on the roof it wouldn't have been enough. They would have sent in the army. They were utterly determined to get us. To this end they were also offering redundancy payments well over the odds to virtually anybody who was prepared to go, irrespective of whether they filled a necessary curriculum post or not.

This reorganisation was supposedly to get the school ready for ARK's new beginning and new curriculum. After less than six months, ARK executives suddenly decide they need another reorganisation, another battle; in the end again with us ensuring no compulsory redundancies. During the Autumn term the ARK head, Annabel Bates is told to leave the premises with virtually no notice before the end of the term. Intelligence reports that this is due to an AQA investigation which corroborated allegations of exam cheating and of school management encouragement and connivance[116]. The letter said: '*I am satisfied that there is evidence of maladministration/malpractice on the part of all named members of staff above'*. Three of the people who were named in this letter were subsequently promoted! Despite attempted cheating, ARK's best educational efforts with almost no Copland teachers (5) left in the school, have still failed to reach the former level of Copland's school results.

The result of what has happened in ARK shows how mistaken Brent Council, in particular Muhammed Butt, was to say that they supported ARK taking over the school as this would make the school better. The proof of the pudding is that ARK have made it worse and the councillors who advocated this were wrong. They have now recognised their error,

---

[116] Subsequently I receive further intelligence that there has been a letter of complaint against her from the Senior Management Team.

but still have to properly repent, **not repeat**, their sins. They also need to stick to and stop back sliding on the position previously wrung out of them.

We have been campaigning hard and long to have the Council produce a document showing the success of local authority schools and how the local authority has continued to help schools despite massive attacks on funding from the Government. In truth, our view is that some paid officers of the council are supportive of the government's academies programme. In the council, the tail wags the dog! This document is conspicuous by its absence and is having a longer gestation period than that of a blue whale.

No sooner had they removed Annabel than ARK demands its third reorganisation with potential redundancies, including, surprise-surprise, Shyam Gorsia.

Things are tough enough when they have more power and we have only our numbers and collective ingenuity to miss - or rather not take - an important strategic move in the life game of chess. So, a battle royal will commence. Not exactly with one hand tied behind our backs, but at least a thumb. We have in depth, good and strategic leadership; Phil Pardoe, NUT Regional Official, Lesley Gouldbourne, Secretary BTA, and Doru Athinodoro, ATL Regional Official and of course Jean and myself. Seamus Sheridan, NUT Rep and Gherie Weldeyesus, ATL Rep will do great work as always getting our members on board and prepared to take action in support of Shyam[117].

Stuart Darke, NASUWT Regional Official is hugely knowledgeable and good, but normally will have his room for manoeuvre completely constrained by Chris Keates. I have heard, however, that she's receiving cancer treatment[118] so I don't know if she's in the position to do her customary micro-managing. Also Ruth Duncan who is the NASUWT executive member is particularly forthright. The point is that the other unions NUT and ATL, not having a sectarian approach, are prepared to strike in support of an NASUWT member and local secretary in the understanding that an injury to one is an injury to all.

---

[117] Shyam gets a reasonable pay off in the end though not as much as he could have done. Both Seamus and Gherie are then put under 'great pressure' with sometimes several observations in one day! Seamus moved schools and Gherie, after hanging on for as long as he could, then left with a settlement. Both are thriving in their new school. All three fought the good fight.
[118] Chris Keates has recovered

Unfortunately, to my knowledge, NASUWT's current sectarian approach means this is not reciprocated.

It will be interesting to see how this one works out. The teacher and education staff unions have still not got their strategy right and it's not just organisational disunity, though that certainly doesn't help.

Another venture – The Left Book Club

Another task on our South African holiday has been my keeping tabs on the progress of Gregor Gall's revising of his book on Bob Crow for the Left Book Club. I'd been approached in 2015 about joining a venture called the Left Book Club, which was seeking to resurrect the Left Book Club Organisation that existed prior to the second world war, and during it, and which was hugely influential in building the socialist climate that led to the NHS and other progressive social legislation and advances.

After a sectarian spat between some of the members involved, unfortunately all too common amongst those that consider or call themselves left, I found myself elected as chair – a sort of *peace and build greater cohesion* candidate. Yes, I know – funny that – me as the *peace* candidate!

Anyhow, I was mightily exercised about there not being a biography of Bob Crow and his great work in the RMT and influence in the wider trade union movement. After the funeral, they also never organised a public meeting to commemorate his work at which people like me and others could show their respect. However, I do go to the funeral or rather gathering outside the crematorium alongside a huge crowd. I suspected that the lack of both a public memorial meeting and a book on his life and work was down to the new General Secretary, Mick Cash, who did not agree with Bob politically. I felt he was not too keen for Bob's legend to be further publicised with the consequent, continued, unfavourable comparison of Bob's abilities and stature to his own. However, through him, we set about trying to get a book about Bob Crow in the form of my suggestion *Bob Crow in His Own Words* to be collated and written by Jan Woolf.

I wrote to Mick Cash numerous of times to no avail. Sorry Mick, the reason it didn't happen primarily in my view is that you didn't want it and obstructed it. If, as General Secretary, you had wanted a biography, even a hagiography, of Bob, it would have occurred. If you did want Bob in his own words, you could have got almost any author you wanted.

Eventually after deciding the Left Book Club would do one, or rather get one done by ourselves, another author produced one. My view was that Gregor Gall, the author, had done a pretty good job, which is not to say I agree with everything he said. For example, Bob Crow was undoubtedly working class not just in origin, but throughout his life. Becoming a trade union General Secretary does not change your class position. General secretaries are not the employer, the executive is, not that it changes their class position either. Nor does the fact that you reach an arbitrary sum of, say, £100,000 pay per annum. A number of very highly paid skilled worker's jobs reach this sum, for example, pilots, oil rig workers, GPs. Similarly, general secretaries of bigger unions tend to be more highly paid than smaller ones, so by the level of pay definitions, some general secretaries would be working class and others not, presumably 'middle' class.

Your class can change. An employer can, for example, go bankrupt and end up having to get a job and sell their labour to another employer. The nature of our pro-business laws means that many employers and the limited companies they set up are serial bankrupts. These serial bankrupts start a business, it goes bankrupt, their creditors often get nothing and they simply sail on and start a new business and so the cycle goes on. Trump is but one example. It's only the employees and their creditors that suffer.

And an employee can become a capitalist. They set up a business and make money out of those employed by them – what is called *extracting surplus value*. This process was described by Marx quite simply in *Wages, Price and Profit*.

My mate Shane[119] has done this and, despite our now different class positions, we are still mates. Friedrich Engels was a capitalist, but financially supported Karl Marx (a hint there Shane?).

It is not how much money you get that determines the difference between working class and capitalist class, though there is certainly a massive difference in the amount of money an average worker gets

---

[119] Unfortunately, Shane's business was destroyed by one of the sharks that regularly destroy businesses by not paying for work done on time or just by continual delaying tactics.

compared to an average capitalist. It is how they get it that counts – by selling your labour power through working for another or others or employing others for their labour power and making money out of them. Some capitalists live by owning shares in companies and getting dividends. This is simply an employer having a *distributed* rather than *individual* ownership, and the money made out of workers being distributed to shareholders rather than being kept by an individual or the few individuals who own the company.

Regarding becoming middle class, again Karl Marx said it all long ago in the Communist Manifesto. *"Our epoch, the epoch of the bourgeoisie, possesses, however, this distinct feature: it has simplified class antagonisms. Society as a whole is more and more splitting up into two great hostile camps, into two great classes directly facing each other — bourgeoisie and proletariat."*

Bob you were a good bloke, indeed a legend. I regret I didn't get to know you better. I heard you speak at a good number of meetings and regularly at the TUC. Entertaining it was, but it was beyond that. You talked common sense. You gave hope and inspiration – as Gregor Gall notes in his book about Bob in his final remarks, *'Crow was fondly remembered in RMT News after his death, being referred to as a 'great General Secretary' because whilst he had weaknesses his strengths vastly outnumbered them. In recognition of this, the most fitting way to end this biography is to recall what Peter Pinkney said in his address to the 2014 RMT AGM. "They say you don't know what you've got until its gone, but in this case that's not true". And to remember it was common to hear non-RMT union members say 'I wish we had Bob Crow as our leader', 'if only our union had someone like him leading us we'd be a damn sight better off', or 'I wish I could join the RMT'. These are surely the best eulogies any leader could hope for.'*

I met him at a small meeting at the RMT headquarters to discuss an up and coming election and what work the Trade Unions Against the European Union (TUAEU) could do. We clashed. I said the really important and necessary work was to concentrate on getting the trade unions, particularly their leaderships and the TUC, to change their stance. He said, in essence that it was too late for that and too difficult. We just had to do as much as we could to educate as many of the general population with leaflets and at meetings to oppose the EU and call for a referendum on membership. In retrospect Bob, you were absolutely right.

Regarding Gregor's book about Bob, I and LBC say *'publish and be damned'*. Silence would be worse. The future will tell all[120].

Dis-graceful.

I'm on the Blue Train known as the 'palace on wheels' writing this on our way back to Cape Town with a planned stop at Kimberly to look at the 'Big Hole' diamond mines' museum.

I have got the runs and I can hear Petra crying in Shane and his mum's next-door cabin, but I'm at peace. I love trains and the cabin is beautifully appointed, an oak veneer I think, bigger, but not as ornate as the Orient Express. It also has its own built in TV which the Orient Express didn't have. The same dressing for dinner; jacket and tie for men and 'elegant' (their word) for women. And, of course, high tea in the afternoon. The relics of British Imperialism cover much of the world as did their empire. Looking forward to the food later, but not half as much as the fact that all drinks, apart from French champagne are FREE! WHOOPEE! I trust I won't let the 'empire' down.

This turned out to be a mistake. I got completely hammered and managed to piss myself. Now I know why they call it getting pissed. Yes, I let the 'empire' down. Piss heads of the world unite. You have nothing to worry about except your trousers.

---

[120] It has. Gregor Gall's book and the edited and slightly changed version we produced for the Left Book Club were published to no legal response. Neither were as successful as they could and should have been in my view because of the long delay in any biography being published after Bob's death for the reason(s) I have outlined.

Chapter Twenty-two
FINALE – FOR ME? FOR DAVIES?

We set foot in Madagascar. It's at the far north end of the island in Diego Suarez. It's not where we were supposed to land. Cyclone[121] Ava has well and truly upset our plans. At one point it was classed as an intense tropical cyclone with winds of over 110 mph with sea swells/waves of 6 metres.

As reported later on the web, '*The cyclone that slammed into Madagascar last week has claimed a total of 36 lives, with 20,000 people displaced by flooding, heavy rain and high winds, authorities said on Wednesday*'.

Our first stop was supposed to be La Reunion, the second time we had tried to get there. This visit was cancelled after the Captain and others analysed the weather conditions. A wise decision as it happens as another cruise ship was stuck in the harbour there for several days unable to leave even for any tours on the island which had to be cancelled because of the severe weather. The cyclone's high winds and consequent flooding from heavy rain caused severe damage there too.

Our next stop was supposed to be two days visiting the Nosy Mangabe and Masoala national parks, a must see for many of the unique species on Madagascar. Unfortunately, the eye of the Cyclone stationed itself very near this area. The Captain took the ship on a long semi-circular path skirting the edge as closely as possible keeping safe and aiming not to lose too much time being at sea and us missing Madagascar's earthly delights. Thus we are at sea for two full days.

Skirting the edge of Ava is undoubtedly better than attempting to go through it but a cakewalk it is not. Four metre swells on a small ship like the Serenissima does not make for a smooth passage. Jean is sick as a dog as are a large number of other passengers. She doesn't leave the cabin or eat for practically the whole time. We know from Antarctica and

---

[121] As you probably know, a cyclone is the same thing as a hurricane and a typhoon. They are different names for the different areas. Hurricanes in the Caribbean and Atlantic ocean, name from Our English word "hurricane" comes from the Taino (the indigenous people of the Caribbean and Florida) word "huricán", who was the Carib Indian god of evil. Their huricán was derived from the Mayan god of wind, storm, and fire, "huracán.". Cyclones in the Indian ocean, probably from Greek kuklōma 'wheel, coil of a snake', from kuklos 'circle'. Typhoon in the Far East name partly via Portuguese from Arabic ṭūfān (perhaps from Greek tuphōn 'whirlwind'); reinforced by Chinese dialect tai fung 'big wind'.

crossing the Drake Passage and going to Pitcairn on the Claymore II that Jean doesn't do rolling seas. I on the other hand appear to be part fish and immune. However, when I first thought about the trip, I thought that it would be nice and smooth circumnavigating the coast and I didn't clock that it was the start of the cyclone season. No wonder it was cheaper – though it still cost an arm and a leg. I'm normally fairly blasé about details of holidays. I just go by do I like the sound of it? Has it got things I want to see and do? Jean or anybody else is better than me at the details of holidays. This holiday has come at the end of my second round of treatment to be followed by immunotherapy. I'd like to claim it was timed and planned as a nice break to help with the recuperation in between the two.

The truth is more prosaic. I as usual pay zero attention to the booking process but also this time super secretary – Miss Organised – also failed. In booking it, it was correctly booked for January but January 2018 and not 2017 as intended. We both fell about laughing when in October 2016 when we were expecting more details about our anticipated cruise, Jean checked the details. Oops wrong year! Anyhow we are here. Just a year late. A cruise like a long plane journey is time out. Time to pick up the story.

Round two

I have just been told that my cancer has returned. Probably more accurately it never entirely went away. This time it is in the lungs. I reflect that this is what my father died of. The lottery of life. I ask for the worst case scenario. How long? She says, "*In young, healthy people like you*"- I burst out laughing – "*it's normally a few years rather than months*". This is the second time I have seen Dr Sarah Partridge, an oncologist at Charing Cross Hospital; utterly charming and caring both times. I presume this is her norm. I can't understand how anyone can keep this up day in and day out. Anyhow greater clarity will come. For a normally planning person it's time to go into overdrive.

But first how did I arrive here – round two and you're out. I was coughing up blood in my phlegm. I didn't know if it was coming from my teeth - messed up by cancer treatment in round one - or from my lungs. Then comes coughing up pure blood; this with a persistent cough and an increasing shortness of breath. I go to my GP. She is worried. I need to see a specialist consultant, but it may be a few weeks.

Sorry I can't do it. I've booked a holiday. I seem to be making a habit of turning down urgent treatment putting holiday first. This time it's Peru. Climbing Machu Pichu was on my list - kick the bucket list as it turns out - but my main aim is going to swim in Lake Titicaca. I realise naturally that there might be some problems because of my breathing/shortness of breath with the altitude but its Titicaca or bust.

Lena and I arrive in Lima – on the coast at sea level. Onto Cusco ancient Inca capital 3,399 meters above sea level. I am seriously breathless and sometimes confused. My sense of direction for example is well impaired. Coca leaves, coca tea, altitude medication and lots of water make the altitude sickness bearable. Off by plane and train to Machu Pichu which is considerable lower at 2,430 metres above sea level and therefore relatively a doddle. An extraordinarily beautiful place built to withstand earthquakes. An architectural wonder of the world. Then to Puno bordering Lake Titicaca at 3,810 meters making it the highest navigable lake in the world.

I approach the hotel receptionist and say, "*I wonder if you could help me please. I want to go swimming in the lake. Could you tell me, or if you don't know, please could you find out for me the best place to go swimming?*" She looks at me in horror. "*No, you can't go swimming here. No-one goes swimming here; it's too cold. If you tried it, it will kill you.*" I respond, "*People do swim here. I've seen it on the internet. I'm not worried about the cold – I've swum in the Antarctic*". She persists in arguing. I make it clear that I came to Peru to swim in the lake. "*I've not come 11,000 miles not to swim in Lake Titicaca. Listen, I'm not being funny but I have looked at the back of the hotel and you've got a long pier out into the lake. If you can't find anywhere I will just dive in off the pier and swim out there.*"

She immediately realised she had someone totally determined, a nutter or both. Some negotiations, and bribing a guide later, I am swimming in Lake Titicaca. It is cold – but not as cold as Antarctica, never mind the north pole. The swim goes fine. I'm cheered by a group of tourists none of whom are inclined to join me.

In the evening I decide to celebrate my triumph. I get totally pissed. Forget to take my coca treatment, my altitude sickness medication, my extra hydration and fall asleep. The next morning, I go down to breakfast. I'm feeling distinctly unwell. After breakfast on the way back upstairs to my room – f… I can't breathe. The air just won't go in. My chest is like a vice – I can barely move. I'm suffocating, unlike the anaphylactic shock a blind panic sets in. Suffocation without doubt is a horrible way to die. I can recall my mother dying in hospital and the look of horror and panic in her eyes when she could breathe no more. Rest in peace Mum.

It passes fairly rapidly and the ability to get oxygen into my lungs, laboriously, returns. With help I eventually make it back to my room. I refuse to see a doctor or go to hospital. I need to get back to England not to be stuck in a hospital in Peru. I've got the TUC Congress coming up shortly after I get back. Eventually but still the worse for wear I 'recover'. Back in Lima it is better but still bad.

Back home I enter the medical merry-go-round. I'm at the TUC Congress and its Saturday 9th September. The phone rings. It's a doctor from Northwick Park. After a very brief introductory blurb, he tells me to come into hospital straight away. I explain that I'm in Brighton at the TUC Congress and down to speak on an important motion. He's not impressed. He explains that I have had a pulmonary embolism. I have more blood clots in my lungs and I could die at any time if I don't get hospital treatment immediately. I say there is no way I'm missing the TUC and if I die, I die. An attempt at negotiation ensues. *"Can't I go into hospital down here?"* In the face of my adamant refusal to return to London he gives in. Go to A&E, say what's wrong and give my number. I explain that a hospital stay is out of the question and he says, *"You should be alright. What you need is the medication"*. In this case blood thinners.

I phone Jean. She immediately sets off for Brighton. As I said every household should have one. To add to the drama there is a bomb scare on the seafront and The Grand Hotel and the Conference centre where the TUC is being held are cordoned off and roads closed, but she finally manages to get to our hotel. I get my blood thinning injections and do my bit at the TUC. Well not actually as I was stitched up out of speaking on the motion I had particularly wanted to speak on.

On our return to London we go to Northwick Park Hospital and they reconfirm the embolism, the blood clots and the need for ongoing blood thinning injections. The consultant says that the scan has also shown up a suspicious area in the lungs and I will need a PET scan. Oh f…ing la de da. It's cancer. Ding-dong. Round two. Is it metastatic i.e. it has it metastasised from my previous cancer in my throat, or not? The result of further analysis scans is that it probably has. Well I'm not naive enough not to know that this means goodbye and good night.

Ironic because it's the second time I've been told I'm going to die. I take it in my stride but the finality of it is underscored by my having to sign a form saying whether I want to be resuscitated or not. I sign. I don't. And then being told that I will be on palliative care. Quick mental adjustment to impending exit. Updated the To Do list … **1) Party 2) More partying 3) Finish book 4) Yet further partying.**

Around half of people in Britain get cancer. Many people have the wrong view of what cancer is. The cancer campaigns tend to use terms like war on cancer as if it were one thing. There are more than one hundred different types of cancer. So, no wonder the all-embracing – 'the cure' – has proved so elusive. In his book *The Emperor of Maladies: a Biography of Cancer*, the author Siddhartha Mukherjee does a majestic and all-encompassing history and review of where we are now. It is not surprising that it won the Pulitzer Prize for nonfiction in the year it was published. In it he asks, '*Where are we in the 'war' on cancer? How did we get here? Is there an end? Can this war ever be won?*' My answer is of course yes. If it is not prevented by a law of nature, it's only a matter of complexity. Therefore there is no fundamental reason why all of the complexities cannot be understood and overcome. A curiosity is that naked mole rats don't suffer, or very, very rarely suffer from cancer. Scientists working on the answers to this will be of fundamental importance to eventually ending this scourge.

Mukherjee's line is more cautious. He writes, '*Cancer is a flaw in our growth*'. '*It is unclear whether an intervention that discriminates between malignant and normal growth is even possible*'. He continues, '*But our goals could be more modest*'. He quotes the aphorism, '*Death in old age is inevitable, but death before old age is not*' then writes, '*But if cancer deaths can be prevented before old age, if the terrifying game of treatment resistance, reoccurrence and more treatment can be stretched out longer and longer, then it will transform the way we imagine this ancient illness…even this would represent a technological victory unlike any other in history. It would be a victory over our own inevitability – a victory over our genomes*'. Mukherjee is a world expert on cancer, but David Deutch is a world leading physicist. My money is on Deutch.

In *The Cancer Chronicles: Unlocking Medicine's Deepest Mystery* by George Johnson, he writes, There are *'six characteristics that a cancer cell must acquire as it develops ... into a tumour'.* 1) *'The ability to stimulate its own growth'* 2) *'ignore signals admonishing it to slow down.'* 3) *'To circumvent the safeguard of programmed cell deaths'* 4) *'defeat the internal counters – telomeres – that normally limit the number of times a cell is allowed to divide.'* 5) *'Must learn to initiate and angiogenesis – the sprouting of its own blood vessels'* 6) *'eat into surrounding tissue and to metastasize.'*

Evolution has built an extremely strong defence system for the body. To advance to the first rung is extremely unlikely. To advance to the 6th rung is fantastically and unbelievably unlikely. However, we need to remember that there are between 30 to 40 trillion cells in the body of an average human and as it only needs one cell to get through the hurdles for people to develop a cancer. The human immune system is fantastically complex. The book *The Beautiful Cure*, goes into it in great detail also explaining how immunotherapy works but that there is so much more to be done and to be found out before its revolutionary potential is fully realised. Before reading this, I didn't even realise that we had two immune systems. The first, evolutionary speaking, was innate and developed within invertebrates and the second was adaptive immunity which developed within vertebrates. I'll leave you to research the different systems. Consider this homework.

As you will realise, I am once again back at Charing Cross hospital. Then lo, a saviour arrives. Dr Lewanski. We chat about everyday things. He says you clearly have a lot left to live for. He must have become aware, through my NHS records, of my union commitments and my insistence on being able to turn up at certain union related events even at the expense of missing important if not crucial medical treatment. He continues; we can't be sure at the moment whether the tumour in your lung is metastatic or not. We are inclined to give you the benefit of the doubt and treat this as a primary cancer on account of your general health and fitness. I laugh once more. Am I prepared to go through another round of chemotherapy, radiotherapy and a new experimental immunotherapy? AstraZeneca was the company offering it to the NHS for free for a trial period. It would otherwise have cost the NHS £100,000 for the year's treatment[122]. If it is taken up by the NHS they will get their money back and more.

Quite frankly I didn't have a family who would not understand, to put it mildly, if I threw in the towel and said fuck it, time to die. I would have done it. Not fear of more radiotherapy – bad, more chemotherapy – indescribable, but do I want serious old age in a bodily knackered position? No. In the circumstances I accept. To cut a long story short. Radiotherapy – better than last time. Quicker, easier, less painful. Unbelievable rapid advance of science. Chemotherapy also better. Immunotherapy for a year with a drug called Durvalumab – seriously bad shits. Towards the end there were even more side effects and I had to stop treatment. But a small price to pay. Dr Lewanski. Get in touch. You are a brilliant guy and literally saved my life. That's worth a pint or two from me. Others would have paid handsomely for you to let me die.

The value of the National Health Service is well illustrated in Ozzy Osbourne's autobiography '*I am Ozzy*'. He has just done a backflip in the air and his quadbike has landed on top of him. "*When I opened my eyes my lungs were full of blood and my neck was broken – or so my doctors told me later. As well as breaking my neck I had fractured eight of my ribs and punctured my lungs … Meanwhile when my collar bone broke it cut through a main artery in my arm, so there was no blood supply. For a while the docs thought that they were going to have to chop it off. Once they were done operating on me they put me into a chemical coma. After almost two weeks they finally brought me out of the coma*". He eventually made a full recovery but he writes, "*My rib cage is still full of screw and bolts and metal rods. When I walk through an airport metal detector a claxon goes off… But I can't complain yer know? I remember when I first went back to America after the crash, I had to go to the doc for a check-up. He took all these x-rays of my chest, put them on the viewing box and started to whistle through his teeth. "Nice work" he said. "Must have been a bit pricey, though. What did it cost ya? Seven figures? Eight?" "Nothing, actually", I said. He couldn't believe it. "What d'you mean?" "NHS" I said and shrugged. "Holy crap" he went. "No wonder you guys put up with the weather."*!! Can we, will we really let them get away with privatising our NHS?

---

[122] By amazing coincidence my cousin's husband was working on the drug at AstroZeneca. He did later leave not liking the large corporate approach.

Lifetime achievement award – better than a knighthood!

I'm sitting outside the main conference area at the last ever NUT conference trying to put the finishing touches to my speech. I receive a text. Kevin Courtney, the General Secretary of the NUT is trying to get in touch with me. I'm due to speak imminently to make an acceptance speech for an award which for me is worth more than an Olympic gold medal or even a knighthood. It is a lifetime achievement award.

I start to look for Kevin and almost immediately bump into him. He says, "*I don't know how you're going to take this, but I've got some bad news for you.*" I think oh fuck, what can it be. I ask, "*Is it that some legal action has been started against me which the union cannot be seen to be supporting me in the circumstances?*" "*No*", he says. "*Is it that there won't be time for me to give my acceptance speech?*" I ask. "*No*", he says. Then he says "*I fucked up. We haven't got the award to give you*". I burst out laughing. He goes on, "*We've got this box There's nothing in it but just pretend. We'll get the award to you and it will be a good one*". I say that I'm not in the least bothered. Don't worry about it. No problems. I just find it immensely funny.

I give my speech. Standing ovation. A good time to peak. The award saga was not yet over. Months go by and my award has not materialised. Surely he can't have forgotten again? If he has, I'll find it even funnier. Speaking to Jean about it I say I'll wait till after Christmas to remind him, thinking that the longer it is, the funnier it will be. Jean tells me not to be so cruel. I arrange to meet Kevin about some other matters and drop it in at the end of the conversation. He is embarrassed. He has forgotten. I said that I am not at all bothered and just find it so funny. As General Secretary he had so much work to do, especially with the amalgamation, so it's not surprising.

But Kevin managed to get me back with his own surprise. At one of the NUT Executive meetings that I attend as an ATL guest and observer, as I was packing my bag in readiness to leave, Kevin announces that he is going to present me with the award. He admits he'd forgotten. Jean says, *unlike you who never admits making a mistake.* There's even an article and photo in the next issue of The Teacher. The award is an engraved glass plaque with the following words, "*For your work for teacher trade unions – against asbestos, corruption and privatisation.*

For professional unity." I am so proud – so proud to have an award with these words.

Nemesis

I receive a letter from The Queen. Well actually The Queen's secretary. It says, *'Her Majesty was sorry to learn that you are currently unwell, and The Queen has asked me to convey her good wishes to you at this difficult time'*. Fancy that. The Queen wishing me well. I had written about my concerns at the repeated delays in bringing the Davies case to trial. I explained I had serious cancer and might be dead before the trial is heard. In the reply it says that my letter has been sent to the Secretary of State in charge of this matter so that *'the points you raise may be considered'*.

I'm now in the Royal Court of Justice. The case is being heard – at last! Several postponements mean that it is now February 2018.

The court case cannot and will not impose any criminal sanction e.g. jail time. However, it can impose financial fines. Prior to the hearing they have been prevented from disposing of their assets. Whoopee! Possibly they will lose their houses. Yippee! I am always worried and generally with good cause that those with power and connections will get away with it. But in this case I would almost be as happy if they did. Let me explain.

Commeth the hour. Commeth the man. Hefin Rees. He gave me at one of our meetings what you call the skeleton case. It has the bones of the Council's case against Davies et al. It is f...ing brilliant. He could not have been more thorough. Every angle is covered including some I hadn't even thought of and the level of repeated proof virtually stomps them into the ground. I think it wouldn't matter what I said in the witness box, or their lawyers got me to say, or for that matter any of our witnesses. The documentary evidence does all the talking and is irrefutable.

This is why I don't mind if they get off; it will only be on a technicality. The facts will show them guilty and I will publish and be damned. They'd sue? I don't think so. And if they did? Truth must out and the devil - or in this case me - would take the consequences.

It's before his lordship Mr Justice Zacaroli. Young. Actually, older than he looks. I find out later he is 42 and not a public-school toff as most High Court judges are, but at the start I know nothing. They, the defence move to disallow any witnesses to hear the testimony of others. This is dire. I desperately want to hear the statements of the accused and even more their cross examinations. To be barred from witnessing this would be a stake through the heart.

The briefs argue. Hefin is stellar. Victory! We can listen to the case. And what a saga of the pond life of the earth it proves to be. At the start of the trial they are cocky, especially Evans. It looks like they've been told they are on to a winner. What else would they say? If they said that you've got no chance plead guilty, the case would be over very quickly. In the event the trial was 32 days long.

Gradually and relentlessly Hefin grinds them down. F...ing brilliant or should that be Hefin brilliant. Is this man more autistic than me? The command of the evidence and the lines of attack are wondrous. I have been a lifetime barrack room lawyer and by all accounts, including my own, pretty damn good. But stand aside for the dancing Wu Li master.

Do give him his due; Judge Zacaroli was also the dog's bollocks. If I had been up before him and guilty, Judge Dread would have been a preferable option. For anyone of a nerdish nature please read the full judgement on my website. For all those not, here are a few of the highlights.

First, indicating the ridiculous sense of entitlement Davies developed after getting his knighthood. He got the school to give him a 'loan' despite the fact he was already on £100,000 plus, for a BMW car. His response to the question of why a state school should give him an interest free loan from the school funds for a BMW was, "*it would make me a more efficient person in driving to meetings, going off to different conferences, so on and so forth. And it enabled me to do that, such things, which would have a beneficial impact on the school. More efficient use of time, getting around, and then coming back.*"

Next, his girlfriend. Michelle Bishop later McKenzie was Davies's secretary. I feel sorry for her, but we all make decisions in life and have to carry the consequences of them. She told me before the affair started that Davies had run his finger over her hand and asked, what did I think it meant? No, I didn't suggest it meant that he wanted to nominate her for a Nobel prize. Later I heard that the missus had come into the school and a public row ensued. True or not, Michelle was shipped out to another school which Sir Alan just happened to be advising/mentoring and she was appointed, surprise, surprise, as a school secretary. Later she was back to Copland as you will see.

A. **Every payment paid to a member of staff in Copland School was justified, in terms of the work they did, the output in terms of the school, the achievements of the school, the achievements of the students and the workload of the member of staff.**

Q. If we look to the next year, 2007 to 2008, page 170, she's now on over £100,000?

A. **Yes, that's what it says. I agree.**

Q. I suggest to you, Mr Davies, that you favoured Mrs Bishop because of the relationship you had with her --

A. **No.**

Q. -- and because she was conducting an important part of what you were trying to do --

A. **That isn't true.**

Q. Let me just finish the question. She was running the payroll system, together with Mr Udokoro, wasn't she?

A. **Yes.**

Q. And the benefit she received from running that payroll system and doing what you told her to do, was that she would get the £100,000?

A. **No, that's not true.**

Q. I see.

The police record from the first criminal trial contained the email correspondence. This was revealed in court (transcript above) as Hefin leads Davies through his emails offering Michelle the job as Bursar, her saying she was not qualified and him telling her not to worry as he'd be on the interview panel. She starts on £25,000 but within three years she is on £100,000 a year – for an assistant accountant job with a two-day accountancy training course!?! You must be joking. Read the extract from the Court Transcript where Davies tries to justify this payment.

In court Michelle said, "*I received mine in good faith as well. I trusted the people that made the decisions above me. As I said to you, that the head was knighted and they were justice of the peace. Why would you not believe such people who were peers in society?*"

Another classic was Columbus Udokoro, the school's accountant and legal adviser. When the heat was on, and advised by his Union Rep, he decided to come clean and admit all at his investigation meeting with the Brent Audit and Investigation Department. He admitted that he knew what was happening was wrong - understatement of the century but probably not the millennium. He admitted that Evans had been forging signatures on crucial documents. His problem was he was looking to be let off for turning Queens evidence or at least getting a less bad outcome. Unfortunately for him, the Council wasn't buying it and wanted the whole lot to go down. Ergo, at the High Court case he had to try and exculpate himself by saying the evidence he had given to the Brent Audit and Investigation team was all a hallucinatory construct caused by a breakdown and mental illness.

Udokoro: *I can remember now, when I've been able to articulate this, is after my cognitive therapy, you're talking about some time and then because when I go home, I tell my wife and my sons, I have three boys, what I am going to -- they say: dad, don't go ... Just ignore me, it's emotional, it's like it's just happening now. So they say that: don't go. So finally, I said, because where I come from, not to go and answer this request, it will look like a coward or you have something to hide. I say: I didn't do anything, but after I've gone to the interview and tell them what they tell me and what letter is sent to me, they said they want me not to go, that: you are not well but you always give this African attitude: I look as a coward if I don't go. He says: it's not the way it should happen because this is different thing, because back home, it can't avoid something like this. You look a coward and people would disrespect you.* (This wobbleshit continues). *So that mentality, that's why -- I shouldn't have gone, knowing what I have known that they did. Sorry. Maybe I'm taking you guys -- sorry, not guys, my Lord, please forgive me. So I'm expressing my feeling. If I may say this, I went to my wife, went back home, telling her, she say: yes, I've been telling you to discuss all this, you have been bottling it up.*
Mr Justice Zacaroli: *Mr Udokoro, I think clearly, when you talk about this, it's upsetting for you.* **Udokoro**. *Yes.*
Mr Justice Zacaroli: *Counsel is asking you some very limited questions about this.* **Udokoro**. *Okay.*
Mr Justice Zacaroli: *Perhaps if you try and just answer the question and then you don't need to give us more information --* **Udokoro**. *Thank you very much.*

You can tell that Judge Zacaroli was not impressed by his Oscar attempt in breaking down with accompanying sobbing 'genuine' crocodile tears as he allegedly recalled his mental breakdown.

He also appears unimpressed by Michelle blubbing about what a terrible and unwarranted experience she had been through as she was innocent. She didn't have a barrister she claimed because she was too poor to afford one – perhaps she should have saved more from her £100,000 salary. She was the only one who didn't have a barrister. Evans had two.

IP Patel, Chair of Governors, he of the brilliant foot shooting admission of the bonus we had no proof of, tried the line as follows (taken from the transcript), *'My Lord, I had to trust him, he was a -- he was the headteacher, doing the good job, so there is no way I can say no, I can't trust my headteacher. And also, he was justice of peace, and also, he was a very honourable person, so how could I, on earth, I would say "Look, I don't trust you"*? Never mind the role of a governor being one of oversight, never mind the Chair of Governors being that of a 'critical friend', he presented his role as sycophant or to put it more crudely, arse licker. It was a line that went nowhere for him or Day, the Vice Chair of Governors who tried similar. However Evans was probably the worst, though IP Patel would have run him a close second. Evans weaselled, and he weaselled. Less cocky as the case progressed. Just an example: '**Mr Justice Zacaroli**: *Dr Evans, I think it is for Mr Rees to organise --* **Evans** (Interrupting): *Sorry, I apologise, sorry. It is, okay. I apologise, sorry, sir.* **Mr Justice Zacaroli**: *--* (continuing) *the way the cross-examination runs. If you don't agree with the form, absolutely feel free to say so and explain why and if someone needs to provide you with a document, they will do.* **Evans**: *Great, okay. I apologise. Thank you.'*

Still always arrogant - a public-school arse extraordinaire - but less so as the case went on. Evans was asked about a house bought in France. **Q**: *'This document is dated 27 March 2006, so it's four days before the year end in the school. This is addressed to a Carlos and it says: "As per my phone call, please transfer from my account, £22,000 to SCP Gachet Louton, 25 Boulevard National, Aymet, France 24500." Giving a French account number. "This should* (be) *the same account as previous. Please make check to make sure no errors. Thanks, Richard. Dr Richard Evans." So you're transferring £22,000 to an account in*

France on 27 March 2006. Can you explain what's happening here, please? **A**. *Yes, my mother had a house in France. She had sold it and we were buying a house in France.*
Q. *And where was the house purchased?* **A**. *In Aymet.*
Q. *And when was it purchased?* **A**. *I'm guessing around this time.*
Q. *And for what amount?* **A**. *I think about 200 -- I don't know, I think about £200,000.*
Q. *And was that without a mortgage?* **A**. *No, it was with a mortgage.*
Q. *You have not disclosed any documents in relation to that property in these proceedings. Would you accept that from me?* **A**. *I haven't been asked to.*
Q. *I see.*

As you read the transcripts of his evidence it is clear he believed he deserved and was owed the money. Hefin did try very hard to pin him down exactly what he was getting the bonuses for, but it seems it was because he was the wonderful Richard Evans. And what's wrong with robbing school children?

Witnesses for the prosecution in order of appearance Mr and Mrs Deshmukh, John Bryant, Phil Allman, John Lewis, Shane Johnschwager, Richard Wildey, Conrad Hall, Andrew Ward, Jo Sattaur, Shaheen Rashid, Valerie Goldie, Arnold Meagher, Martin Bailey, Ken Gaston, Michael Sudlow, Paul Butterworth, John Galligan, Faira Elks, Anna McCormick and me of course. Well done. We are all heroes and heroines. All it takes for evil to triumph is for good men, and women, to keep silent.

We wait and wait for the final judgement. With only a few hours' notice on 16th August I manage to get to court and hear that they have been found **GUILTY!** We plan to celebrate. The hearing for the sums to be recovered, interest and costs is scheduled for between 17th and 19th October. More than enough time to plan a great party.

It's the evening of October 19th. The band, Loose Change – my brother David's band - has arrived. People are piling into the venue with huge smiles, enjoying the welcome glass of bubbly. Ex Copland staff, our trial witnesses, the Fraud squad police who worked on the criminal case, Hefin and his team, Councillors including the Leader Muhammed Butt, journalists who publicised the case and Brent education unions members. The atmosphere is electric, joyful. Davies et al will be paying back the money stolen. The Legal team estimate Davies personally will have to pay back £1.6 million when everything is added up.

We start with the thank you's. Shane and Dave can't be there. Both abroad – Shane on a school trip as he is now back teaching. Dave is married and lives in Italy. But they get the first thank you which they richly deserve. I make it clear that without Shane I wouldn't and couldn't have done it.

A bottle of champagne for the key people like Val Goldie for her 'crown jewels' evidence. Lorraine King and Alex Wellman who did so much to publicise all the goings on in the local newspaper. Tim Ross for his brilliant articles in the Evening Standard and that iconic picture of Davies leaving Copland after being suspended. Some give unexpected but brilliant speeches like Richard Ward on behalf of the Fraud squad team who supplied so much of the crucial evidence. I introduce them by saying, "*In the social class I grew up in there was a saying 'all coppers are bastards'. But you most definitely are not. You are all heroes.*" Richard spoke about how they were in tears when the criminal case collapsed and how thrilled they are now that finally Davies et al have got their just desserts.

Speeches from Mary Bousted, NEU Joint General Secretary who has recorded a congratulatory video as she could not be present. People are thrilled that she is prepared to do this. The Chief Finance officer Conrad Hall who detailed all the work of Brent officers in prosecuting the case.

The penultimate group are Hefin, QC and his legal team, Jennifer Thelan and Arnold Meagher. Hefin gives an erudite and entertaining speech with the audience hanging on his every word. To top it off he presents Jennifer his junior, with her red bag. You only get given one in your life. The red bag with the owner's initials monogrammed in gold, is an ancient tradition. It is considered to be a prestigious honour to receive one from your QC. In giving her this highly deserved award Hefin is recognising Jennifer's excellent work on the Davies case. This honour was not lost on the audience who loudly applaud.

Finally, an emotional Cllr Muhammed Butt who, with tears in his eyes, laments what this had done to the lives and educational experiences of the children at Copland, which had included his own. He is presented with a beautiful crystal bowl which is to acknowledge the Council's brave decision to take on the case. The citation read, *'Presented on 19th October 2018 to Muhammed Butt and Brent Council for service to education in bringing the prosecution of Alan Davies et al and for regaining the money they wrongfully misappropriated from Copland School'*.

Funnily enough, when the bowl was transferred to the glass case containing the Council's award in Brent Civic Centre, it was turned the wrong way around so you couldn't read the inscription. An accident of course. We pointed this out and it was turned the right way around. It can have had nothing to do with the fact that it includes the words, *Presented by Hank Roberts, Brent President on behalf of the National Education Union.* Of course not.

After the speeches and buffet, we enjoy the entertainment. One of the BBC news clips from when I had blown the whistle and Davies had said he was worth it – people fall about laughing. A game of *Who wants to be a Copland Millionaire*, and a Hitler downfall video subtitled with all the up-to-date happenings related to Davies and Co. Both the audience found thoroughly entertaining. Thanks so much to Shyam for all his technical wizardry. Before the band strike up, we are treated to a song written specially by Bob Groome, Joint Norfolk NEU Secretary, taking the piss with new lyrics to the Ian Dury song, *What a Waste*. Great compliments for the band who keep us dancing to closing time. It is a fantastic way to celebrate such a hard fought and outstanding victory.

After a few more months the costs are decided. Arnold sends us the Judgment. Highlights are: The Judge found that the fiduciary duty i.e. the financial responsibility for proper use of school funds was owed by Davies, Patel and Day. They got hit the hardest. Davies has to pay £1,395,839 (including damages and interest) plus 75% of the Council's assessed costs incurred against him. Patel and Day have to pay between both of them £552,729 (including damages and interest) plus 65% of the Council's assessed costs incurred against them. With the others as the responsibility lay with the holders of the fiduciary duty, they were hit for considerably less. Evans has to pay £46,091 (including damages and interest) and Udokoro the sum of £22,429 (including damages and interest). McKenzie has to pay £9,374 (including damages and interest).

Richard Evans has had an easier ride than he deserves but at least now he'll never be a Minister of Education. What can I say to Davies et al? You're finished. To the crooks and parasites that have followed on this path? You will be too. Forgive and forget? You must be joking.

Academies: A Charter for Theft and Corruption

When this robbery occurred, it was the greatest robbery in the history of education in the UK. They filched more than the great train robbers. But the almost 10 years since, it has been massively exceeded.

One that actually got convicted was Sam Kayode, a Nigerian accountant and part-time pastor in the United Kingdom. In 2016 he was sentenced to nine years in prison for stealing £4.1m from Haberdashers' Aske's schools. Out of the £4.1m, only £800,000 was recovered. Described as "*dishonest*" and "*greedy*", the court heard how Kayode bought lavish gifts for his wife, Grace; a second 'wife' in Nigeria, and two other women in the UK. He bought luxury cars, including an Audi TT sports car and an Infiniti car with the money. For over seven years, he stole from the accounts of Haberdashers, locking himself in his office to work late "*after arriving in a Mercedes, wearing £500 Gucci shoes and carrying a Louis Vuitton briefcase.*"

I suspect Bright Tribe academy chain's boss Michael Dwan may prove to have exceeded the £600,000 of taxpayers' money he is presently accused of 'pocketing'. This with manoeuvres that even Davies and Evans and Co didn't come up with. For example, using the real names and business addresses of suppliers and building and repair firms, they manufactured false receipts for work never done and supplies never sent. Of course, the firms had no knowledge of this. A representative from one of the firms concerned said he had never ever been into the county let alone the school. The Panorama expose '*Profits before Pupils? The Academies Scandal*' 10/9/18 by the BBC was incredibly powerful.

As I predicted in a document I wrote way back in 2001, Willesden High School – the Start of the Privatisation of State Education, *'What is being proposed is quite simply privatisation of a state school, but in a particularly flabbergasting manner. First, an asset (our asset) worth many millions is being virtually given away to be owned and run privately. As Harold Macmillan (Lord Stockton) said regarding Margaret*

Thatcher's privatisation, more "family silver" is being given away. In addition, £8 million worth of new building and refurbishment is being given by the Government (our money). And all of the day-to-day running costs will be paid by the Government (our money). And what will this cost the private sponsor who will be given it to 'own and run'? A one off £2 million. It is being given away for a song.'

Of course, now they don't have to put any money upfront. After a storm of protest most academies are leased for 125 years at a peppercorn rent. The whole world of academies and in particular their land issues have a murky shroud around them.

Michael Rosen wrote on his blog on 15 March 2014 asking, *'Hey Gove, where have the title deeds of our state schools gone?'* He says, *'Thatcher sold state assets - Michael Gove gives them away - and some of the companies he gave them away to - just happen to have very prominent Tory party members on the boards - with us even paying all legal fees.'* He ends with *'Serious investigations need to be asked as to how Michael Gove can have "lost" the title deeds for £10 billion of state assets without a trace - after councils kept them safe for decades!'*

These figures are of course for 2014 – five years later how much more is it now?! Any updates on what happened regarding this please inform me.

The main strategy of their attempt to turn state education into a commodity and to make profit out of it, involves getting all schools out of local authority control and gaining control themselves. They knew from the start that this would take a gradualist approach. A salami approach, one slice, or in this case one school, at a time. Initially bribery was involved. Giving them, whilst cutting back on school funding generally, the reward of extra money if they became an academy. Later also using compulsion, the punishment of forced academisation. They have suppressed and ignored any democratic expressions of opposition and simply ridden out strikes no matter how many days. Striking alone, though good and can succeed, is very often not enough. In their relentless persistence they have captured huge swathes, maybe now a majority, of our state education system.

They then thought they might be able to capture the rest in one bite. In 2016 George Osbourne announced in his budget and Nicky Morgan, then education secretary wrote a white paper saying that all schools would be compelled to become academies by 2022. Such was the backlash particularly from Conservative councils that the plan was shelved. However, they returned to their step by step approach. At one time it looked that in the midst of such all-encompassing and manifold crises they might put their assault on hold. But Damian Hinds in January 2019 announces a drive for more academies and free schools making it plain they will not stop. So we know their strategy. All out continuing war until they get their goal. The total abolition of the state education system. It is their number one strategic priority in education.

What are our strategies and priorities in the light of this? It must be that our number one priority is to prevent them from succeeding in doing this. If they do there will be no school teachers pay and conditions document to set the standard for school. No Pay Review Body, never mind an alternative Burnham type body. All our other concerns – workload, testing, observations, inspections already worse in academies - will become worse still in a completely privatised education sector. This does not mean that you shouldn't campaign and fight against these worsening conditions, especially if you are in an academy. You should, but you need to identify the main strategic thrust and respond with your own to defend it. Fortunately, the response to threats to academise is growing. Of those attempting to convert - which are not being forced - many more are being defeated. Even a few forced academy attempts have failed. This fight needs to be our, the NEUs, fundamental strategic priority. A plan and framework with local regions and national assistance and guidance needs to be drawn up and provided.

In Brent we have had some magnificent campaigns. You already know about Tent City and Copland. There have been many notable campaigns, involving parents in particular. Gladstone Park primary was one, but the staff were reluctant to raise their heads. The St Andrew and St Francis battle, led by ATL rep John Roche, where staff were appalled that their school was being forced to academise, took action. Parents were key to the high-profile campaign, in particular Anna and Irene who were stars and organised the many other parents who came and supported the staff. Fifteen days of strike action, a lobby of the DFE, marches etc raised the profile of anti-academisation. Though in the end the school became an academy, the campaign was recognised nationally. John is now the joint NEU secretary in Brent and a great addition to the team.

There is one more that I must recount. Having successfully stopped the school becoming an academy a few years before, the governors of The Village school, a brilliant new school to replace asbestos riddled Hay Lane's building costing Brent £29 million, decided to try again. It was to join Woodfield, another special school already an academy, to become a Multi-Academy Trust.

Disgracefully this was supported and promoted by Councillor Sandra Kabir who was Chair of Governors and the Brent Labour Group Whip! She is stuck in a time warp of continuing to support New Labour and Blairites privatisation i.e. the self-same agenda as the neo-liberal Tories. Not unaware of, but in fact opposed to, her Labour Leader Jeremy Corbyn and indeed the Party's membership's stated opposition to privatisation. Unfortunately she was supported by Councillor Muhammed Butt. A massive campaign against this was launched.

Photo courtesy of Pedro Perez

Going against the overwhelming opposition of staff, the local MP, councillors, the local Labour Party and the community the Governors still voted to convert by a majority. So worried was the Head by the widespread opposition that she organised a security firm to turn up with dogs to stop members of staff – or their supporters – going in to observe the meeting.

But the opposition did not stop. Over the months of the campaign staff took thirteen days of strike action, invaded the Brent Civic Centre more than once, organised petitions, wrote many letters of protest to the Leader of the Council, parents, Governors, newspapers and the DfE. They were joined on their picket lines by supporters despite the freezing weather, singing songs and hearing inspirational speeches from national union officers.

The staff have been magnificent making brilliant homemade banners and writing song lyrics. The title to their lead song was *There's Something Shady Going On*. Woodfield staff also joined the opposition.

Our Scurrill sheets came back into fashion. See examples on my website. They make a great read particularly exposing the financial going-ons at Woodfield. I also sent details of this to Brent Council, the DfE, and Barry Gardiner, MP. The Education and Skills Funding Agency (ESFA) were forced to get involved and had to conduct an investigation. The conversion was delayed and delayed and delayed. If it does succeed it has already been delayed for nearly a year[123].

The ESFA report has now come out and exposed a 'litany of gross failings' including paying £400,000 of school funds to two consultants. They found 'lack of transparency' and 'conflicts of interest'. Despite this outrageous use of schools funds no prosecutions ensued. This is commonplace in the academy system. So corrupt has our society has become that this is par for the course and people overpaying themselves hugely from public funds is now commonplace.

Special mention must go to Jenny Cooper[124], NEU school Rep and Brent H&S Officer who bravely led the struggle and Oscar Ayyadi the joint Rep. Paul Horsewood has now taken over as her joint Rep and continues the fight.

The Future of Education

A new era is dawning. Resistance to academisation is growing. But we need to put the stake through its heart.

Long term we need to break the legislative constraints. Get back to where our action and pressure on government leads to improvements in trade union rights and education, not erosion. We must call for the

---

[123] Unfortunately, it became an academy on 1st March 2019.
[124] I have just heard that Jenny has won the TUC H&S Rep of the Year. The second time someone from Brent has won this, which makes us very proud.

renationalisation of education and reject state subsidy for private ownership as well as outright ownership.

I think the time has come to widen our ambitions for a future education system still further. Instead of state education being absorbed into the private it should be in the other way round. In their new book *The Engines of Privilege: Britain's Private School Problem* by Francis Green and David Kynaston it says this on the fly cover. '*Britain's private, feepaying schools are institutions where children from affluent families have their privileges further entrenched through a high-quality richly resourced education. There is an irrefutable link between private schools and life's guided path: Private school to top university to top career*'.

'*In a society that mouths the virtues of equality of opportunity of fairness and social cohesion, the educational apartheid separating private schools from our state schools deploys our national educational resources unfairly and inefficiently ... reproduces privilege down the generations and underpins a damaging democratic deficit in our society. Accessible, evidence-based, and inclusive Engines of Privilege aims to kickstart a long overdue national debate*'.

Ditto with religious schools. This will undoubtedly require a phased approach, but we will never have a 'national education service' without it.

Great, let us make it so. Think big. It's part of laying out what we want and what we need from a national education system. And similarly, what we want and need from a national system of union organisation in the education sector. A watchword for both should be unity.

Chapter Twenty-three
THE FUTURE - WITH SOME RETROSPECTION

Got myself elected to the new NEU executive - actually returned unopposed - so I've got a final two years to make trouble. Sorry I mean advance the interests of education and the working class. My main task will be to try and ensure that the line – we need a break from trying to promote further unifications because we have to concentrate on getting the amalgamation right, embed the union, got too much to do, maybe we can return to it in a couple of years – is not followed.

No, we don't want to settle down. Get in a rut. Take our time. The situation demands that we must further strengthen our forces as urgently as possible. NASUWT, NAHT, ASCL, UCAC yes and even Voice. We should also embrace UCU, with further and higher education a semi-autonomous section of a single education union. We should be in a federated relationship with the EIS of Scotland. One union for education. From the cradle to the grave. Over 1 million strong. A mighty and united force. A principle of our organisation should be, if you are in the building you are in the union.

It was an absolutely correct decision for the NEU to decide to organise education support staff as well as teachers. We need to use the lessons we have learned, to give an example and lead to the whole UK trade union movement. There should be no competitive recruitment between unions in the TUC. 'Industrial unionism' should be our core organising principle. When you transfer from one sector to another - say education to health - your union membership would be automatically transferred to the appropriate sector. There would obviously still be room for distinct employment groups, like the example of radiographers in a united health union or the pilots in a united transport union to have semi-autonomous or even autonomous organisation.

This is not an original idea. A previous TUC General Secretary John Monks had this idea and tried to organise change in the document he and the TUC produced entitled *Meeting the Millennial Challenge*. Unfortunately, his brilliant and prescient strategic plan for how to strengthen the movement came to naught. In my view the self-interest of those at the top was undoubtedly an obstacle. If you're used to being a General Secretary and at least to a fairly large degree in charge, many indeed probably most would not want to share the leading role.

This makes the decision of Kevin and Mary all the more noble, indeed outstanding, to support the move to unite ATL and NUT. It's not completely necessary that a General Secretary supports a move towards greater unity for it to succeed but it is more than useful.

Doug McAvoy previous General Secretary of the NUT was really against it, but such was the strength of feeling across the union in favour of it that he felt in the end he had to publicly be seen to support it. We proposed conference motions and they were passed not only supporting professional unity per se but demanding that certain things be done. For example, a slogan supporting unity go on all our literature. And that a pamphlet be produced arguing the case for financial, organisational and benefits of professional unity. It was done.

When in 2002/3 it looks liked all three unions ATL, NUT, NASUWT were going to unite and it was a done deal, he came up to me in the conference and says, "*Well done Hank you must pleased with yourself*". I reply, "*Yes but it's been lots of people involved.*" It must have been hard for him; he disliked me and I returned the compliment. Mentioning him leads me to recall a funny incident concerning him. The NASUWT and the NUT were at full spat with each other over tactics related to teacher shortages among other issues. In my view the NASUWT had started it. To be honest dear old Nigel de Gruchy was the more sectarian - he wouldn't talk to me then, now he does.

So I was speaking at the executive trying to stop the constant retaliatory tit-for-tat. I particularly remember this so you've got it word for word. I was trying to explain that nobody ever won an argument by insulting the person they were arguing with. I gave an analogy. I said, "*It's like if you are arguing with someone about whether the sun goes around the earth or the earth goes around the sun and they say the sun goes around the earth. You don't say no you fat twat, the earth goes round the sun. Gratuitous insults do not help you win the argument*".

Now what I didn't know is that the word twat has a very different meaning down south where I grew up compared to up North. Down south twat simply means idiot whereas up North it means c--t. What I also failed to appreciate was that all of the other executive members couldn't believe their ears because they thought that I was deliberately taking the piss out of Doug McAvoy – because he was fat and that I was pointing this out, and also his twatness because he was a twat.

I wasn't. In my mild autism which sometimes shows itself in not understanding allusion, especially in humour, I had no idea that what I was saying might be taken as an insult. That said Doug was undoubtedly fat. As to a twat I didn't think then, and I don't think now, that he was an idiot. He was a clever but on occasions a pretty nasty bit of work. He used to bully many of the executive if not most by showing them up and humiliating them in executive meetings. He had the advantage always being able to have the last word in delivering the General Secretary's report or answering questions on his report. I had an advantage though too. I didn't give a flying fuck about being humiliated. The very next opportunity I'd carry on exactly as before. Regarding the second interpretation of the word I refuse to comment on the grounds I could incriminate myself and/or its sexist.

McAvoy was also a right winger. He and his big mate Peter Robinson, who managed Stoke Rochford, the NUT's stately home training centre in Grantham, allowed it to be used for meetings by the UDM (Union of Democratic Miners). They were a blackleg breakaway from the NUM. McAvoy and Robinson were also involved in a CIA supported front, the Trade Union Committee for European and Transatlantic Understanding, and allowed them use of the building too. This was revealed in Private Eye. I produced a synopsis of it and distributed it to the whole executive thinking something might be done about it.

Further, I remember one Executive committee where the executive rebelled when McAvoy tried to insist that what he said as general secretary goes. Tony Brockman, a past President, pulled out of the bag an obscure rule that the executive could meet in committee. This committee had the power to make decisions itself. Doug stormed out of the meeting and ordered all staff to follow. We met in committee like in the French Revolution. Unfortunately, despite these actions the executive as a whole never had the cojones to try and sack him.

The worst episode was when his mate Robinson was found out to be financially ripping off Stoke Rochford i.e. the Union. The alleged financial irregularities came to light post McAvoy's retirement. By then, I have been informed, he had fallen out with Robinson, as he did with most people. No court action was taken. When I later found out, I had a row with my friend, past National President Malcolm Horne, who said that it was deemed not to have been in the best interests of the union because of the consequent bad publicity. My view is never cover up corruption because publicity would harm an organisation. It does more harm if you cover it up. Especially if the cover up is exposed as often, well at least sometimes, it is.

Allowing one individual to have too much power is always a potential problem. The saying is that power corrupts and absolute power corrupts absolutely. Power gives the potential for the abuse or misuse of that power and the greater the power the greater the potential for this to happen. The collective normally knows more and better than the individual as discussed in *The Wisdom of Crowds: Why the Many Are Smarter Than the Few* by James Surowiecki. Finally, always remember that the price of peace - or in this case democracy – is eternal vigilance.

The famous handshake between Doug McAvoy and Nigel de Gruchy at the debate.

Every dog has its day, however. And McAvoy had his. I spoke to a journalist John Carvell from the Guardian and suggested that it would be a great idea if he could get McAvoy and de Gruchy to have a debate on professional unity. I had tried and failed. He succeeded. It was a great and well attended debate.

Brian Williams, UNIFY (PU 2000 then) Honorary President NASUWT speaking at the debate.

McAvoy spoke well. But his trump card was at the end of the debate. He said that Nigel keeps on talking about how bad and wrong the NUT is. "*I have in my hand*" and he held it up for dramatic effect, "*an application for a job with the NUT by one - Nigel De Gruchy.*" It brought the house down. He won the vote 2:1. Credit where credit's due. It was a bravura performance.

Identity Politics and Political Correctness

After quite a bit of thinking because I knew that entering this area would be like picking up a hot potato, I have decided that I have no alternative but to enter the arena of identity politics and political correctness. It's started to be commonplace at the TUC, at Conference and in the media; I just can't stand it anymore. I am aware that any popularity I have gained over professional unity will disappear into the mist but needs must.

I proposed the following motion below to Brent NEU for annual conference 2019. We had a debate. There were objections of course but it was overwhelmingly passed.

Ending divisiveness, building unity
Conference notes with alarm that
1) TUC membership has declined from 13 million to 6 million.
2) That in the 16-24-year age group membership density is down to 7.8%
3) That even in the NEU our youth % membership density is declining.
4) Most trade unionists living standards have declined by up to 20%

Conference commends the Union for building professional unity and our aim of becoming a sectoral union as a route to rebuilding and strengthening our position

Conference also notes the decline in class consciousness and understanding within our own ranks especially among our younger members, but also in the wider movement.

Conference believes that the burgeoning of identity politics has caused too much concentration on separate identity groups and focus on what divides us rather than what unites us i.e. our position economically as members of the working class and employees in the field of education with all the massive problems that confront us.

Conference calls on the Executive of the National Education Union and local districts to discuss our work and actively, with a view to building common ground and developing greater unity, to arrest and reverse our economic and educational decline and producing a strategy to do this.

It didn't get prioritised as I thought it wouldn't, but I have crossed the Rubicon. Years before in 2007, the following motion brought by Brent Branch of ATL, was actually passed at an ATL conference. My seconder Azra Haque, just happened to be a Muslim teacher.

Supporting union integration to assist combating discrimination
That ATL believes integration of members on an equal basis within our trade union is as important and worthwhile an aim and practice as it is regarding pupils within the classroom. Conference therefore rejects 'identity politics' in its organising and believes that ATL should not fund delegates to attend conferences called for black workers, LGBT workers, disabled workers etc: Conference fully supports our funding of attendance at conferences open to all members opposing any and all forms of discrimination and discussing what members can do about it collectively.

This was the rationale we provided as to why the motion should be passed. *'The only way that we will have a united approach to issues such as racism and homophobic bullying is for us to work in a united way. We all need to be fully aware of issues not just those directly affected so that we can all campaign to combat them.'* This is just as true today as it was then. Unfortunately, this line was not taken up by the trade union movement generally.

I was reminded how absurd it has got by the furore that unfolded over Jeremy Corbyn allegedly mouthing stupid woman about Theresa May. For this he was labelled a sexist.

Let's deconstruct this. Could Theresa May reasonably be labelled stupid by a reasonable person? My answer is yes. Is she a woman? My answer is yes. Is it an attack on the whole female sex? Self evidently not. Similarly, can you not refer to a man as stupid without it being sexist? Differential treatment seems to me to be the essence of sexism. If all women have some differential protection from certain words this is in essence sexism as it would be if it only applied to men.

Have I got this wrong? If so, please write and explain.

Next, look at the women's equality movement. It is not one of all women having to fight against all men. Many progressive men do now and have done in the past supported the fight for equal treatment for women.

When the Ford women went on strike for equal pay for equal work they were supported by their union, opposed by some men and equally opposed by some women. When the suffragettes were fighting for the vote and equality, progressive men supported them. Founded in 1908 the National League for Opposing Women's Suffrage was a women's organisation that was against the vote for women. That was supported by conservative men.

Then we come to racism. The term 'race' was invented by the colonialists to label foreign and conquered people as inferior to the needs of people to justify their utterly inhuman treatment and exploitation. Defined in Wikipedia as such: *'Modern scholarship views racial categories as socially constructed, that is, race is not intrinsic to human beings but rather an identity created, often by socially dominant groups, to establish meaning in a social context. This often involves the subjugation of groups defined as racially inferior, as in the one-drop rule used in the 19th-century United States to exclude those with any amount of African ancestry from the dominant racial grouping, defined as "white". Such racial identities reflect the cultural attitudes of imperial powers dominant during the age of European colonial expansion'.*

'This view rejects the notion that race is biologically defined.'

The line adopted by the NUT in their booklet *'Race, Education and Intelligence: A Teacher's Guide to the Facts and the Issues'* 1978, was that there were no races and no scientific justification for the term. A recent position was put forward by David Reich, a geneticist, in his book *Who We Are and How We Got Here: Ancient DNA and the New Science of the Human Past.* I will try and summarise a highly complex - and rapidly developing - situation. Of course, it is best to read the book yourself.

- The average difference between individuals from within any population is around six times greater than the average difference between populations.
- Nonetheless, we cannot deny the existence of substantial average genetic differences across populations.
- As recently as 2012 it still seemed reasonable to interpret human genetic data as pointing to some 'immutable' categories such as 'east Asians', 'Caucasians', 'west Africans', 'north Americans' and 'Australasians', with each group having been separated and unmixed for tens of thousands of years. Instead,

the current position shown through research is that populations of the world are mixtures of highly divergent populations that no longer exist in unmixed forms but in population mixtures forged mainly over the last 5000 years.

- That sub Saharan African populations have the greatest genetic diversity, so we would expect some individuals in these populations to be outliers in their ability. An example and explanation is given regarding sprinting ability. In the Olympic 100 metres every finalist since 1980 has west African ancestry.

This can be explained in two possible ways she says. One, a small increase in average sprinting ability i.e. a change in the normal distribution curve due to natural selection. A small change can make a big difference. 0.8 – standard deviation increase in the average sprinting ability in west Africans would be expected to lead to a hundredfold enrichment in the proportion of people above the 99.9999999ith percentile in Europeans. Another explanation is simply a wider genetic pool.

West Africans have on average an approximately 33% higher genetic diversity than Europeans.

The point is, where science leads, we should follow. **But** cautiously and ever checking and always ready for a paradigm shift caused by further developments in scientific understanding. It is not so much that it will necessarily have arrived at the ultimate truth but that it has proven something previously believed false. It is worse than pointless to deny reality. The study of genetics shows us that there are not just genetic differences within human populations that give some certain advantages or better put, sometimes potential advantages, but there are also some small but significant average differences across certain sample populations. The book goes into those so far found. The author asks how we should deal with this and any other differences that might be found in the future.

He writes, '*The right way to deal with the inevitable discovery of substantial differences across populations is to realise that their existence should not affect the way we conduct ourselves. As a society we should commit to according everyone equal rights despite the differences that exist among individuals. If we aspire to treat all individuals with respect regardless of the extraordinary differences that exist among individuals within a population, it should not be so much more of an effort to accommodate the smaller but still significant average differences across populations.'*

In science there is no *'inevitable'*. Only degrees of probability. We are one species who can not only interbreed with genetic variants but make, where possible, a habit of it.

Angela Saini in her book *Superior: The Return of Race Science* makes many thoughtful points on this issue. She is also gracious enough to say that *'David Reich is not a racist'*. His and other work showing massive levels of ancient and ongoing constant and massive human migration back and forth undermines biological concepts of different human races. It is a social construct and a mistaken one and one that we should aim to socially deconstruct. Those that don't are in my view being guilty of primarily what they accuse others of. Not discrimination but separatist thinking.

To quote from her book, '... *We only have to go back a few thousand years before we reach somebody who is the ancestor of everybody alive today. Go back a few thousand years more, and everybody who is alive is either the ancestor of everybody alive today (if they had descendants who survived), or nobody alive today (if they didn't)'.*

We now know that not even Neanderthals were a completely separate species. We bred with them. If anyone could have been considered a separate species or subspecies it was them. Now they are gone - though they have left their genes behind.

In my view 'identity politics' makes a fetish of dividing people which helps reinforce the perceived problem. Looking at the issue of allegedly different races or ethnicities as an example: take black members union conferences. Apart from all the nonsense of arguments over various definitions – you are black if you have one drop of black blood in you (I thought the blood groups were A, B, AB or O and Rhesus positive or negative) and if you are of Chinese origin say, you are still categorised as black. Or not, depending on what the current trend is or the particularities regarding the organising of that event.

As trade unionists we should not have conferences costing the union time and money for people to sit around and discuss their identity, or identities. If people want to do that, I have no problem with it, but it should be in their own time and at their own personal expense. We **should** have conferences to discuss discrimination and what we can do and should do about it. And these conferences **should be open to all** not just to those who are being discriminated against or face potential discrimination. **An injury to one is an injury to all**.

Further, how are we going to change those with attitudes of intolerance and supporting division without involving them. We do need to rebuild an identity. It is a class identity that, much to our detriment, neoliberals have been successful in weakening.

A final point on genetics. Genetic analysis, for example, in the future could show that a ruling class, taking advantage of their power to selectively breed to get an average IQ significantly higher than those below them, could use this to arrogate all the bounty of the world, to themselves. They could say that they have earnt and deserve it by their cleverness and therefore carry on doing it, and worse. My response to that is how clever do you have to be to pull a trigger on a gun? And if you don't know you'll soon find out if you carry on behaving like that.

We need more challenge to these new proposed orthodoxies.

National Education Museum – another project

Having an interest in the history of education and its development in the UK, starting with my doing Economic History as one of my A levels, I noticed that there was no National Education Museum or National History of Education Museum in the UK. I thought that I should do something about it and discussed it with a colleague Veronique Gerber years ago, but I had too much to do, fighting to unite the unions, fighting against ARK academies, exposing asbestos scandals and financial swindlers.

Anyhow in twilight years I have finally got together with others to set up a National Education Museum. It is not an impossible task for us to create such a Museum. We know it can be done. It is not easy, but it is eminently feasible. We have made a big step forward on the road. The National Education Museum is now registered as a charity by the Charity Commission.

Our proposal is to set up an independent National Education Museum covering the whole history and development of education from nursery to higher education and lifelong learning. The objects of the Museum are to *'advance the education of the public by the establishment and maintenance of a museum and educational facility relating to the development of educational provision in England and Wales and elsewhere'*. Some of our key aims are to inform, educate, enlighten and entertain the general public, including those pupils and students in education and to have a museum housed in a building and fully resourced online. We aim to collect, store and display relevant materials such as general education artefacts, paintings, photographs, documents, banners, books, and pamphlets. Got anything relevant? Donate it or loan it to us. Join our supporters' group.

The Museum will place special emphasis on promoting the value and benefits of a good, broad and balanced education for all. Links will be made to other school museums and education exhibitions housed in museums around the UK. There are excellent examples, the British Schools Museum in Hitchin and the Ragged School  Museum in London just to mention two. The aim is to have a fruitful relationship and not be in competition!

This project will not be reaching full fruition for perhaps 100 years. I and the others starting it will be long dead. I do have a suggestion for its final premises befitting of its status and importance. The present Waterstones Bookshop facing Trafalgar Square. Yes, it will need the whole premises. There is an important and interesting and, in my view, exciting story to tell.

But we need to start somewhere, and we have. Portsmouth. We have formed a subcommittee of interested people in that city, including Keith Gardiner, Graham Barbrooke, Sheena Wright and Amanda Martin, incoming President of NEU and Trustee of the NEM, who are actively looking for premises. Our daughter Kathy and her partner Ross are also involved. Through them we held a successful exhibition and presentation meaning we now have the Leader of the Council and others fully on board.

If, by virtue of good luck or fortune or even by dint of your own hard work, you've got a reasonable sum of money saved consider becoming a founder patron. It's not cheap. In fact, £2500. We are looking to have 100 founder patrons to raise £250,000. You and your family's name will be carved on marble or granite that will prominently displayed. Any small donations would be most welcome too of course. Many thanks to all those union branches have already made donations.

Second Postscript

Finally, where are we? What to do to change things and what will happen if we don't?

In the book *Why We Can't Afford the Rich* by Andrew Sayer, he shows, as inequalities widen, and the effects of austerity deepen, in many countries the wealth of the rich has soared.

There was a huge increase in equality that was achieved in the first part of the 20th century up until the late 1970's. There was a fundamental reversal of this started under Thatcher and increasing for the rest of the century up to today and doing so at an ever-increasing pace. Both processes are linked. In fact it is the outcome of one process. The balance of class power. Improving in our favour in the first part, declining in the second.

Accompanying the first was an increase in trade union membership and activity and concomitant improvement in long term wages and conditions, and laws and other legislative measures such as pension increases, establishment of the NHS etc.

Accompanying the second, and no doubt a causal factor, was a decline in trade union membership and density - virtually halved - and in real pay and conditions and a weakening or abolition of legislative structures that aided greater equality. For example, abolishing the closed shop where everyone in the work place was required to be in a union. Pensions have been cut and in some cases been closed down completely.

All this has been accompanied by an astronomically increasing share of income and wealth going to the superrich. As stated, we talk here not about the 1%, but the 0.001% and smaller. In a chapter in his book

Sayer writes, under the heading *'The Rule of the Rich'*, *'Economic power is also political power. The very control of assets like land and money is a political issue. Those who control what used to be called 'the commanding heights of the economy' –* and increasingly that means the financial sector – can pressure governments including democratically elected ones, to do their bidding.

He continues, *'They can threaten to take their money elsewhere, refuse to lend to governments except at crippling rates of interest, demand minimalist financial regulation, hide their money in tax havens and demand tax breaks in return for political funding. Investigative journalists have revealed the circulation of individuals between political posts and positions in key financial institutions, and the role of powerful lobby groups in maintaining the dominance of unregulated finance, even after the crash. Prominent financial institutions have been involved in illegal money laundering, insider dealing and manipulation of interest rates, yet in the UK no one has been prosecuted and, where banks have been fined, the fines have not been imposed but arrived at by negotiation as 'settlements'! They have infamously pocketed gains while the losses they have incurred have been dumped on the public, who have suffered substantial drops in income and services as a result.'*

The UK super rich

Do you know how long it would take to count to one billion at a rate of one per second? Answer: 31 years, 251 days, 6 hours, 50 minutes, 46 seconds. And to think many of these people are multi-billionaires. Sorry but their wealth is obscene.

In 2016 the top six UK billionaire's resident in the UK were all foreign nationals. Top: Alisher Usmanov13.3 billion, Russian
Second: Leonard Blavatnik, Russian
Third: Hinduja Brothers, Indian
Fourth: Lakshmi Mittal, Indian
Fifth: Roman Abramovich, Russian
Sixth: John Fredrickson, Norwegian born, Cypriot citizen

The first domestic ranking billionaire is at eighth place and is the Duke of Westminster with £7.8 billion. In 2010 Britain had 53 billionaires living here. By just 2014 it had risen to 104 resident billionaires. Sayer writes, *'These individuals take advantage of a rule unique to the UK and Eire that allows those who can claim to be linked to some other domicile, to escape UK tax on their income and capital gains in all the rest of the world providing they do not bring the money into the country'.*

In *Moneyland: Why Thieves and Crooks Rule the World & How to Take it Back* by Oliver Bullough, he points out '*In the ten years after 2000, the richest one per cent of the world's population increased its wealth from one-third of everything to a half'*. You don't have to be a genius to work out if this trend is continued, especially as it is occurring on an ever more rapid basis, what the situation will be like in the next ten years, the ten after that and the ten after that. In a single lifetime these people will have pauperised the world and taken almost everything for themselves. He describes what he covers in his book. First how Moneyland conceals wealth. Second how Moneyland enables the powerful to steal. Third how Moneyland defends both its citizens and their wealth. He says, '*Moneyland can let you get away with murder, and it has'*. Fourth he lays out how the citizens of Moneyland like to spend the cash they hide in it and what these increasingly '*outrageous spending habits'* are doing to the world. Read it. It's a fascinating story and fully justifies the book's title.

In addition to the superrich breaking every law and rule to strengthen their rule and further enrich themselves, they are perverting the rule of law and the system further down the pecking order. They want to encourage across the whole of society the idea of breaking rules and breaking laws to achieve individual self-advancement. This is a support for, and not a challenge to, their rule. Look at the crime rates and the retribution rates for committing crime. Getting worse and worse. In the twelve months to March 2019 7.8% of recorded offences resulted in a charge, down from 15% in 2014/15. Overall recorded crimes rose by 8% to nearly six million in the same year.

Finally, in a trilogy of books that expose utterly despicable actions on a grandiose scale, is another one that shows how the superrich have captured the state machines of the world to get them to protect them from the effects of any further crash as they did in the 2007/8 crash but this time they have a new plan. The book is entitled *The Road to Ruin: The Global Elites Secret Plan for the Next Financial Crisis* by James Rickards. He exposes that the governments and multi billionaire elite have a plan to deal with the next financial crisis which is virtually inevitable and as the former governor of the Bank of England Mervyn

King has said in his own book *The End of Alchemy: Money, Banking and the Future of the Global Economy*, it is very likely coming sooner rather than later, and agrees it is virtually inevitable. It is of course to make us, ordinary people, pay for their crisis but this time because it could be even bigger and even more dangerous, they have devised a different way to try and deal with it.

This time the plan is to freeze all assets. On the back cover of his book Rickards writes, '*In preparation* (for the next upcoming collapse) *the global elites have been secretly hoarding cash and hard assets. Even now legally unorthodox regulations are allowing regulatory agencies to freeze all assets with a few keystrokes in a self-proclaimed emergency are quietly sliding into place'.*

Once all assets are frozen, they can impose what are termed 'haircuts' on people's money of whatever size and nature are needed. The money will already be held by governments, so they do not have to raise taxes and print money to bail out the superrich companies and individual con artists. They already have our money frozen. They just help themselves to the required amount and hand it over to the thieves and crooks who now run the world. To prevent immediate riot and revolution the large mass of the poor will not be targeted. They haven't got the money anyhow. The superrich will have already found ways around it. This will obviously exempt them: after all they and their elite apparatchik servants invented it.

You think that accessing your cash is as simple as tapping in some numbers at a cash machine. '*Is it really*?', Rickards asks. He then goes on, '*ATMs are already programmed to limit withdrawals on a daily basis. You may be able to access $800 or even $1000 dollars in a day. If the daily limit is $1000 dollars banks can easily reprogram the machines to drop the limit to $300, enough for gas and groceries. It's even easier to turn off the machines as happened in Cyprus in 2012 and Greece in 2015. The Troika (*refers to a decision group formed by the European Commission (EC), the European Central Bank (ECB) and the International Monetary Fund (IMF)*) who had assumed control just took funds to recapitalise the failed banks – the bail in. Greek depositors also experienced how easy it was to lock down their money in the Greek debt crisis of 2015'.*

People forget or think it is not going to happen here. The truth is as Rickards says, 'The 2012 Cyprus bail in was the new template for global bank crises.' If your money is held digitally instead of in cash, they can control it and take it, easily. This is why our Government and governments around the world are organising to move away from cash payments being the normal method of payment. When I visited Sweden one of the leaders in this process, I was surprised to see shops that had signs saying no cash as opposed to some places in the UK saying no cards. Use of cash for purchases in Sweden is becoming a rarity. In the UK a majority of payments are now made electronically and not by cash and this process is advancing fast.

Professor of Economics at Kingston University Steve Keen has written a book Can We Avoid Another Financial Crisis? At the end of his powerful book – he predicted the last crash – he says, 'So, to answer the question this book poses, no. We cannot avoid financial crises ... because of excessive private debt and excessive reliance on credit' that 'have already been set. We could dramatically lessen the impact of these crises ... if they were willing to use the state's money creating capacity to reduce the post-crisis overhang of excessive private debt. But because they are not, crises are ... inevitable.'

Don't say I haven't warned you. A crisis is coming. If you can, store some cash, don't keep it at home – safely please. Also have some stored basic provisions. How sad it is that in the 21st century we have arrived at this. Doing the above cannot be the ultimate solution. Because if we, and more importantly in a way they, survive this coming crisis you can bet your bottom dollar there will be another and then another as has been the pattern of our entire lives. Or of course a nuclear war starts, and these people manage to utterly devastate and destroy the country another way.

A recent book by Daniel Ellsberg entitled, The Doomsday Machine: Confessions of a Nuclear War Planner, not only shows how nearly we came to have the world devastated by these people, but that they are still a clear and present danger.

History shows us that war is the norm when one dominant great power is being challenged by another rising power which threatens to eclipse them. In this case the US and China with the likelihood I would say of Russia becoming involved on China's side. This becomes closer to reality with Trump announcing in his state of the union address in January 2019 that the US will officially withdraw from the nuclear missile treaty with Russia. A move that could start another arms race but also allow the US to better prepare for a war against China.

To repeat the earlier Margaret Mead quote. '*Never doubt that a small group of thoughtful, committed citizens can change the world; indeed, it's the only thing that ever has*'. We have to act to stop what is happening. I am confident that we will. I have faith in my colleagues, friends and the workers across the world. The alternative for our kids, grandkids and great grandkids is too appalling to contemplate. At the end of Ellsberg's book, he has a quote from Martin Luther King which I think is entirely apposite.

"We must now move past indecision to action ... If we do not act, we shall surely be dragged down the long, dark and shameful corridors of time reserved for those who possess power, without compassion, might without morality, and strength without sight ... Now let us begin. Now let us redirect ourselves to the long and bitter, but beautiful, struggle for a new world".

Good advice.

So, remember **THERE'S NO JUSTICE. JUST US AND WHAT WE CHOOSE TO DO ABOUT IT**. The bottom line; **what you choose**. We can change the world. **We have but to try**.

'Hope is the fuel of progress and fear is the prison in which you put yourself.' Tony Benn 1925 - 2014

More comments about the author

- *Driven by an unfailing sense of what is right and fair. A powerful ally; fearless, direct, honest and contemptuous of those who abuse their power.* **Mark Baker**, Former ATL National President

- *Hank is a stubborn bugger at times and the world is a better place for it. Keep it up mate, there are more battles to fight and wars to be won.* **Graham Clayton**, Former NUT Senior Solicitor

- *Hank has devoted a large part of his life to campaigning for one education union and has been undeterred by numerous false dawns and setbacks. With the creation of UCU and NEU, the achievement of unity is now in sight thanks, in no small measure, to Hank's indefatigable efforts.* **Alan Carr**, Former President AUT, & National Treasurer AUT and UCU

- *Hank has been a tireless but not uncontroversial campaigner on many issues over many years. He has an amazing ability to win over both friends and foes to his point of view. A stout defender of public-funded and democratically controlled education for the masses, I have very much enjoyed working with him - for most of the time anyway!* **Peter Pendle**, Former ATL Deputy General Secretary

- *Professional unity was only pious talk before Hank started putting that talk into practice. It took great character to stand up to officials who put their interest above the profession, denouncing him as a traitor, infiltrator, or simply deranged. But then, Hank is indeed a "character"!!* **Tony Brockman**, Former NUT National President

- *In the 50 years we've been comrades, I've never known a dull moment, exasperating and infuriating, yes! – but always challenging, positive and energising. Hank brings to life Mao's adage, "It's Right To Rebel!"* **Bill Greenshields,** Former NUT President

- *If I ever got myself into trouble, there is absolutely no one I would want in my corner more than Hank.* **Kath Alexander**, Copland colleague

- *Hank's determination to expose the corporate theft of our publicly funded education system is unsurpassed. His work in defence of state education is a beacon to all activists who want to take up this fight.* **Mike Phipps**, Lecturer and author

- *Loud applauds for the amazing Hank Roberts for exposing and bringing the Copland School's head, Alan Davies, and his gang of perpetrators, to justice successfully. His contribution will be remembered for a generation to come!* **Cllr Ketan Sheth,** Brent

- *What a tremendous struggle and a wonderful achievement. Exposing corruption so thoroughly. It is a clear reminder of how entrenched the whole system is and what dedication and determination it takes to defeat them.* **Clare Maloney**, NEU

- *Hank is forever a legend, a man of integrity and sound conviction.* **Dalian Adofo**, NEU

- *Just keep on going. There are many more wrongs to right.* **Pat Daly**, Copland colleague

- *The fall of the Davies regime shows that if good people all pull together, we can beat the cheats, but we need a catalyst and for that we all owe Hank.* **Dave Donaldson**, Copland colleague

- *A success like this is vanishingly rare and gives us all a needed lift. Well done to Hank for his persistence and sustained courage.* **Cllr Claudia Hector**, Brent

- *A terminally ill teacher was the face of his campaign to get us to understand the legacy of asbestos. The fine judgement about when to make issues individual and when to keep them formal is a great gift. Hank has used it to powerful effect, but never for his own ends.* **Ian Timpany**, NASUWT Officer

- *I think I have had more fun with you than anyone I've known since my teens on our nights out. I sure as fuck love you.* **Murray Sharp**, Camden Crew

- *In the striving for a single teachers' union, you have been extremely successful - one more hurdle to surmount and you will have done it.* **Professor Peter Mortimore**

- *Hank and Jean are a formidable team. They and their ilk should be the celebrities in today's world – struggling for equality and social justice.* **Anne Brown**, Education for Tomorrow

- *Thank you for keeping up the fight.* **Julie Pardoe**, Copland colleague

- *Great to have brought such a wide range of people with different skills, ideologies and experiences together to fight for a common goal.* **Martin Brown**, Education for Tomorrow

- *Well done Hank. Some have had many sleepless nights because of you.* **Gherie Weldeyesus**, Copland colleague

- *Hank is definitely on the spectrum and thank goodness for that! Otherwise he would not be able to stand the slings and arrows aimed against him.* **Rupert Dunn**, Camden Crew

- *The legend that is Hank Roberts: By day Defender of the People, by night the original Rock'n'Roller. All hail the Hank!* **Tina Chignoli,** Camden Crew

- *A battle well fought. Great work Hank.* **Val Goldie**, Copland colleague

- *Never give up being an awkward b*****d. We need more of it (you!).* **Ann Humphries**, Copland colleague

- *What do I say? The best brother anyone could have.* **Pete Roberts**, Brother

- *There's no stopping him.* **Johnny Beetlejuice**, Camden Crew

- *Passion and determination for a just and fair world - the backbone of Hank's life. A modem day Robin Hood who's really made a difference to the lives of so many. Calling out those who damage our education system means it's not always been an easy ride.* **Amanda Martin**, NEU National President

- *A battle well won - doing what's right for the kids. Keep up the good work.* **Shyam Gorsia**, Copland colleague

- *To stop him, you'd have to kill him.* **John Bougher**, Camden Crew

- *You have done great work for so many vulnerable people and stuck a pointed stick up the powerful.* **Geoff Scargill**, Former ATL Official

- *Fight on like you do.* **Ian Murch**, Former NUT National Treasurer

- *A truly altruistic guy, I'm pleased to call a friend.* **Patsy Bellingham**, Camden Crew

- *The longest suicide note in history.* **Eoin MacMahon**, Copland pupil

- *Hank - may the cause of unity triumph.* **Fred Jarvis**, Former NUT General Secretary

- *An exemplary comrade. Long live the struggle.* **Bernard Regan**, Former NUT National President

- *A fearless warrior.* **Fawzi Ibrahim**, Former NATFHE Treasurer, author

- *Hank's unflinching, no holds barred style includes the campaign for professional unity and the significant and determined part he has played.* **Jerry Glazier**, NEU Executive

- *My brother-in-law: an inspirational maverick with an unyielding, high spirited moral compass behind whom sits a great wife and doyenne.* **Clare Erasmus**, Teacher and author

- *Hank the younger always asserted that persistence pays. Hank the elder is living proof of the assertion.* **Dave Blundell**, Former UNITE Chair UCL

- *A shining beacon of the labour movement in Brent. He is someone from who I have been able to draw inspiration, and I hope his actions and deeds continue to inspire many others.* **Cllr Jumbo Chan**, Brent

- *Hank has never allowed other people's perceptions of what is possible prevent him from taking action. Sometimes the most obvious path is the most difficult - that has never stopped Hank from taking it.* **Greg Foster**, NEU Secretary

- *Hank is a thinker who embodies the primacy of practice. Rare, and valuable!* **John Rigby**, NEU Officer

- *Hank's extraordinary combination of courage and determination should inspire us all as we seek to transform our broken education system into one for the many and not the few. We all have much to learn from his story.* **Professor Howard Stevenson**, Nottingham University

Printed in Poland
by Amazon Fulfillment
Poland Sp. z o.o., Wrocław

49319488R00179